WOMEN, PHILANTHROPY, AND SOCIAL CHANGE

Civil Society: Historical and Contemporary Perspectives

Series Editors:

Virginia Hodgkinson
Public Policy Institute
Georgetown University

Kent E. Portney
Department of Political Science
Tufts University

John C. Schneider
Department of History
Tufts University

WOMEN, PHILANTHROPY, AND SOCIAL CHANGE:

Visions for a Just Society

Edited by

ELAYNE CLIFT

Tufts University Press
Medford, Massachusetts

Published by University Press of New England
Hanover and London

Co-sponsored by

TUFTS | **University College**
of Citizenship and Public Service

Tufts University Press

Published by University Press of New England
One Court Street, Lebanon, NH 03766
www.upne.com

Library of Congress Cataloging-in-Publication Data

Women, philanthropy, and social change : visions for a just society /
edited by Elayne Clift.
p. cm.—(Civil society)
Includes bibliographical references and index.
ISBN–10: 1–58465–492–9 (cl. : alk. paper)
ISBN–13: 978–1–58465–492–6 (cl. : alk. paper)
1. Women—Charitable contributions—Cross-cultural studies. 2. Women in
charitable work—Cross-cultural studies. 3. Women philanthropists—Cross-
cultural studies. 4. Social change. I. Clift, Elayne. II. Series.
HV541.W644 2005
361.7'082—dc22   2005006845

*I have to cast my lot with those who day after day, perversely,
with no extraordinary power, reconsititute the world.*

Adrienne Rich

✺

*True financial freedom can only be achieved when generosity
toward others is part of every breath you take.*

Suze Orman, The Nine Steps to Financial Freedom

CONTENTS

PREFACE

Not so long ago, the phrase "women and philanthropy" seemed an oxymoron to me. How could those two words be joined? Programmatically, women were seldom the recipients of anyone else's generosity, and didn't we lack the resources to be philanthropists ourselves? In the world of women-centered nonprofit organizations where I worked for many years, we barely managed to subsist on grant money and it always seemed that we were asking Daddy for a dime. Those dimes were hard to come by, and they frequently were given with stringent conditions and only grudging recognition of our work to improve the lives of women and children. The last thing we wanted to imply in this paternalistic system was that our projects were actually about social change.

It was working with women like Esther Peterson, Virginia Allen, Catherine East, Mildred Marcy, and Estelle Ramey, to name just a few, who gave of themselves unstintingly in cash and kind, that first revealed to me the passion and power of women's giving. In the heyday of second-wave feminism, these forward-thinking women taught me that we really could make a difference. Their contributions of time, unceasing effort, and money resulted in the birth of organizations such as Business and Professional Women (BPW), EMILY's List, and the Women's Political Caucus, as well as smaller scale, less obvious successes that led to a higher quality of life for all American women and many of our sisters abroad. This was also the time when women's funds began to flourish locally and nationally to ensure the safety, dignity, and empowerment of the women they served in their various communities.

Of course, had I done my homework, I would have known that the women I respected were following in the footsteps of other pioneers who had appreciated long ago that social change rested on the shoulders of forward-thinking women. For example, I later learned that Lady Byron had given financial support to Dr. Elizabeth Blackwell's New York Infirmary for Women and Children in the 1850s. Sophie Smith endowed the first women's college in 1875, which bears her name to this day. Elizabeth Peabody, a Boston Brahmin, lent her support to Sara Winnemucca's school for Native Americans, and Caroline Harrison, a president's wife, raised money for Johns Hopkins Medical School, but only after ensuring that women were admitted on an equal basis with men. William Randolph Hearst's mother Phoebe made sure that UCLA had a women's sports program. Heiress Katherine McCormack gave Margaret Sanger $40,000 at dinner one night so that she could continue her birth control research. Alva Belmont used Vanderbilt money to keep Alice Paul's National Women's Party afloat and left it $100,000 when she died in 1933. And the list goes on.

Sitting on the Council of the Vermont Women's Fund as I have done since 1999 has afforded me further opportunity to explore the realm of women and philanthropy, now from a grant-making rather than a grant-seeking perspective. The lessons I've learned have been many and varied. I have seen what a difference even a small sum of money can make in birthing a vital service or program. I have witnessed what just a little bit of technical assistance can mean in growing that service or program. I have watched women emerge from workshops and events strengthened in their own resolve to join the community of women worldwide who give of themselves to change their environments for the better. I have also seen what a difference it makes when women hold the purse strings. Priorities change. Social constructs and political policies change, however slowly. The very foundations of society, and the structures that sit upon those foundations, change.

This reality was made clear to me, and thus the seed for this book was planted, when I attended a conference of the San Francisco–based Women's Funding Network in April 2000. It was there that I first began to contemplate the potential for large-scale, far-reaching social change via women's philanthropy, and to understand how global that movement is. I am deeply grateful to all the women I talked with at that conference, as I am to the many women who subsequently saw the value of a book such as this one, and helped to bring it to fruition. It is my hope now that the women, and men, who read this collection will join in honoring—and supporting—the vital work of women's funds and individual philanthropists wherever and however they are making a difference for all of us as we strive together for appropriate, timely, and progressive social change.

EC
September 2004

ACKNOWLEDGMENTS

The poems "Dear Mrs. Bethune" and "Working Wonders" by Davi Walders are reprinted by permission of the author from *Gifts: Poem Portraits of Gifted Individuals Who Valued Giving* (Maryland: Orbit Press, 2001).

I am deeply grateful to each of the authors whose work appears in this collection. Their dedication to this project has been profoundly reward-ing given the many demands on their time and expertise, and it has been my honor and pleasure to work with them.

For their encouragement and guidance, I also wish to thank Pat Alea, Marge Craig Benton, Sallie Bingham, Mariam Chamberlain, Rebecca Chekouras, Harriet Denison, Sue Dvora, Joanne Hayes, Margo McCloud, Gail McClure, Adele Smith Simmons, Sally Ver Schave, Abby von Schlegell, Davi Walders, and Leslie Wolfe. I also thank Marsha Rose for her helpful editorial suggestions and Mary Ellen Capek for her unfailing support and good advice.

Special acknowledgment and heartfelt thanks go to Ellen Wicklum of University Press of New England. No writer or editor could ever hope for more supportive and cheerful stewardship.

And to A.A.—Viva!

DEAR MRS. BETHUNE

DAVI WALDERS

Invest in the human soul. Who knows, it might be a diamond in the rough.

Mary McLeod Bethune, 1875–1955

I have wandered far trying to write this—
hot South Carolina afternoons, live oaks dusty
above slow salt rivers near where you were born,

taking paper into old churches, jotting notes
during sermons and hymns. North, too, trying
to find traces of you at the Bible College

where you dreamed missionary dreams until
they said, "We don't send Negroes to Africa,"
damning a calling that demanded to be heard.

I have driven between Daytona speedways
and tattoo parlors looking for the library
you built on the town dump (the only land

you could get), passed fancy beach hotels
where you brought students to sing for rich
guests before you passed the hat (the only way

to keep the college open). You see, Mrs. Bethune,
I've been looking for you here in Washington,
too, in committee rooms and old office buildings

where you cornered and cajoled, wrote and coaxed
through the war years to get funds to the young,
the Black, the under-represented and unseen,

living in and beyond an apartheid world (tea with
Eleanor, dinner with Franklin), tapping the cane
he gave you for "swank" as you dazzled and disarmed.

So what I can't understand is why, even here
and now, it's still so hard to find you.
Not a word about your statue in guide books,

not a mention of the first memorial of a woman
in a public park, the first statue of an African
American in Washington, the first, the first,

the first. . . . Well, after all this searching,
Mrs. Bethune, here I am in this small park
finally looking up into the bronze immensity

of your face, your gaze focused beyond the Hill
where House members harangued you, beyond a city's
dirt and common wrath, toward the brilliant

horizon you always envisioned, still waiting.

The philanthropic work of Mary McLeod Bethune, daughter of slaves, includes
founding and supporting Bethune Cookman College and beginning the National
Council of Negro Women.

WOMEN, PHILANTHROPY, AND SOCIAL CHANGE

INTRODUCTION

Women's Values, Women's Vision
The Power of Giving Women

SUNNY FISCHER

J ane Addams, the social reformer who founded Hull House as a standard for American settlement houses and for providing respectful and helpful human services, also had some strong ideas about "charity." In 1902 she wrote:

> Probably there is no relation in life which our democracy is changing more than the charitable relation—that relation which obtains between benefactor and beneficiary; at the same time there is no point of contact in our modern experience which reveals so clearly the lack of that equality which democracy implies. We have reached the moment when democracy has made such inroads upon this relationship, that the complacency of the old-fashioned charitable man in gone forever; while, at the same time, the very need and existence of charity, denies us the consolation and freedom which democracy will at last give.

Jane Addams understood the limits of "charity," and its dangers. She warned that "indiscriminate giving" could have "disastrous results." The most effective kind of giving, she said, is work that leads to justice. It is this perspective that seven decades later inspired the women's funding movement, a movement that emerged from yet another time when most traditional institutions were being challenged.

The 1960s and 1970s were a time of consciousness-raising, organizing, and recognizing the issues that faced women. Inspired and taught by the civil rights movement, the personal was becoming political, and more and more women began to develop strategies to change the way women were treated in the workplace, schools, the media, and at home. Women began to establish and work in programs that understood that services and policies had to be tailored to women's needs. It was becoming clear, for example, that "universal" social services and religious institutions were telling women to return to abusive husbands and "work it out." They were no more effective in helping rape victims, or running job training programs that, if they served women at all, were doing so without including child care options. Alternatives *had* to be created, and if they were to be relevant, women would have to create them.

At the same time, women and men with inherited wealth and progressive ideas were becoming involved in social justice organizations and had started foundations of their own to support these efforts. The Vanguard Foundation, the Haymarket People's Fund, and the Wyndham Fund, just to mention a few, became models for other public and private foundations working for social change. The way they did their work was fundamentally different from most existing philanthropy.

Growing out of the experience of raising funds for the civil rights movement, for environmental concerns, and other social justice issues, women knew that to create the changes necessary for women's equality, they had to raise the funds themselves. Of course, there was a long and inspiring history of women raising funds for equality. For example, the suffragists did it very effectively. Jane Addams and Susan B. Anthony were mothers of us all in framing the arguments for women's equality, and they were masterful at raising the funds to nourish the movement. Other examples of early women philanthropists appear in the preface to this book.

It was only in the early 1980s, however, that substantial numbers of women began to organize in earnest to increase the amount of money going to women's organizations through self-developed philanthropies. Carol Mollner and Marie Wilson, in "History as Prologue: The Women's Funding Movement," describe our beginnings and pose key questions that came up at the time, and that continue to arise. In April 1985, the twenty funds that were forming or already established, met in Bethesda, Maryland, immediately before the Council on Foundations meetings in Washington, D.C. Out of this meeting came the National Network of Women's Funds, which is now the Women's Funding Network (WFN).

Those three days of the first WFN meeting in April 1985 were pioneering, I realize now, as I look back on the conversations, the learning, and the shared hope. Coming together, we took solace in our commonalities— our values, goals, and concerns—and discovered our differences. Eventually, we learned to celebrate both. We took Jane Addams's words to heart: "Social advance depends as much upon the process through which it is secured as upon the result itself." I was at that meeting to represent the

Sophia Fund, one of the first private women's foundations in the country, founded by Lucia Woods Lindley, and the Chicago Foundation for Women, which Marjorie Craig Benton, Iris Krieg, and I had been organizing for two years. Several of the other attendees who shared complicated stories of establishing funds are represented in this book: Tracy Gary, Helen LaKelly Hunt, Katherine Acey, Marie Wilson, Carol Mollner. They are joined by women who, with the founders of the early funds, have enriched and broadened the work in the almost twenty years since we struggled to discover the themes, the strategies, and the language to birth the women's funding movement.

Mollner and Wilson, early leaders of the movement, write with honesty about the labor and delivery. Their chapter creates the roadmap for the rest of the book, and for the women's funding movement, citing the commitment to continue to try "to become organizational models of truly inclusive and powerful philanthropic organizations." Their history of those days and the ensuing years is testimony to the struggles and the successes of the way women work for social change.

As Tracy Gary says in her chapter, "Lessons Learned: Strategies for Success in Education and Endowment," "Together we have helped to launch a movement for nothing short of social revolution, and the full consequences have yet to be realized." As a founder of one of the first, larger public foundations, the Women's Foundation of San Francisco, Gary has provided a summary of what we've learned in the past twenty-five years; it serves as a primer for those wanting to start a women's fund.

Much of what we learned about women's funding took years of study, experimentation, and replication. We knew the truth of what Elizabeth Cady Stanton had said (echoed later by Virginia Woolf): "Woman will always be dependent until she holds a purse of her own." In the chapter, "Putting Our Money Where Our Mouths Are: Sharing Earned Income," Peg Talburtt, Judy Bloom, and Diane Horey Leonard describe how individual women who have earned their own wealth are becoming more interested in creating social change through their giving. No one described in this chapter fits the "Lady Bountiful" image, those well-intentioned foremothers who brought charity to poor families without much thought as to the reasons for the poverty. Many modern businesswomen (examples are in this chapter) are "driven by social change as the perceived goal of giving." One donor's efforts, for example, are "aimed at [civil rights] organizations that work to change laws and behavior, especially the educational elements that change people's attitudes." In Zaineb Salbi's chapter, "Think Big, Spend Small: The Impact of Woman-to-Woman Small-Scale Support," Salbi describes how small-giving made a difference to Women for Women

International and to Soroptomist International. The support from individual women was very important, but more important was "the attitudes and values" that informed and shaped the giving. Those willing to give their resources to other individuals—building on each other's successes and learning from the failures—made enormous differences in the lives of women, their families, and their communities.

In 1985, we had no idea how much technology eventually would affect the women's funding movement. Most of us were happy to have basic computers; many still used typewriters. Fax machines were rare and e-mail unheard of. In "The Future of Funding: E-Philanthropy and Other Innovations," the overriding context for the chapter is, "if you want to change the world, fund women," and do it with all the tools that are currently at hand. Christine Kwak, Gail McClure, and Anne C. Petersen tell us how far we've come from index cards and Smith-Coronas, and explain the benefits of using the Internet—another tool that didn't exist twenty years ago—for raising funds. They also predict how youth philanthropy, global giving, and venture philanthropy, among other trends, will affect the women's funding movement.

Those early days of the movement were the testing grounds for ways of thinking about women and philanthropy, for experimenting with language and context. Early on, even before she earned her doctorate in feminist theology, Helen LaKelly Hunt was deeply interested in women's spirituality. Helen often brought that perspective to the new movement. She and Kanyere Eaton say in their chapter, "We Are Our Sister's Keepers: Role Models, Success Stories, Inspiration," that "the struggle for social justice, economic equality, and the eradication of violence is sacred," and that "much of the work that takes place on earth to promote the rights of women is rooted in the deepest and most compassionate aspects of world religions." They go on to write about the work of the Sister Fund, their foundation, in the context of biblical narratives, to illustrate the archetypal power of sisterhood.

From a more secular perspective, Chris Grumm, Deborah Puntenney, and Emily Katz Kishawi describe in "Women's Biggest Contribution: A View of Social Change," the way that women's funds move away "from a deficiency or needs-based model to a paradigm that emphasizes the undertapped potential of women and girls to contribute to social change." Their chapter is a summary of where the ideology of the movement is today. Using practical examples and research results, their discussion about how to use "challenges as though they were opportunities" is particularly useful for those in the movement who get stuck either in dogma or daily tasks and miss the extraordinary power of the work that "operate[s] with a feminist consciousness."

A "feminist consciousness" should lead directly to the ways that women can work together. Kimberly Otis, the former director of the Sister Fund, provides her own personal history, one that mirrors the experiences of many others working in women's philanthropy. Her chapter, "Partners and Stewards: Fostering Healthy Collaboration," is a sensitive reflection about how women's funds "emphasize the development of true partnership and careful stewardship in a field that is notorious for power relationships that are unequal." While never denying the amount of work and depth of the challenges, Kim Otis presents the opportunities of different methods of collaborative giving and cites many useful examples from sharing office space to collaborating to send representatives to the Beijing Women's Conference.

Novelist and social critic Rebecca West wrote in the 1920s: "Charity is an ugly trick. It is a virtue grown by the rich on the graves of the poor. Unless it is accompanied by sincere revolt against the present social system, it is cheap moral swagger. In former times it was used as fire insurance by the rich, but now that the fear of Hell has gone . . . it is used either to gild mean lives with nobility or as a political instrument." Though our language might be less inflammatory (we do, after all, have to persuade donors to invest in us) and our context different, the strength of West's argument cannot be denied. "Charity" is ephemeral, often allowing the benefactors to feel good rather than effecting any change in a social system that perpetuates the need for charity in the first place. Women's foundations almost always respond to the need for services that women, especially women in crisis, must have available. But, they often overlook efforts that create social change, that eliminate barriers to advancement for women. Rarely did traditional philanthropy provide a model; a notable exception, however, is the Ford Foundation.

An early funder of WFN, Ford, through its goals to "strengthen democratic values, reduce poverty and injustice, promote international cooperation, and advance human achievement," has been for decades in the forefront of civil rights funding, including women's issues such as reproductive rights and domestic violence. Barbara Y. Phillips is Ford's current program officer responsible for grants and activities related to women's rights and gender equity. She begins her chapter, "The Ford Foundation: A Model of Support for Women's Rights," with descriptions of some of her grantees. Phillips goes on to articulate the comprehensive approaches that Ford takes in its funding—looking at the interrelationships among women's health, nutrition, and contraceptive practices, for example. Ford's programs are challenged to "craft new legal theories with innovative companion remedial proposals to confront structural inequality, and to develop strategic law-related plans responsive to the deep and continued significance of race, class, sexual orientation . . . as they intersect with gender." Though Ford's program exists within one of the largest foundations in the country, its analyses and approaches are indeed models for all women's funds, and its goals are the goals of the entire movement.

We knew in those first days of the movement that we needed to be inclusive of women from all backgrounds, including race, religion, occupation, region, nationality, and sexual orientation. We recognized that most of us were in our forties at that conference, but it took another decade before many funds made a concerted effort to bring in younger women. In fact, Tracy Gary says that the "time has come for the women's funding movement to help the next generation of women philanthropists and leaders to create their own organizations and set their own agendas." Essential to the future success of the movement is to enable new organizers, activists, and donors to offer new ideas and new ways of working.

Kalpana Krishnamurthy has been in the forefront of teaching us how younger women approach the work of women's funding. In "The Next Wave: Feminism, Philanthropy, and the Future," she reports on the concerns of the third-wave feminists and their recognition that ". . . fewer dollars were making it to the innovative programs that Third Wave Direct Action members were leading across the country," even from women's funds. Conversations among four young activist philanthropists led to the founding of a fund specifically for young women—and the Third Wave Fund was born, adding to new ways of working for social justice and the growing list of women's funds. Stephanie Yang, in "Voices of Young Women: The Development of Girls' Funds," provides a deeply personal, poetic description of how she first came into the movement, and how she and other young women have "become like sisters, united by a common goal. Each time we are together, we become more confident to speak, to trust our instincts, to create solutions for our world." She reassures us all with her sensitive narrative that the future is in good hands.

"My first instinct when I was thinking of giving all my wealth away was to throw all my stuff out the window. Now I think there are more strategic ways to give and I'll gradually give more and more." This from a young woman called "Pam" in Cynthia Ryan's compelling chapter, "From Cradle to Grave: Challenges and Opportunities of Inherited Wealth." The issues of class were and are ongoing conversations. Reconciling the tensions among women of different classes who have similar goals and values may be one of the most important contributions the women's funding movement makes to social change. Disparities in wealth in a social change movement, especially one that must address money in almost everything it does, can sabotage the larger goals of the cause, if not addressed with sensitivity and mutual respect.

"People of wealth have several emotional and psychic challenges to grapple with: guilt for having unearned income, fear of spending it all and having nothing left, concerns about competency regarding money management and sound investing, worries about approval or disapproval because of money, the quest to find one's rightful place in the world," Ryan says. She goes on to discuss gender differences and issues of wealth, and includes several personal stories from wealthy women. For some funds, where a lower-income woman may find herself the only woman in the room who has to earn her own income, this chapter could be the basis of bridging class distinctions, or, at least, finding a way of talking about them and understanding the challenges of bridging the gaps.

Mary Ellen Capek has been researching women and philanthropy since the beginning of the women's funding movement. In her contribution, "Documenting Women's Giving: Biases, Barriers, and Benefits," she explodes the myths about differences in how men and women behave as donors. Because of the dearth of research on the patterns of women's donating behavior, and because old stereotypes die hard, Capek comes to the conclusion that ". . . none of the existing data prove conclusively that women give more—or that women give less. Based on the survey data available, gender is not a reliable predictor of philanthropic behavior; nor does it account for significant differences among givers." Giving, she suggests, is based on complicated variables. Her review of the literature, statistics on giving and givers, and sensible and creative strategies for raising funds for women's programs are especially useful content for anyone in the field.

A good companion piece to Capek's chapter is "Women as Donors: Old Stereotypes, New Visions," by Jo Moore and Marianne Philbin. Both authors were involved in the Chicago Foundation for Women and are now consultants to many organizations including women's nonprofits. They bring a practical sense of the field to their thoughtful essay on women's motivation to be donors and their expectations for their gifts. "Asking and giving is about relationship-building," they write, "and in fact, the classic cycle of donor relations parallels the steps women instinctively follow when reaching out to individuals with whom they're interested in becoming friends."

Katherine Acey, who attended the first conference of women's funds and has been a long-time advocate and funder, writes in "Backbone and Bite:

The Place of Volunteerism in Women's Giving" that it is "volunteers—overwhelmingly women—[who] are the backbone of the women's funding movement. It is their time, money, skills, and most importantly, diverse lived experiences that inform, sustain, and give our foundations the necessary bite to navigate the rich terrain of women's philanthropy." She recounts over four decades of working as a volunteer, or with those who give their time, how important it is "to show up if we care about what happens in this generation and the next." Her history of the Astraea Foundation for Justice and the Lesbian Action fund is a fine example of an all-volunteer board (before they could hire Katherine as the first paid staff in 1987) who brought their talents, values, and commitment to creating a risk-taking, inclusive, successful fund for social change.

In 1985, at the first conference of women's funds, we had representatives from one international fund—Mama Cash, from the Netherlands. At this writing, as Patti Chang and Kavita Ramdas note in "Giving Globally: International Perspectives," the Network has grown to include over twelve funds across the world that focus on funding social change for women. In fact, they have met as a separate network to discuss the many issues women across the world experience. Their chapter contains many examples of "The Global Women's Movement," from women in China who started the first hotline when the Chinese government claimed domestic violence was a "western phenomenon," to a group in Croatia working to strengthen the rights of lesbians. They also list the reasons many donors resist giving globally and provide persuasive ways of countering the concerns. The global reach puts all of our work into perspective, and shows us how much more we need to do.

Yet, we have come a long way since those spring days in the barest of settings. Rarely today in our communities do we hear questions and criticisms we were plied with then as we were starting to organize women's funds. "Why separate out women's issues? Everyone needs help." "Special interest philanthropy isn't good philanthropy. You need to see the issues of the whole society." "If you have more than one women's fund in a city, you're not going to find enough organizations to support." The collective assets of women's funds in 2004 are over $190 million (according to WFN) and growing. They have brought to the attention of traditional philanthropy not only credibility to funding women's issues, but a democratic and social change process. We are not a movement that will rest; too many women and communities all over the world suffer still from the oppression of poverty, violence, and discrimination. And we have not answered all the important questions or unraveled all the troublesome knots. Marsha Shapiro Rose's chapter, "The Other Hand: A Critical Look at Feminist

Funding," describes three cases of women's funds struggling "to maintain an activist position and a simultaneously critical perspective." Can we raise money and hold on to feminist ideals? Rose posits that using a constructive feminist lens, we can avoid the dilemmas that threaten our work.

Carol Mollner and Marie Wilson sound the challenge in the first chapter of this book that is echoed throughout. It is a quote from Barbara Ehrenreich, who spoke at the 1997 Women's Funding Network conference:

> The first goal is of course equality—for women, and among women in all our glorious diversity. What we've learned is that this goal will not achieve itself through some inevitable process of human progress. The forces of misogyny and racism are organized and ascendant right now— and will be overcome only by pushing and organizing and struggling as if our lives, and our dignity, were at stake—which they are.

This book, then, is a memoir, a guide, and an inspiration to continue our work.

PART I

THE WOMEN'S FUNDING MOVEMENT

Part I recalls the history of the women's funding movement and examines women's philanthropic motives and practices. It explores some key lessons learned in the Women and Philanthropy community to date and offers perspectives on the unique contributions of volunteerism, the value of partnerships, and the vision of youth. A critical analysis of the women's funding movement also is provided.

HISTORY AS PROLOGUE:
The Women's Funding Movement

CAROL MOLLNER AND MARIE C. WILSON

- Can we be activists and fund controversial projects without losing our funding base?
- Can we develop a common language around diversity and inclusion?
- Should we focus on annual gifts, endowments, or workplace fundraising?
- Can we influence other funders to increase grantmaking for women and girls?
- How do we educate ourselves—and others—about how our issues are shaped by our race or class? Our age, sexual orientation, or physical abilities?
- Who are our allies? How do we tell our stories? How can we stay connected?

In April 1985, an eclectic group of women gathered outside Washington, D.C., to grapple with these and other questions at the first conference of women's funds ever to take place. Over seventy women from twenty funds in the United States, joined by funds in the Netherlands and France and some individual women donors, came together at that groundbreaking event to share experiences, learn new strategies, and explore creation of a new association of women's funds. The conference marked the beginning of a powerful new movement that would change, literally, the face of philanthropy and provide critical financial resources for women and girls all over the world.

The women's funding movement had roots in both the women's and civil rights movement. The women's movement of the 1970s had made women more aware of the need to take control of their resources, whether a weekly paycheck, family budget, trust fund, or inheritance. The organizers of the 1985 conference recognized the criticisms directed at the women's movement for being perceived as excluding working class women and women of color. They envisioned a women's funding movement that would take a giant step forward by embodying inclusiveness in all its operations.

In her keynote address, Dana Alston, first woman president of the National Black United Fund, looked out at the seventy women from funds around the world and declared it a "truly historic event. . . . To me, the message of what we're doing . . . is that women, like blacks and other minorities, are overcoming the limits that have been imposed by our society, limits that we've internalized and that have kept us from realizing our potential. And the message of women's funds is that we have the strength within ourselves to help the many women who are struggling today because of poverty and discrimination and abuse."

Many of the attendees were seasoned in philanthropy. Yet they were dissatisfied with the general lack of attention to women's issues and the exclusion of the emerging women's funds because they were dubbed "special interest." They challenged the notion that organizations representing 52 percent of the world's population could be a special interest, particularly when their funding missions addressed the broad issues of economic justice, violence, environment, human rights, health, and education.

Daily sessions gave way to late-night discussions that focused on the issues that would consume the funds for years to come: the work on racism, classism, and board diversity, exploration of a range of effective fundraising strategies, discussion of what women's funds needed for the future, and how funds could continue to network with each other after the conference ended. Boundless optimism and a growing sense of power and possibility filled the rooms. Several women reported that their funds had received their first million-dollar contributions. Others had developed broad-based pools of women donors of all income levels. What we all shared was our passion for getting critical resources to change the conditions for women and girls in our communities.

We had our tensions—our ambivalence about money and having power, both particularly challenging within organizations whose core missions were about raising, giving, and managing money. We had our disagreements about values, purpose, and strategies. We struggled over how to find common language to discuss the impact of racism, classism, and homophobia. For many, the conference opened a new world.

Conference planners and participants struggled with how much the conference should focus on discussions about raising money and developing joint efforts (such as a national workplace federation) to strengthen the funds, versus how much to focus on diversity and inclusivity; that is, how to best reflect feminist values and create social change funds. Some saw these themes as a dichotomy, while others understood that working simultaneously on raising money and developing diverse and inclusive leadership signaled the commitment to social change that they were about.

While most of the women present shared the belief that combating oppression was integral to the women's and women's funding movements, they didn't really have models for how to proceed. But they vowed to succeed. One early organizer described the process as "struggling perfectly . . . trying every minute, every day . . . going back to the drawing board over and over . . . keeping on working till they get it right . . ."[1] Women's funds have not fully achieved this vision, but most are committed to continuing the work to become models of truly inclusive and powerful philanthropic organizations.

Participants at this early conference drew strength from building connections instead of working in isolation. They wanted to create a national network to facilitate communications, information-sharing, and problem-solving. At the end of the conference, they selected a steering committee with specific mandates: to plan a second conference, develop a purpose statement and criteria for membership in an association of women's funds, develop a diversity statement and guidelines for a representative structure, create a mechanism for ongoing communications among the funds and a clearinghouse for information, and provide leadership in and attention to diversity and the "isms."[2] That enthusiasm and purpose led to the formation of the National Network of Women's Funds (since renamed Women's Funding Network) and sparked the burgeoning growth of women's funds throughout the United States and other countries.

The Context for Building a Movement

The growth of women's funds occurred within a climate of severe government funding cutbacks, the feminization of poverty, an escalation in violence against women, and the documented lack of substantive amounts of philanthropic dollars going to women's and girls' programs, particularly those seeking to address sexism, racism, and homophobia and their effects on women's and girls' lives. To provide a steady and meaningful level of resources for these issues, women decided they had to do it themselves— taking bold steps to raise, contribute, and manage ambitious levels of financial resources.

The women who gathered outside Washington, D.C., weren't the first to raise or give money for issues important to women. For centuries, women of all classes held bake sales, contributed volunteer time, saved pennies,

EXPOSITION TO A CONFERENCE: HOW DID IT ALL START?

During the years of organizing around women and philanthropy, sexism was blatant within the philanthropy establishment. Early research and several episodes at the 1974 meeting of the Council on Foundations (CoF) had shocked activists. So one of them, Eleanor Peterson, then Executive Director of the Chicago-area Donors Forum, convened a "women only" meeting the following year at the CoF conference. It turned out to be a "standing room only" event.

This event led to an exploratory session by fifteen women focusing on women's roles in the philanthropic sector. In spite of differences of opinion, participants achieved consensus on the need to keep up the momentum, and to organize both a plenary session for the 1976 annual meeting of the CoF, as well as a pre-conference session on women. We established ourselves as the Planning Committee for Women in Foundations.

Congresswoman Martha Griffiths, lead speaker for the 1976 event, gave a detailed account of the numerous ways in which women and girls were being ignored and short-changed in the allocation of both public and private resources. Along with attorney Marilyn Levy, she made the case for funding women's programs and for the particular responsibility of women and men in private philanthropy to do so.

A new planning committee was endorsed, and another pre-conference session was planned for the 1977 CoF annual gathering. This committee, which included two men, began to develop the objectives, functions, and organizational structure for what was to become Women and Foundations/Corporate Philanthropy (WAF/CP), now Women and

charged for speeches, and organized other creative approaches to raise money for schools, hospitals, children's homes, settlement houses, anti-slavery and anti-war movements. A few groundbreaking women in the early twentieth century encouraged women of wealth to use their money to support the women's suffrage movement. But for the most part, women donors operated in isolation from each other, and there was little funding—by anyone—for women's and girls' issues. Many wealthy women gave in their husbands' names, and to their husbands' institutions.

In the 1970s, the second wave of feminism brought new money for women's concerns, as national women's organizations were formed and legislative successes grew. Government money was secured to help women with job training, workforce placement, child-care and transportation, college and continuing education. Later, due to effective organizing by women, the first battered women's shelters were opened and funding began to trickle out for domestic violence and sexual assault programs.

EXPOSITION TO A CONFERENCE (CONTINUED)

Philanthropy. One of our first research efforts focused on the filters that precluded women's professional advancement, perhaps the first formal research ever conducted on the "glass ceiling."

During its first year as a new corporation, WAF/CP relied heavily on volunteers. It committed to a set of goals—education and communication, networking, advocacy, and monitoring of the philanthropic sector. The two primary objectives were to increase the level of funding for women and girls, and to enhance the status of women as decision makers within private philanthropy.

In 1978, WAF/CP began researching and publishing important information about the real and woeful status of funding for women and girls, showing that the aggregate level of private philanthropic funding directed to females was 0.6 percent. We also developed regional networks. By 1979, seven regional groups had been convened from coast to coast.

WAF/CP built an increasing number of influential programs and publications, such as "Welcome to the Club—No Women Need Apply," first printed in 1981, which laid out unequivocally the discrimination against women in private clubs. By providing its fiscal agency, the Women's Funding Network was nourished into independence.

Those early years of WAF/CP were a learning experience for all of us. In spite of many challenges, we succeeded in making significant change. Yet, as is made abundantly clear from this book, our work is far from done and the challenges of social change continue.

Jing Lyman, Founding member, Women and Philanthropy

But by the mid-1980s, government priorities changed and funding dwindled. The women's organizations remained and women began to look to foundations and corporations for funding. What they found was a new trail to be blazed.

In the early 1970s, a small group of foundation program officers conducted a survey seeking to determine the amount of foundation giving for women and girls. The survey documented that only 0.6 percent of foundation giving—mere pennies—went to women, even though women were becoming the majority of foundation staff. This survey prompted the creation of Women and Foundations/Corporate Philanthropy in 1977 (renamed Women and Philanthropy in 1995) with a mission to increase philanthropic dollars for women and to support women working in the field of philanthropy. Program officers in a handful of foundations worked with supportive male colleagues to create funding initiatives for women. But the dollars were still a meager part of total foundation giving, and they went mostly to national organizations. Programs for women and girls at the state and local level still struggled along with little access to resources.

"Necessity is the Mother of Invention"

By 1980, a dozen women's funds had formed. The three oldest—the American Association of University Women Educational Foundation (1888), Zonta International Foundation (1919), and the Business and Professional Women's Foundation (1956)—drew on large membership bases to raise money for scholarships, research, and grants for women and girls.

The first of the new wave of public women's foundations was the Ms. Foundation for Women, founded in 1972. The founders of Ms. *Magazine* had such difficulty in raising money that they decided to donate the magazine's profits to a new grantmaking foundation. Not surprisingly, the challenges of supporting a progressive feminist magazine meant there was little profit to help the new foundation. Organizers soon began raising money from foundation and corporate grants and individual gifts from women and men.

Other early, new-wave women's funds illustrated the diversity of organizational structures, missions, and geographic scope. Astraea National Lesbian Action Foundation was founded in 1977 to advance the economic, political, educational, and cultural well being of lesbians. Astraea embraced a strong commitment to multicultural values and developed programs to benefit lesbians, gay men, and all women and girls nationally and eventually internationally. Women's Sports Foundation was started in 1974 by Billie Jean King to ensure equal access to participation and leadership opportunities in sports and fitness for women and girls. In 1975, Women's Way was founded when seven agencies in Philadelphia serving women and children banded together to form their own fundraising coalition. They were weary of dealing with an uncertain future, operating on a shoestring, and being barred from traditional funding sources because of their size, or because they were considered "controversial" for supporting issues like reproductive choice. A few private foundations, created by women of wealth to support women and girls, were also established by 1980. Sadly, several other women's funds started in the 1970s closed their doors, succumbing to challenges described later in this chapter.

The San Francisco–based Women's Foundation started in 1981 and quickly became a group to which other women turned for help in starting their own funds. Prompted in part by the many requests for information and assistance, representatives of the Women's Foundation circulated a background paper calling for a national conference of women's funds and the formation of an association of women's funds. They met with other women's funds during a joint conference of the National Black United Fund and the National Committee for Responsive Philanthropy, and out of this discussion, the organizing for the 1985 conference was initiated.

Women of wealth throughout the country were also beginning to step into the public spotlight to put their dollars to work for women's issues. Some created private women's foundations. Others worked on the start-up of public women's funds. Some worked around the country to organize EMILY's List ("Early Money Is Like Yeast"—it makes the dough rise), which channels money to pro-choice women running for political office. EMILY's List is among the largest political action committees in America. These women of wealth continued in the best tradition of fin de siècle women donors ("Lady Bountifuls"). But they also stepped into the public world and began to connect to the issues all women face—safety, health, economic discrimination, racism, and so on. By joining a movement of women giving to women, women of means began thinking about their own lives and values. They recognized that this movement benefited them, and that they in turn could be an important part of a broad-based movement for social change.

Growth of Women's Funds

By the time of the 1985 conference, about thirty-five women's funds were in some stage of development. Among them were the first women's funds established in community foundations, joining public and private foundations and federations as another organizational model for women's funds. One of these was the Minnesota Women's Fund (now the Women's Foundation of Minnesota), the first statewide women's fund and the first to set out to raise a multi-million dollar endowment.

Following the 1985 conference, women's funds grew at a rapid rate. Many would flourish, and some would never gain momentum, eventually going out of business. In the last half of the 1980s, inspired by the excitement and growing visibility of the movement, another twenty-five women's funds were created. Start-ups of women's funds continued at a rapid pace throughout the 1990s. During this decade, about sixty-five new women's funds were formed. At least thirty more funds quietly explored start-up. Some were private foundations, quickly beginning to make grants; others were public funds that are still in the exploratory stage.

The growth in the number of women's funds prompted many women to point with enthusiasm to the growing spread of the movement, while others questioned whether duplication of geographic funding areas was good or bad, and whether there were enough resources to sustain all of these funds. For women's organizations seeing the funds as a potential new source of support, and for communities without a women's fund, the expansion looked like a wonderful thing. But for other women working in organizations struggling to find funding, and for women in funds already operating in the areas in which new funds were forming, the expansion raised concerns about whether there were sufficient dollars and donors to support all of these organizations.

Many of these early fears have been alleviated, as women's funds have demonstrated their ability to expand the pool of donors giving to women's concerns. The funds nurture and cultivate new donors. They educate foundations and corporations either to give more to women's programs directly, or to make a grant to the women's fund and thus use the fund as an effective intermediary to get dollars to grassroots groups.

The late 1980s and the 1990s saw the rise of an exciting new aspect of the movement: the expansion of international women's funding. The Global Fund for Women, based in California, and Match International, based in Ottawa, Ontario, began funding grassroots women's groups around the world. Astraea began an international funding program. New women's foundations were started in Canada, Mexico, Nepal, Guyana, and other places around the globe. Women from these funds reported exciting stories about innovative work to change conditions for women in their countries. They challenged and inspired women from the U.S.-based funds with their courage in taking on the power structures and the controversial issues—such as supporting reproductive choice for women—that some in the United States were reluctant to touch.

Some funds participated in the United Nations' Fourth World Conference on Women in 1995 and the concurrent International Nongovernmental (NGO) Forum on Women, helping to develop a far-reaching Platform for Action and strengthening links among women worldwide. Funds that couldn't go to the meeting engaged in local discussions about building international connections and strengthening a global women's movement. They explored issues such as child labor and low wages for women in developing countries, and how to organize against U.S. companies profiting from such practices.

Along with the growth in the number of women's funds came growth in dollars for the movement, as existing women's funds strengthened and diversified their fundraising strategies and more funds were formed. In 1985, fourteen public women's funds reported raising $4.7 million and five years later, thirty-seven funds reported raising $11.8 million. In 1998, fifty-eight women's funds raised $45.1 million, illustrating growth of the movement as a whole.[3]

The money raised was channeled into grants and allocations, program support and building endowments. Increases in annual grantmaking by women's funds paralleled the increases in fundraising. In 1985, of the fourteen funds that reported raising money, only eleven were making grants or allocations, together awarding $1.2 million that year. By 1990, thirty-three funds reported giving over $4.9 million in grants and allocations. That figure grew to over $14.7 million by fifty women's funds in 1998.[4]

These dollars are targeted to organizations and projects working for equity for women and girls. Often, women's funds provide the first funding these organizations get—helping important work get started and eventually secure other financial support. Dollars from women's funds are being directed to end violence against women and girls, and to foster economic justice, small business development, health and reproductive rights, civil rights and social justice, leadership and empowerment, arts and cultural expression, and general advocacy and services. Some funds focus grantmaking on efforts to challenge and change the power structures of society, while other funds are more comfortable funding traditional service programs. These programs benefit women and girls in all parts of the globe. And they do more—they are changing all of society, making our communities better places for everyone to live.

Women's funds demonstrate exciting new models for grantmaking, supporting strategies for change created and led by women who have experienced the challenges, who understand the issues, and who recognize promising approaches. A handful of other progressive foundations utilize similar grantmaking processes. Yet women's funds have developed this model even further, bringing new voices to philanthropic decision making by engaging people diverse in race, class, sexual orientation, disability, age, and experience. Grassroots activists, low- and middle-income women, women of inherited and earned wealth work together to create new ways of addressing community needs.

Addressing the 1995 women's funds conference, "Social Change and the Women's Funding Movement," Chandra Budhu, past board member of the Canadian Women's Foundation and Women's Funding Network, described the value of bringing people together to create change: "Gender is not enough. Race alone won't do it. None of the other ways we look at diversity is enough alone. It is the intersection of them that gives us the clarity to look at our world and find solutions."

Women's funds combine innovative grantmaking with strategic program work. Ideas generated in one fund become the seed that blossoms in many communities. The Minnesota Women's Fund collaborated with the University of Minnesota on research about girls. The Ms. Foundation took that research and Carol Gilligan's work to create Take Our Daughters to Work, which has become one of the largest public education projects in the country. Young Women for Change, a program of the Michigan Women's Foundation, made a grant to the nonprofit group Communities for Equity that sued the Michigan High School Athletic Association over Title IX discrimination and won in federal district court in 2002. Many women's funds launched innovative girls' grantmaking programs, and several independent girls' funds were created. In these funds, girls serve on boards, grantmaking, and fundraising committees. The funds are developing a new generation of strong and confident young women, challenging and changing societal stereotypes that keep girls from reaching their full potential.

Overcoming Internal and External Challenges

Early organizers faced daunting internal and external challenges in creating women's funds that would survive and thrive. Essentially, they had to become entrepreneurs in adapting models and devising new strategies to create successful funding institutions. The task was never easy and about a quarter of the funds failed. But the challenges presented opportunities too, and those who met the challenges thrived, building new resources for women and girls, changing roles for women, changing the field of philanthropy, and changing communities.

Externally, the funds faced hostility and resistance, both to the idea of raising money for women's concerns that were marginalized by society in general, and to the idea of creating specific funds by and for women, which were dismissed as having a "single issue" focus. While some foundations and individuals were highly supportive, these views were strong in the foundation and corporate community, where some described women's funds as ineffective "do-gooders" and others as "too radical." One seasoned fundraiser noted that raising money for the women's fund was the hardest fundraising she had ever done. She was struck by the different standards used for evaluating requests from the women's funds, compared to how requests from other organizations were evaluated. Women's funds had to be smarter and more persistent with fundraising, using tried and true methods as well as developing creative new ones.

Many women had to educate themselves to stop asking for small gifts. They had to build confidence in asking donors to give large gifts consistent with the importance of the work they were seeking to finance. Even women with substantial resources often were uncomfortable giving large gifts, particularly to women's organizations. Women's funds set about educating women about giving, encouraging them to use their power to create change through philanthropy. They sought to go beyond the traditional view of who is a philanthropist. They worked to educate women of all economic levels about the difference that they could make through their giving, to develop a regular habit of giving, to stretch their level of giving, and to give to what matters most.

Women's funds created new models, such as donor circles and collaboratives, to leverage both learning and resources. In these funding circles, a group of donors come together out of concern about an issue. They pledge money for a pooled grantmaking fund and study the issue to determine how to have impact through their grants. Many of the donors continue their own funding and involvement on the issue afterward.

Funds reached out to girls with financial and donor education programs too. The Women's Fund of the Milwaukee Foundation launched the "Little Women's Fund Program" designed to help girls develop the skills and resources to become long-term philanthropists. Donors make a permanent charitable gift in the girl's name. When the fund reaches maturity, half of annual net earnings go to the Women's Fund endowment and the young women use the other half to make donor-advised gifts. While the fund is maturing, girls aged five to seventeen participate in an educational program designed to increase awareness of community needs and issues and build advocacy skills.

Women were inspired to give by the examples of other women. Wealthy women traveled around the country to describe their own consciousness-raising and their commitment to making a difference through their giving for women and girls. Women of varied means provided inspiring examples. For instance, poor women in a Minnesota women's shelter pooled their meager resources to join in building a statewide endowment. They said that, alone, their contributions wouldn't look like much given the ambitious goal of the fund. So they collected contributions in a lemonade can, and together contributed $58 for the fund. Their model encouraged women to ask for bigger gifts and inspired other women—many with substantial resources—to stretch their own giving in the same spirit.

Internally, fundraising challenges were heightened due to tensions around class, women's ambivalence about having power, and conflicts about money—all magnified in funds striving to create inclusive organizations with money as a central focus. Some funds didn't grow because they didn't have clear or ambitious fundraising goals. Others had big goals but lacked effective fundraising strategies. Some were too timid—asking for "small gifts" when it was big dollars they wanted. There were conflicts about donor source—some were uncomfortable asking individuals for money, focusing almost solely on foundations and corporations. Some viewed wealthy people as the only appropriate donors and fundraisers. Others believed that women of more modest means could be effective fundraisers and important donors. And some made distinctions about "good" money and "bad" money—to them, good money came from people with modest means, while money contributed by wealthy individuals was less valued.

Such conflicts derailed effective fundraising, causing some funds to close. Most, however, were able to work through these issues, creating successful fundraising models and building a growing cadre of effective women fundraisers and philanthropists, evident in the growing assets of women's funds. Many of these women also took what they learned and put it to use by helping other organizations raise needed resources.

Values intersected with fundraising on several critical issues. Many funds joined in the ongoing debate about what was "clean" money: Could they ever take money from tobacco companies? From *Playboy*? Was any money really "clean" if traced to its roots? Were compromises justified, if the money was going to important work benefiting poor women and others needing assistance? Many developed internal policies to avoid money that came directly through women's exploitation—such as the pornography industry—but otherwise were willing to accept money from a broad array of sources.

While most funds were forthright in making reproductive rights a part of their values, others were fearful about the impact on fundraising. What would they do with women who were anti-choice? Would pro-choice statements limit their ability to raise money? Conversely, should they take money from women who put restrictions on use of the gift for pro-choice work? Most funds affirmed their pro-choice values and many developed guidelines for fundraising; they were willing to accept money directed toward specific purposes, but not money that prohibited women's options.

Long before diversity became a topic in philanthropic circles, women's funds made the commitment to create a different model. The first conference of women's funds set out a framework of values around diversity and inclusiveness. From their founding, most women's funds sought to put these values into practice. The work was never easy. Internal tensions around race, class, sexual orientation, disability, age, and other issues continue, as women's funds work to achieve a vision of becoming truly inclusive, multicultural organizations, while not really sure what such an organization would look like, how it operates, or how to realize its vision. It is a work in progress. Many point to the leadership of women's funds—most executive directors are white—as a sign that there is still a long way to go. While boards and staff are increasingly diverse, top leadership in most women's funds still reflects mainstream philanthropy.

Some funds have debated whether to have women who are openly lesbian on their board, staff, or in their funding priorities, again fearing an impact on fundraising. Others argue that denying acknowledgment or participation by lesbians—or refusing to fund lesbian organizations—is counter to the core mission and values of women's funds. They argue that if you looked at the founding leadership of the women's funding movement, lesbians have been at the forefront. After one fund said that it would never make a grant to a lesbian project, lesbians met at the annual women's funds conference and decided to take a stand. They stood up so that their sisters would know they were talking about a great many women in the room. Some straight sisters stood with them in a sign of solidarity and support. They believed that denying a part of the core constituency was not only counter to the values of women's funds, and would send a message that women's funds weren't really different from many existing institutions. Although most funds affirm these values, lesbians today still do not feel fully welcome in all women's funds.

Women's funds face other internal challenges, many heightened by the fact that their core work is about raising, managing, and dispersing money. Some struggle to set a common agenda and to set aside the individual agendas of each of the founding parties. Measuring success is a challenge—how much should success be defined by grantmaking, convening, fundraising, changing community attitudes, or other accomplishments? Defining effective board and staff roles and developing real partnerships were often troublesome. Many women's funds lost early board and staff leaders, who dropped out feeling under-appreciated, unrecognized, underpaid, overworked, and burned out.

Resolving power and control issues among women of diverse class backgrounds was critical to positive development of women's funds. In some funds, the grantmaking and fundraising programs operated in almost total isolation with little trust among the people involved. Some viewed fundraising as the most important work of the fund because it brought in the money to do everything else. Others looked on grantmaking as the most important work, with fundraising the dirty work necessary to support these programs. Investing appropriately in both fundraising and grantmaking, and recognizing the equal values of these and other parts of the funds' work, was critical.

Addressing the 1990 conference of women's funds, writer Judy Remington observed that many women's organizations deal with women's power, victimization, empowerment, and equality by "running with the brakes on." Uncomfortable with power, they hold leaders back, instead of having them go forward, held accountable to bring others along. Remington challenged women's funds—and other women's organizations—to examine the meanings, limitations, advantages, and ramifications of their principles as the first step in transforming their organizations and propelling them into positions of social leadership, influence, power, and success.[5]

That work has been an ongoing part of the women's fund experience—frustrating to some, exciting to many, and hopeful for the future of the women's movement and society at large.

The Legacy of Three Decades

Women's funds have entered a new millennium with an impressive legacy built upon the seeds planted at that first conference.

- *Sustaining a movement.* Women's funds demonstrated creativity and entrepreneurship in building a new base of financial support for long-term work for social change. Women raised more money than ever before—money channeled to sustain critical women's and girls' issues and movements that had the least access to resources.

- *New donors.* Women of diverse backgrounds learned to be bold and strategic donors, effective fundraisers, and powerful social change agents. Women's funds identified women of means who were already giving money, cultivated new donors, and linked these women to each other and to a movement of progressive change.

- *Innovative fundraising.* Women's funds developed new mechanisms—such as funding circles and collaboratives—for raising and giving money.

- *New institutional models.* The funds created new institutional models for philanthropy, with diversity on boards and staffs, and closer partnerships among grantseekers, grantees, and funders. They broke down a big wall that had existed in philanthropy, by demonstrating that grantmaking will be much wiser when people most affected by issues take part in creating solutions.

- *Educating communities.* Women's funds raised feminist issues in the broader community, advanced gender-specific funding strategies, and demonstrated the importance of direct local funding, laying the groundwork for how many large foundations now do their funding.

- *Leveraging resources.* In addition to the dollars they raised directly, women's funds encouraged other funders to increase their giving to women's organizations.

- *Fostering new leadership.* The funds developed leadership among women and girls. Women from the funds have moved into leadership positions in other foundations, businesses, nonprofits, politics, and a host of arenas.

- *Building connections.* Women's funds helped to strengthen the connections among women around the world working to create a more just and equitable global society.

Through what they support and how they operate, women's funds are creating important shifts. Funding work to challenge the power structures of society at large is an investment in building a better future. Engaging women of diverse class backgrounds in raising and managing money is proving transformative as women of diverse backgrounds convene to accomplish a common vision. Self-determination evidenced in women's funds' grant-making processes is a powerful model for the philanthropic field.

For all their differences, women's funds have built a much-needed new base of financial support for women and girls. They have fueled a discourse around money, feminism, self-determination, diversity, inclusiveness, and the interconnectedness of oppressions. That discourse is helping to shape new institutional cultures and new ways of changing societal structures. An early Women's Funding Network report describes the values that underpin the women's funding movement: empowerment and self-determination, leadership by women of diverse backgrounds, connections and collaboration, creativity and resourcefulness, a vision and passion for justice, a belief in the value of democratizing and diversifying philanthropy, and the desire to use our resources boldly to make philanthropy a tool for progressive social change.[6] Many women in the funds continue to work toward their vision of social change—"struggling perfectly . . . trying every minute, every day . . . till they get it right . . ."

Barbara Ehrenreich, speaking at the women's funds 1997 conference, called on women to work with renewed intensity and vision. "Our first goal is of course equality—for women, and among women in all our glorious diversity. What we've learned is that this goal will not achieve itself through some inevitable process of human progress. The forces of misogyny and racism are organized and ascendant right now—and will be overcome only by pushing and organizing and struggling as if our lives, and our dignity, were at stake—which they are."

Women's funds will continue to work with passion, boldness, and vision—because they must. It is inherent in their collective spirit, and they know that there is simply no other way to move forward.

ACKNOWLEDGMENT

Grateful acknowledgement is made to Helen French for her assistance with this chapter.

NOTES

1. Christina H. Joh, "Diversity in Feminist Organizations: A Case Study of the Women's Funding Network's Commitment" (master's thesis, Hubert H. Humphrey Institute of Public Affairs at the University of Minnesota, 1997).

2. First Women's Funds Conference, 1984, 1985 (unpublished background papers).

3. Women's Funding Network, http://www.wfnet.org, "Facts about Women's Funds, 1998 Financials."

4. Ibid.

5. Judy Remington, "Running with the Brakes On" (unpublished address to the National Network of Women's Funds Conference, 1990).

6. National Network of Women's Funds, "Changing the Face of Philanthropy, 1985–1992."

7. Joh, "Diversity in Feminist Organizations."

DOCUMENTING WOMEN'S GIVING
Biases, Barriers, and Benefits

MARY ELLEN S. CAPEK

We've heard the stereotypes, maybe muttered a few ourselves: "Women don't know how to manage money." "Women don't trust they'll have enough for their old age." "Women only get involved in organizations they care about." "Women don't give large donations." "Women give less than men." "Women give more than men." "Women really care about causes they support, men just give for status." "Women have a hard time asking for money."

We can all add to the list. But what's beyond the stereotypes, and what does research tell us about women as donors? Not much. Few sources of reliable data accurately document patterns of women's donating behavior or account for giving differences between women and men. Indeed, much of what has been published in the last decade—research as well as journalism—misinterprets the scant survey data available, recycles stereotypes, and generalizes inappropriately from anecdotes and case studies.

Given so little available data, distortions might be understandable in popular press accounts: stereotypes of sex and wealth sell papers. But distortions also show up in professional publications like *The Chronicle of Philanthropy*, which several years ago reported in a front page article: "Cultivating Philanthropy by Women: Female donors now have the means, but they're still not as willing as men to part with their money." The real surprise is not that reporters and researchers are raising questions about gender differences in money management or philanthropy, but that so much information is *premised* on unproven and seldom-challenged gender-linked stereotypes.

Common sense suggests that before giving patterns are attributed to gender differences, other personal information that influences individual giving be accounted for: amount of disposable income and savings, age, health, number of dependents, other financial responsibilities for family and friends, pension, control of financial planning and investments, and "age" of wealth ("new" money or "old"). Also important: personal connections to the institutions or projects that people are asked to support, what specifically they are asked to give to, how they are asked, for how much, by whom, and if in fact they *are* asked.

Survey Data

One of the most frequently recycled stereotypes comes from people misconstruing data made available by Independent Sector. Earlier editions of their *Giving and Volunteering* study, which had been a door-to-door national survey of 4,000 people conducted by the Gallup Organization, was cited frequently to prove that married women gave less than their spouses.[1] As several experts note, however, "the most definitive thing one can say about the results is that women [who answer the door] say their households give a little less than men [who answer the door] say [their households give]."[2] Under the best circumstances, data about personal giving is difficult to collect by door-to-door polls. And married households often experience "the grocery problem": how to keep track of "your groceries, my groceries, and our groceries" when the buying, cooking, and eating is shared.[3] In married households as in any multiple-person household, giving decisions can be individual, joint, or assumed joint, with one giving for both or others without the other(s) knowing. And under the best circumstances, people forget or guess or exaggerate to look good.

The results of door-to-door strategies are open to different interpretations. Do married men give more, or do they "exaggerate household-giving levels"? Do married men give less, or do "married women give less and assume their husbands give the way they do?"[4] The point is that none of these interpretations can be determined conclusively from available data. The results are opinions, not linked to records of the actual dollars contributed. For the 2001 edition of *Giving and Volunteering,* Independent Sector switched from door-to-door surveys to a phone survey and stopped reporting the results from female and male respondents for a household as "female" or "male" giving.[5] But ambiguous analyses from earlier versions and giving stereotypes still persist. The reality is that almost no significant gender differences emerge in these surveys: The 2001 survey, for example, shows only very slight differences in women's and men's giving: 88.4 percent of households with women responding show average contributions as

3.2 percent of household income, compared to 87.8 percent of households with men responding, with contributions averaging 3.1 percent of household income.[6]

When researchers at Boston College's Social Welfare Research Institute (SWRI) did in-depth tracking of household giving in a year-long 1997 diary study of a sample of Boston households—a methodology more likely to yield accurate reporting—they found women giving more: "Women respondents report more [giving] for themselves and their husbands than men respondents report for themselves and their wives."[7] When Gallup went into the field to conduct their next year's *Giving and Volunteering* survey, the Institute asked Gallup to re-interview its diary sample and found that numbers cited by women respondents were even higher and numbers from men respondents even lower than the totals recorded in the weekly diary reports.

In non-married households, giving patterns show few differences between men and women. If anything, single women seem to give more often and give a higher percentage of their income than do men, but even these patterns seem to be leveling out.[8] The point is that none of the existing data prove conclusively that women give more—or that women give less. Based on the available survey data, gender is not a reliable predictor of philanthropic behavior; nor does it account for significant differences among givers.

Although the *Giving and Volunteering* data do show giving differences among white, black, and "nonwhite/nonblack" women, the available tables do not refine these numbers by marital status or income level—or by marital status, income level, and gender for racial/ethnic groups. Additional runs of the data yield samples that are too small for statistically reliable analyses. A 1987 survey of black women's philanthropy reveals few overall differences between white and black women, but the data show black women giving more frequently in the middle range of income levels than white women. [9]

Another difference in *Giving and Volunteering* data that *is* worth noting documents that blacks and Hispanics "are not asked to give at the same rate as the rest of the population." Furthermore, "findings clearly show that . . . these groups are even more likely to give when asked than other groups in the population."[10] This observation is confirmed by a number of the people of color interviewed for this chapter. One Hispanic organizational leader notes that many Hispanic donors, women and men, mistrust "organized" philanthropy, particularly community foundations, because, as she quotes one Hispanic woman of wealth, "they don't know me nor do they take the time to ask."

Stereotypes

Even though research problems and misinterpretations have been documented widely for a number of years, researchers and those who write about philanthropy still generalize from little reliable data. One scholar, for example, points to different incentives that inspire men and women to give, claiming male donors are attracted by the prospect of visibility while female donors shun the limelight, giving their largest gifts anonymously.

This kind of assertion reveals several lapses of logic. Obviously, if gifts are anonymous, it isn't known that more women than men give anonymously. Nor is it known why they give anonymously when they do. While anecdotal evidence exists that suggests some women do shun the limelight, others clearly do not. Indeed, like many of their wealthy male counterparts, they relish having their names on buildings or endowed chairs. At least thirty-seven gifts of ten million dollars or more listed in *Giving USA 2004*, for example, are attributed to eighteen individual women (although only one to a women's organization, Daughters of Hawaii, and none to women's colleges).[11]

Experienced practitioners who raise large donations from both men and women point out that people who made their money themselves (women as well as men) will be more likely to use their money for recognition and status. Visibility in giving or shying away from the limelight are more likely class-based attributes in giving, functions of the "age" of the giver's money, and the reasons for the gift, not functions of gender per se.

When studies do control and account for even some of the facts or variables cited earlier (e.g., age, income level, number of dependents, religion, home ownership, and associational patterns), differences between women's and men's giving behavior appear to lessen. When studies do not control for the complex range of giving variables, results are circular and generate superficial conclusions that merely reinforce the stereotypes used to lay out the hypotheses of the study. One example—which summarizes selective consumer research on gender, money management styles, and attitudes toward money—finds that males are "more prone to feel involved and competent in money handling, and take risks to amass wealth. Females have a greater sense of envy and deprivation with respect to money . . ." Only in his conclusion does the author note that his research carried "certain limitations": "There is overlap in money attitude profiles of males and females . . . [and] the small samples used . . . precluded the introduction of important demographic and psychographic variables to control, test and improve further the predictions obtained."[12] Without such variables, his conclusions are essentially useless. Worse, they perpetuate simplistic stereotypes about women, men, and money. Where the analyses of giving data include such refinements as tracking donations over time and regression analyses that account for more variables, there is a "lack of statistically significant difference between gift-giving women and men"—in this case, in a study of male and female alumni contributions to a large public university over a fifteen-year period.[13]

If anything, women may prove to be more generous than men. Although previous laboratory tests for differences in men's and women's economic behavior have generated mixed results, double-blind experiments conducted by a team of economists funded by the National Science Foundation indicated that "women, on average, donate twice as much as men . . . when any factors that might confound cooperation are eliminated."[14] But lacking more reliable research that takes into account the broad range of factors that affect giving, the jury is still out.[15]

Estate Bequests

Estate tax returns, which as of 2002 must be filed for estates with gross assets of $1,000,000 or more, are the only available data source for tracking individual differences in charitable behavior by gender. The 2001 IRS data in *Giving and Volunteering 2004* reported less than 18 percent of estate tax returns listing charitable deductions. With few exceptions, using estate tax data to document gender differences in giving, however, is notoriously unreliable because of the "widow effect": women live longer than men.[16] Women's bequests may reflect their husbands' wishes as much as their own. There is no way of knowing more from the data. One study projecting wealth estimates from estate tax data excludes locked trusts from the analyses (trusts that do not allow the inheritor any flexibility in disposing of assets).[17] Even assuming widows in these data do have some control, however, there is still no way of knowing if they are following their husbands' or husbands' advisers' advice rather than their own inclinations about distribution of assets. These caveats obviously will lessen as more women with their own earned wealth manage their own money and leave their own bequests, but there are at present no ways for determining women's "exclusive" donative behavior from the data available.

Where the Money Goes

Gender patterns in bequests are interesting. *Giving USA 2003* cites 1998 data that found that married men and women were about equally likely upon their deaths to leave charitable bequests (5.9 percent of women, 6.7 percent of men). Widows and widowers were also comparable: 23 percent

Table 1. Bequests by Women and Men, 1998–2000 IRS Estate Tax Data
(Percentage of Estate Tax Returns that Included a Charitable Bequest for a Subsector)

	Women	Men
Religious organizations	13.1%	7.3%
Health	7.4%	3.5%
Education	7.0%	5.1%
Other	6.8%	4.1%
Human services	5.9%	3.0%
Philanthropy/volunteerism	2.2%	1.3%
Arts, culture, and humanities	2.0%	0.8%

of widows left charitable bequests as did 23.2 percent of widowers). Single women, however, as well as separated or divorced women, were far more likely than their male counterparts to leave a charitable bequest: 44.4 percent of single women compared to 32.4 percent of single men and 28.3 percent of separated or divorced women compared to 15.1 percent of separated or divorced men. Women also left almost twice as much to religious organizations as men did. Table 1 lists bequests in order of priority.[18]

So Why Do People Give?

What is known about motivations for giving in general? And what makes people keep on giving and even increase their support for the same organizations or projects?

Motivation is one of the messiest attributes to measure because the data are often self-reported and subject to some of the same caveats noted earlier about the survey data: women and men both want to look good. They may not acknowledge self-interest. They may not know why they give other than to "do good." They may be moved momentarily by an emotional direct-mail appeal yet not convinced to keep on giving when the organization tries to convert that emotional responder to a sustaining contributor.

Are there gender differences in this range of motives? Here too the literature abounds with stereotypes. Of the research reviewed, some of the most fact-based assessments come from sociologists Paul Schervish and Susan Ostrander.[19] Schervish paints the big picture: "What motivates the wealthy is very much what motivates someone at any point along the economic spectrum . . . from heartfelt empathy to self-promotion, from religious obligation to business networking, from passion to prestige, from political philosophy to tax incentives."[20]

Schervish formulates what he calls an "identification model of charitable giving" or "consumption philanthropy." He hypothesizes that "the level of contributions depends on the frequency and intensity of participation, volunteering, being asked to contribute."[21] Charitable giving derives from "forging an associational and psychological connection between donors and recipients.[22] The key to philanthropy, as Schervish describes it, is "not the absence of self . . . but the presence of self-identification with others. . . . Donors contribute the bulk of their charitable dollars to causes from whose services the donors directly benefit." Hence the greatest portion of giving and volunteering takes place locally.[23]

This version of "consumption philanthropy" among the wealthy— donors giving to schools, health facilities, arts organizations, and churches that meet their and their families' needs—has been analyzed by others as reinforcing class status and privilege, especially by women donors who have inherited or married into their wealth, not earned it themselves.[24] But while not discounting the force of this class-based identification, Schervish suggests a strategy for building on it because it is there that "identification between donor and recipient is strongest": "The basis for higher giving and volunteering is in large part a function of the mix and intensity of the network of formal and informal associations both within and beyond one's local community."[25]

The "Capital" behind Giving

More research needs to be done on differences between younger and older donors of wealth. But based on available data, young donors' experience fits the patterns that Paul Schervish and others have formulated. More than differences in levels of income and wealth ("financial capital") or intrinsic generosity ("moral capital") or even religion, age, gender, and race, what matters most in predicting and describing people's philanthropic behavior—according to Schervish—is people's "associational capital," their networks and felt connections and the persuasive invitations they receive to give to institutions to which they feel connected. As one young donor noted, "it's about a personal connection."

Schervish's analyses, based on interviews with both women and men of wealth, echo many of the observations growing out of a set of 1992 focus groups of women donors conducted by the University of California, Los Angeles Development Office.[26] The women in the UCLA focus groups sound much like the women and men Schervish interviewed. The point is that dimensions that the UCLA focus groups attribute to women's special gender concerns—personal involvement, wanting to make a difference, recognition, wanting to see the results of giving, feeling responsible for giving—are as true of many men as they are of many women.

Unfortunately, no focus groups were conducted for a matched sample of UCLA male donors. As I hope this chapter makes clear, analyses of gender differences must account for other variables. In the UCLA analysis, for example, important but unstated variables are implicit in the development office's not taking women seriously. To repeat the cliché, they "just didn't get it." Women were not asked. If they were asked, they were not asked to give to a project or program they connected with. And if they did give, they were not credited for the gift in their own names. The women's thoughtful responses in the UCLA focus groups and in support groups that followed, therefore, do not reflect gender differences in giving so much as gendered "norms" at work in bad fundraising practices.

"Associational capital," a term that explains the results of the UCLA focus groups as well as those in Schervish's study, is a useful concept. While appealing to common sense, it also helps to account for patterns of giving reported among ethnic and racially distinct communities. A 1997 study of midwestern African American philanthropy by Cheryl Hall-Russell and Robert Kasberg documents the importance of broadening our definitions of philanthropy.[27] Other researchers and practitioners who are part of or work with communities of color also point to the diverse forms of giving that get left out of analyses of philanthropic behavior for both women and men, white and of color: taking financial responsibility for other family members and neighbors; providing loans to family members or community people in need, or for "self-help" business start-ups; feeding, caring for, and otherwise providing emotional support, including time spent talking to or tending sick, elderly, or distressed family members, friends, and neighbors— sometimes taking in or raising other family members' or neighbors' children as their own.

When analysis of the Boston diary study attempted to quantify these expanded definitions of giving, the authors found that, intentionally or unintentionally, participants actually tithed (the Middle English term for "tenth"), contributing an average of 10 percent pre-tax family income per family in the study. This amount is significantly higher than other philanthropic survey assessments, the most recent of which pegged individuals' average giving at 2.2 percent of income.[28] Not only did diary participants make outright gifts of cash, they "extended an average of eleven loans per participant . . . and praised, congratulated, or similarly encouraged other people, on average, more than 460 times per participant during the course of the year."[29] Such expanded definitions of philanthropic behavior are also helpful in analyzing the depths of people's motivations for giving.

Susan Wiedman Schneider, another researcher, notes "it's a truism of fundraising that a woman will first get involved with a project and then give money."[30] This attribute also can be labeled a "truism" for most philanthropy. Citing Schneider, researchers Susan Ostrander and Joan Fisher argue that "what seems to us most important . . . is *not* whether individual women or men in fact exhibit . . . consistent and established gender differences. . . . What is important, rather, is that a number of practitioners—mostly women and some men—are actively engaged in re-making and re-organizing how philanthropy has been conceptualized and practiced."[31]

Women's Resources

Before women's potential as philanthropists can be better understood, analyses need to account for stumbling blocks that women donors experience. But first it is important to provide basic background data about women's resources, what they have and what they do not have.

Income

Inequities still abound. Median income for men aged fifteen and older who worked full-time, year-round in 2003 was $40,668, virtually the same median annual income they earned in 2002. Women with similar work experience saw their earnings decline 0.6 percent to $30,724, their first annual decline since 1995. As a result, women working full-time, year-round earned 76 cents for every dollar in 2003, down from 77 cents for every dollar in 2002.[32]

This seems to be a reversal of what had been a steadily narrowing gap when wages rose from 62 percent in 1979 to a high of 77 percent in 1993, although sampling or measurement error could account for the shift. A more detailed June 2004 Census Bureau report based on data collected in the 2000 Census for full-time workers in more than five hundred occupations shows men earning more than women in all twenty of the highest-paid occupations for both sexes as well as in all twenty of the lowest-paid. Overall, among full-time, year-round workers, women's median earnings were 74 percent of men's.[33]

The wage gap is worse for women of color. In 2000, black women's median weekly earnings were $429, only 64 percent of the earnings of white men, and in one year, the average black woman earned approximately $12,000 less than the average white man, adding up to $420,000 in a black woman's lost income over a thirty-five-year career. The median full-time earnings for Hispanic women in 2000 were $20,527, only 52 percent the median earnings of white men.

In general, women's average annual earnings benefit less from higher levels of education than men's annual earnings do, but even with this dis-

crepancy, more education does pay off, and as more women continue to increase their educational levels (women currently constitute the majority
of college graduates), their income will continue to increase—not as much
as men's incomes, most likely, but increase nonetheless.

The point here is that while women still have not reached pay equity
with men, indeed are slipping, the amount of women's income has in fact
increased significantly over the last several decades. In 2000, over 1.35
million women reported earning incomes of $500,000 or higher (41 percent
of the 3.3 million Americans reporting incomes of $500,000 or higher).[34]
The median weekly salary for women lawyers in 2003, for example, was
$1,413, which although still less than their male counterparts (87.3 per-
cent of what male lawyers earned), still represents some level of disposable
income available for charity.[35] While women and children still constitute
the majority of the poor in this country, women themselves are becoming
a source of increasingly sizable resources.

Women-Owned businesses

As of 2004, there were over 10.6 million businesses at least 50 percent
owned by women that generated an estimated $2.5 trillion in sales and
employed an estimated 19.1 million people. Between 1997 and 2004, the
growth rate of women-owned businesses was nearly twice that of all firms.[36]
And women of color are a significant part of this trend: A 2001 study released by the Center for Women's Business Research projected an estimated 1.2 million businesses owned by women of color in the United States
by 2002, employing more than 822,000 people and generating $100.6 bil-
lion in sales. Of this number, the Center estimated 470,344 Hispanic
women-owned firms, 365,110 African American women-owned firms,
358,503 Asian or Pacific Islander women-owned firms, and 77,483 Native
American or Alaska Native women-owned firms. Between 1997 and
2002, the number of these firms was estimated to grow by 39.3, 16.7, 44.6,
and 44.6 percent respectively.[37]

And women business owners are philanthropically active. According
to the Center for Women's Business Research, 70 percent volunteer at
least once a month, 31 percent contribute $5,000 or more to charity an-
nually, and 15 percent give $10,000 or more.[38]

Net worth

Just as stereotypes abound about women donors, information about women's
wealth or lack of it also suffers from stereotypes and distortions. Contrary
to popular assumptions, women, especially widows, do not control the ma-

jority of wealth in this country. At most, the data available document that top female wealth holders control about 40 percent of top wealth holdings. However, the good news is that women—married, never married, divorced or widowed, women across age groups, women of diverse racial and ethnic backgrounds and different education levels—do have assets and often higher net worth than is commonly assumed.

Similar to the constraints in assessing the *Giving and Volunteering* data, most existing national data sets used to measure wealth are compiled by interviewing "heads" of households, making it difficult to extrapolate resources belonging to individuals within the household. One survey conducted every five years by the University of Michigan's Institute for Social Research, the Panel Study of Income Dynamics (PSID), has worked to refine interview questions and coding to capture "who owns what" in married or partnered couples.[39] Most available data sets, however, deem the "head" in married-couple households to be male and in same-sex households the older person—and assume that assets within the household or "primary economic unit" are jointly held.[40] Except for persons living alone, most available data include estimates of all assets generated in households. The caveats noted earlier about a "widow" effect on estate bequest data also apply here. Even with individual data from widows living alone, no available national data sets track who in a married or partnered couple made the decisions that determined how a trust was set up or assets managed.

One of the few reliable analyses that computes individual-based wealth is a series of IRS studies that use an "estate multiplier technique" to project from Federal estate tax returns to a national sample.[41] Because these and other data sets are aggregated, designed to protect confidentiality, with the exception of popular compilations such as *Forbes* or *Fortune* "wealthiest" lists, no one can name with certainty all or even most of the women millionaires in the United States. (As of 2004, only sixteen women headed companies on the Fortune 1,000 list.) By relying on IRS projections, however, and by extrapolating data included in several large national data samples, analyses can piece together a picture of women's net worth.

In 1998, there were an estimated 6.5 million adults in the United States aged eighteen and older each with gross assets of $625,000 or more, holding an combined net worth of almost $10.2 trillion. Of these wealth holders, 61.2 percent were males, with combined net worth of almost $7 trillion (62.4 percent of the total top assent pool). Female top wealth holders in 1998 numbered more than 2.5 million, holding a combined net worth of $4.2 trillion, 60 percent of the wealth men held and slightly over 41 percent of all top wealth holders' net assets. Almost 1.1 million of top female wealth holders in 1998 were married, 28.5 percent widowed, 13.9 percent single, and 10.7 percent divorced, separated, or marital status not determined.

So what can be concluded from this overview of the numbers? The bad news is that women, even widows, still control significantly less net worth than men. The stress here, however, is not on gender disparities (although it is important that more original research and analyses of existing data be done to determine what these differences are). The emphasis here and in previous sections of this chapter is on the reality that women do have money, less than men but comparatively more than women had even just a few years ago.

The IRS data summarized in table 2 estimate that from 1992 to 1998, the number of top female wealth holders increased faster than the number of top male wealth holders—one-third more women than men in six years. And although women top wealth holders still own approximately 40 percent less wealth than top male wealth holders ($4.2 trillion compared to $7 trillion), the increase in top females' net worth also outstripped top male wealth holders' gain in net worth in six years, 133.3 percent compared to 118.8 percent in the same period.[42] So, women not only have money, their net worth is increasing.

Women also know how to give. And they give generously, especially considering their net worth relative to men's. To cite just a few examples: Wellesley's 1993 capital campaign raised $341 million in gifts, pledges, and in-kind contributions and broke records for per capita giving among all liberal arts colleges.[43] In 1997, Vassar completed the most successful fundraising campaign of its kind—also a record breaker—and a majority of the money came from women.[44] Women alumnae from a large public university were found to give as generously over a fifteen-year period as

Table 2. Increases in Male and Female Top Wealth Holders' Collective Net Worth from 1992 to 1998

	1992	1998	% gain
Total male wealth holders			
Number	2,402,056	3,997,000	66.4%
Net worth (trillions)	$3.2	$7.0	118.8%
Total female wealth holders			
Number	1,289,163	2,533,000	96.5%
Net worth (trillions)	$1.8	$4.2	133.3%

the university's male alumni.[45] In 2002, EMILY's List members contributed over $9.6 million to pro-choice Democratic women candidates, making EMILY's List the leading funder of congressional candidates.[46] As of 2003, EMILY's List had helped elect fifty-six Democratic congresswomen, eleven senators, and seven governors. Finally, to cite just one more example, which needs follow-up research, women may be the majority of donors to at least some local workplace giving campaigns.[47]

Women clearly give and give generously to many organizations. Yet the key question remains: Why is fundraising so difficult for so many women's organizations? For answers to this question, we turn from data to analyses of perceptions and trends synthesized from interviews.

Stumbling Blocks for Women Donors

Although no systematic research documents specific answers to the question of why fundraising is so difficult for so many women's organizations, interviews with key experts and a review of related research point to three basic dimensions to the problem: women donors' self-perceptions and attitudes; organizations' skills and constraints in raising money; and larger social, political, and economic forces that affect both.

Women Donors' Self-Perceptions and Attitudes

First, there is the problem of donors' perceptions of disposable resources. People in general tend to underestimate their levels of discretionary wealth and capacities for giving.[48] While responding to a question about reasons for not being more philanthropic, for example, 21 percent of very wealthy participants in a 1996 survey by Bankers Trust Private Banking acknowledged concern that they might need their money for themselves. Moreover, 48 percent cited "confidence that I will not need the money" as a factor that would increase giving. Interestingly, women generally attributed less importance to these and other reasons for not being more philanthropic than did men.[49]

It generally is agreed that women earn less on average and own less wealth than men. It is also known that some women, especially older women who have not earned their own incomes or generated their own wealth, have less experience managing their own money than men. Hence, they may well be less confident of their disposable resources. And given the length of time women have been in the work force in large numbers, and the persistent dearth of women at senior executive positions in large organizations, it is probably accurate to assume that many women do not have pension security comparable to same-aged males. Add to these facts other financial realities, such as women's often diminished financial well-being following divorce, and as the SCF and IRS numbers document, many women may understandably hesitate to trust their own disposable resources.

These concerns obviously will affect women's philanthropy for any giving they might undertake, not just their giving to women's organizations. But what about giving to women's organizations? The women donors listed in *Giving USA 2004* did not make their gifts of a million dollars or more to benefit women's organizations. Why not? As seen in the estate tax data, women bequeath the most to educational, medical, and scientific institutions. Could it be less threatening, less controversial to contribute to a college or university, even a women's college, than it is to contribute to a women's organization? And there is usually an alma mater connection: The college or university, if it has done its work, will have maintained strong, often sentimental ties to its alumnae and mobilized alumnae networks. For that reason, compared to free-standing women's organizations, women's centers or organizations affiliated with colleges or universities probably also have an edge in fundraising from alumnae.

This chapter argues, however, that major stumbling blocks for women giving to women's organizations are a consequence of lack of accurate information, on the one hand, and on the other, negative fallout from controversies that plague feminism and the women's movement—especially those controversies generated or inflamed by the media and public policy initiatives outlined below.

Paul Schervish notes that a "serious obstacle [for both men and women] is that potential major donors simply do not appreciate fully enough how effective charitable organizations are in generating valuable outcomes."[50] If people do give generously to organizations they connect to—organizations that tap their "associational capital" and "first-hand" connections— then clearly the challenge lies in strengthening women's (and men's) links to other women's organizations through information. Are women's college alumnae who give to their alma maters any more likely to give to a women's or girls' organization than other women? More likely to give than women alumnae from coeducational colleges or universities? These answers are not known. But all women have not embraced the goals or visions of the women's movement, and it cannot be assumed that women give to organizations just because they are women's organizations. In fact, there is clear evidence that they do not.

But there also is a constituency of women and men donors who do support the advancement of women and girls: feminists who grew up with the women's movement; women who themselves have experienced discrimination; and men and women whose daughters experience discrimination or who themselves have come to understand income and opportunity disparities as part of larger patterns of systemic discrimination that disproportionately affect poor women and children of color. And for those women and men who are not dissuaded from giving by financial uncertainty or fear of controversy, who might be more inclined to invest their "associational capital" in a women's organization—even one that does not provide one-stop shopping for planned-giving services—the question of effectiveness in fundraising rests with the organization.

Women's Organizations' Skill and Constraints in Raising the Money

In 1991, EMILY's List tapped these educated, activist donors in a remarkable convergence of events: the controversy surrounding Anita Hill's testimony at Clarence Thomas's Supreme Court nomination hearings and a pending spot already scheduled on the CBS news program 60 *Minutes* for EMILY's List. As an organization, they had experience—and start-up capital from founding donors and previously successful fundraising—to set up enough phone banks to handle the deluge of calls they expected from women who wanted to take some form of concrete action.

Another key to EMILY's List's success is targeting smaller-dollar donors who are given a list of potential candidates to support, often from donors' own districts. EMILY's List evokes the ideal combination of national passion with a local focus—and they also wisely set minimum threshold amounts (separate checks written for $100 each to at least two different candidates) in addition to the membership contribution to EMILY's List itself.

EMILY's List built their direct-mail lists from names of other women (and men) donors. Betsy Crone, development consultant and one of the group of women who helped found EMILY's List, points out the importance of sharing donors: "a donor is a donor is a donor." Which is to say, unlike "pie" thinking (you get a bigger piece, I get a smaller piece), Crone prefers "yeast" thinking. Not only "Early Money Is Like Yeast: it makes the dough rise" (the EMILY acronym), but people who give to five or more other organizations are the most likely to give to EMILY's List.[51] Considerable anecdotal evidence also suggests that sharing donors encourages donors to give more to more organizations and, conversely, that hoarding donors diminishes opportunities for both donors and organizations.

Other effective fundraising qualities are also apparent in EMILY's List's success. As development executive Karen Stone notes, EMILY's List "had clearly defined goals, a sense of community, and value-driven excitement that appealed to the marketplace."[52] Indeed, Crone thinks that much of the success of EMILY's List is a clear focus: She claims that she can describe the organization's purpose and goals in three crisp sentences. Getting more women elected to political office is an obvious need, readily documented. But even though the need has been documented for decades, funding did not begin to match that need until EMILY's List emerged.

So, if EMILY's List can do it, why is it so hard for other women's organizations to raise money? Different perspectives on this question emerge from conversations with researchers, fundraisers, foundation executives, and other practitioners. But a common denominator can be found in realities that need to be noted about women's organizations themselves: women's organizations are both diverse and innovative; budget constraints affect performance; and stages of development have an impact.

Women's organizations are diverse. Researchers can no more talk about all women's organizations than they can talk about all women. The 1992 *Directory of National Women's Organizations* published by the National Council for Research on Women lists 478 national women's organizations alone, not counting any local, regional, or state chapters.[53] The 1997 *Encyclopedia of Associations* lists almost three thousand regional, local, and state-based women's and girls' organizations and chapters across the country and over two thousand international organizations.[54]

In the research informing this chapter, analysis was limited to U.S. women's organizations whose mission is the support and empowerment of women and girls—organizations, in short, that name the problems of women's and girls' well-documented needs. Even that definition ranges widely, however, from organizations that provide services for basic human needs like shelter, freedom from violence, and health maintenance to organizations that provide professional association, women's and girls' education, religious affiliation, research and policy analyses, legal remedies, and/or social transformation.

While some women's and girls' organizations have existed for a century or more, many are new, a rich "harvest of the new women's movement."[55] An estimated eighty-seven percent of women's funds in this country formed since 1980, 61 percent of those since 1990, with twelve funds forming since 2000.[56]

Women's organizations are innovative. Like other so-called progressive nonprofits, a number of these newer organizations have been experimental in structure. Responding to 1960s and 1970s concerns about non-hierarchical leadership, racial equity, and redistribution of power, their efforts to do things differently have made many progressive nonprofits crucibles for experiments in institutionalizing diversity. With varying degrees of success, women's organizations and other progressive nonprofits have incorporated complex understandings of equity into their leadership and day-to-day management structures, often with special attention paid to race, ethnicity, sexual orientation, class, and other qualities such as physical ability that are often ignored in "traditional" organizations.

It is also probably safe to claim that many women's organizations, typical of social movement organizations, tend to be both idealistic and ambitious. A number of researchers and practitioners interviewed reflect the assessment that, as a movement of institutional experiments, women's organizations often have been laboratories that yielded important organizational innovations, especially in their emphases on racial, ethnic, and class diversity at the board level as well as in institutional management and staffing. And at least some of their innovations surfaced during the 1980s in larger corporate settings, for example, flat, nonhierarchical organizational charts that stress team-building and institutionalization of family/work balance as good business sense, to name just two corporate innovations of the last decade seldom credited to women's organizations.

Such innovations are not without cost, however, taking tolls both on leaders and on budgets.[57] It takes time and patience to do consensus management. Innovations in board governance, for example, with the aim of promoting more diversity in decision-making, chew up scarce people-resources that might otherwise be spent on fundraising. At start-up, such organizations may find themselves continually experimenting with structure, often without the guidance of tested models to follow. And they may continue to struggle with innovation as they develop—all the while trying to fit into funders' and donors' more conventional blueprints for accountability and evaluation. As a result, experimental organizations often are not acknowledged for the innovations they have achieved so much as they are labeled "unprofessional" or "naive" for not fulfilling more conventional expectations.

Budget constraints affect performance. Many women's organizations, like other idealistic groups, start with and survive on shoe-string budgets. There is seldom enough core support and capacity-building grant money to go around. And the lack of available capacity-building grants from foundations often translates into lack of sufficient money to hire an experienced development staff, which results in the lack of resources to stabilize, much less institutionalize, women's organizations with endowments.

There is more than enough blame to go around. The lack of adequate development staff to do research often means that women's organizations do not know whom to ask and are not asking for large enough contributions when they do ask. And when they do donor research, as one young donor pointed out, it was sometimes intrusive. But she and other young donors also noted that they were seldom asked or asked for enough. More than half a dozen professional women interviewed, none of them wealthy, also noted that while they often receive direct-mail solicitations, they seldom are asked personally for contributions to women's organizations, and when they are asked, by mail or in person, they are not asked for enough. To a person, each said she could have doubled, even tripled the amount she has been asked to give. It's a vicious cycle: Organizations need money to get money.

Moreover, the very vision and energy and idealism that launch a women's organization often leaves its mission messy, hampering its ability to explain succinctly what it does. Some of the women and men interviewed noted that in solicitations that they received from (a variety of) women's organizations, the appeal was for good work "all over the map," not for a targeted cause that might capture their imaginations. Such unfocused self-presentation—which can be attributed to lack of communications or public relations skills or, in at least one case described as "we're all in this together, you're a woman, support us"—squanders many organizations' potentially valuable "associational capital" and seriously misreads or underestimates their audiences.

Stages of development have an impact. When a new organization is struggling with such innovations of leadership and staffing as consensus management and shared power, it runs the risk of becoming inward-focused and consumed by internal conflict. Organizations at this stage of development have a hard time letting others in and an even harder time reaching out to volunteers and donors, especially if donors are accustomed to being "treated like donors" with a certain amount of deference and solicitation.

Women's organizations that do get beyond this awkward inward phase still may not be clear about the effectiveness of their work or able to publicize their accomplishments. "They don't brag enough," one woman noted, or set themselves apart. Indeed there is often redundancy and even intentional overlap of organizations doing work in the same area, such as reproductive rights—an overlap that in some cases organizations' founders claim help them raise more money as separate institutions. But the multiplicity and duplication of effort often annoy prospective donors who may not have a grasp of the subtle differences, shared expertise, or ongoing collaborations among the groups.

Both the innovations and the handicaps are evidence of dynamic institutional behavior and present intriguing areas for research. Yet sophisticated research on women's organizations is only starting to emerge.[58] The lack of more research is itself an interesting epistemological lacuna in the organizational theory and organizational management literature. But the reality is that there is even less of a research base for women's organizations than there is for women donors. Additional research could yield data on leadership; on successful efforts to institutionalize diversity; on fundraising pressures faced by local, state-wide, and national organizations; on the impact of direct-mail fundraising on both organizations and donors; and on the advantages of linking both locally and nationally in larger fundraising and media cooperatives. Based on research cited earlier, however, one can conclude that any organization or coalition of organizations able to combine the appeal of local connections and national passions with demonstrated impact and media outreach would produce better results through collective fundraising efforts than through any single local or national organization.

Even without a larger research base, however, it is important to chart the political and economic climate within which most women's organizations and other nonprofits operate. This climate is, in effect, a nonprofit version of the "Federal Reserve Bank" that over the last several decades has rocked their "Wall Street" and created a "bear (bare) market" in associational capital for women's organizations. Indeed, it is this bear (bare) market's economic and political climate that shapes donors' impressions as much as the work the women's organizations themselves do in reaching out to new donors. Moreover, understanding this climate—and figuring out how to counter it and even take advantage of it—is an essential key for developing new strategies to involve donors.

Cultural Phenomena that Affect Giving to Women and Girls

Over the last few years, federal support for nonprofits and community-based organizations has declined. Women's organizations across the country may be among those hardest hit. While some of these realities reflect what may be fallout from this new social climate, there is some evidence that these transformations have come about, in no small part, because of sophisticated, successful media and legislative agendas.

A conservative climate. Women's organizations, like many nonprofits, increasingly are affected by both fundamentalist Christian and economically conservative organizing efforts, on issues such as abortion rights, the "politically correct" debates, immigrant rights, affirmative action, and welfare reform. The list goes on.

Having learned from both the civil rights movement and the women's movement, conservative think tanks and grassroots organizations developed—and funded—successful strategies that have kept many women's organizations on the defensive, playing catch-up and not moving their own agendas or reaching out to enough funders. Precious financial resources get diverted to counter still one more round of lobbying and media efforts.

Conservative foundations like the Lynde and Harry Bradley Foundation, the John M. Olin Foundation, the Sarah Scaife Foundation, and the Smith Richardson Foundation, among others, stabilize well-funded conservative nonprofits like the Heritage Foundation, the American Enterprise Institute, the Cato Institute, the Hudson Institute, the National Commission on Philanthropy and Civic Renewal, the Philanthropy Roundtable, and others. The foundations are long-term partners who provide crucial core support and funding for their grantees' research, media initiatives, lobbying, and grassroots efforts.[59]

Many of these efforts are responsible for successful media and legislative initiatives like the "p.c." controversies, third-trimester abortion challenges, illegal immigration spotlights, "race-blind" state-based anti-affirmative action ballot initiatives, anti-homosexual rights drives, and "welfare-to-work" campaigns as well as other initiatives like devolution (shifting programs from the federal level to state governments), privatization of social security, and medical savings accounts.

The overarching agenda of many of these efforts is to limit the role of the federal government in favor of market forces. But implicit in many of these efforts are gender concerns. Among some of the conservative fiscal agendas are religious agendas that attack abortion and homosexual rights and promote a narrow view of family values. These efforts seek to reassert control over the family and over the workplace. For example, women of means are encouraged to remain at home while the same agenda pushes poor women into the workforce (usually in low-paying jobs) as assistance programs require.

Providing more extensive analyses of these dynamics, motives, and consequences is a topic well beyond the scope of this chapter. But it is important to note them, especially the dynamics that produce such disparate results for poor women of color—or to use the current research language, dynamics that link gender, class, and race/ethnicity—because they are implicit, if not explicit, in many of the recent attacks on social services, welfare programs, and affirmative action initiatives.[60]

Smart philanthropy. Conservative funders are organized. The Philanthropy Roundtable, a growing membership organization with 430 institutional and individual donors, is intent on shifting philanthropy away from what they view as social activism.

Compared to the breadth of philanthropy in the United States, economically conservative philanthropy seems relatively modest. From 1999 through 2001, for example, seventy-nine conservative foundations made more than $252 million in grants ($126.3 of that from just five foundations) to conservative nonprofits, 66 percent of them public policy organizations— less than what some of the largest United States foundations each give away in one year.[61] But conservative philanthropy is aimed at building conservative organizations. Most conservative funding is in the form of general support or loosely designated project money. Conservative funders provide more than three times what most other foundations allocate for general support and basically unrestricted grants, with foci on building strong institutional grantees. And they stick with their grantees over decades.

The fact of such stabilizing funding can be seen as at least one component in the growing strength of conservative organizations, as opposed to the lack of core support that afflicts so many social service providers and progressive social change nonprofits. Unrestricted funds are the hardest dollars for nonprofits to raise. Moreover, the prevailing length of time for most progressive foundations' support of grantees seems to be limited to two or three years. Then, as one program officer noted in an interview, it's on to the next progressive "program *du jour*." On the other hand, the availability of core resources has helped conservative nonprofits fulfill their missions, develop legislation, exploit state-of-the-art technology, launch effective media campaigns that hit their marks, and create a fertile climate for attracting individual donations to their own causes. Unlike their social change counterparts, with solid core support from their philanthropic partners, conservative nonprofits as a group have become both stable and effective.

Negative images discourage donors. What does this have to do with raising money for women's organizations? While there is no way to document cause and effect, at least one "climate" impact that has been measured is the public perception of nonprofits that are classified as "public/society benefit (i.e., civil rights, social justice, or community improvement organizations)." These are the private nonprofits inspiring low levels of confidence among those responding to the *Giving and Volunteering* Gallup poll.[62] Only 30.5 percent of respondents have "a great deal" or "quite a lot" of confidence in these organizations. Worse, 20.8 percent of respondents cite "very little" confidence, ranking these nonprofits only slightly higher than "federated charitable appeals (e.g., United Way), beset by scandal in recent years, and "international/foreign organizations (i.e., culture exchange or relief organizations)."

Many women's organizations, including women's funds, are under attack. Politicized media and the growth of tabloid journalism have helped to stigmatize the poor and women who support women's issues. Many of the constituencies targeted—women on welfare, pregnant immigrant women, women students, feminist scholars, and abused women and children—are the very populations that most women's organizations serve and women's funds support. It is not surprising to reach the conclusion that disturbing media-generated public images like these can shake the confidence of traditional women donors. This makes it even more difficult to engage such donors as those who participated in the Wellesley and Vassar campaigns, even EMILY's List donors, to become supporters of grassroots women's organizations, national policy institutes, or women's funds. The challenge for women's organizations is to turn these attacks around, to document the distortions and unfairness implicit in these attacks, and to use them as counter fundraising strategies.

Internalized "norms." Finally, the phenomenon of internalized norms needs to be examined. Differently put, these unnamed standards, unspoken principles, and implicit assumptions that define what "most of us" regard as "normal," and often without our paying attention, simultaneously shape what is regarded as "not us," different, not normal. These norms underpin successful attacks on immigrants and the poor.

Just as foundations often consider women and girls a special interest group, women themselves (white women, women of color, straight women and lesbians, young and old) tend to internalize cultural norms of white middle-class masculinity (especially youthful-looking, physically able white middle-class masculinity). How does this internalization affect donors? Since most people give to organizations that they feel connected to, a lack of identification with an organization's constituency poses an especially crucial stumbling block for women donors.

If women and girls are a special interest group, which group is not considered "special interest"? And which group is understood to be normal? More than two decades of sophisticated research document how intrusive, subtle, complex, and deeply rooted is this male (white, straight, middle-class, physically able, Western) norm.

These norms dictate "generic" masculine pronouns, the singular "he" that is supposed to stand for both "he" and "she." They delineate our images and language of the sacred. If we are not careful, they underpin medical research protocols, where until very recently researchers extrapolated treatment for menopausal women from research that was conducted on white male college students. They condition how women "without men" are seen—for instance, a never-married woman college president is never "safe" from rumors of "lesbian," a label that could wreck her career. In spite of over a decade of efforts to diversify organizations, especially for-profit corporations, "Norm" is still thoroughly in charge of many "traditional" institutions. And "Norm" shapes how women see themselves, even though many may have struggled for years to find their own voices and speak for themselves.[63]

This analysis is not about bashing men. Quite the contrary. It is about naming bizarre, contemporary manifestations of ancient behavioral vestiges that damage all of us, men and women alike. Many theories attempt to account for how gender norms evolved—hunter/gatherer divisions of labor; men's jealousy of women's ability to give birth (and jealousy of images of goddesses that celebrate women's fertility); the convenience of exploiting physical strength for power over others—and many more. But for the purposes of this analysis, suffice it to say that these often unacknowledged gender dynamics shape our families, our institutions, *and* our perceptions of ourselves. As Michelle Fine once quipped, referring to the results of her research documenting how women students are sidelined in law school, "It's in the air conditioning."[64]

It's in the air conditioning? How does all this apply to philanthropy? A colleague described her experiences as a program officer in a major foundation: "Women hesitate to fund women. They see funding women as self-interested, selfish. And even worse than being seen as aggressive, women avoid being seen as selfish." Women's own internalized, diminished sense of women and girls as "special interest," even when they understand their pressing needs, is a substantial complication in raising money for women's organizations. Added to that complication is one that arises from the current status of the women's movement. People are tired of hearing the "same old feminist stuff," as one respondent noted. The ERA was defeated, and unlike the heady, early days of *Ms. Magazine*, it takes a cataclysmic public event like the Hill/Thomas hearings to make the "click" happen.

The need for new language. Whether from successful conservative media campaigns or over-exposure to complaints of discrimination, many women and men alike have lost patience with rights language and identity politics. Others challenge that: "They may be sick of hearing it, but I'm sick of the problems." Yet few women's organizations have resources to pay for the focus groups that advertisers use to find the hot buttons and language that work to sell their products. Clearly more needs to happen if women's organizations are going to come up with the images and arguments that consistently make the case for funding women and girls.

Given the systemic and ancient roots of the problems, it is obviously not an easy case to make, but one theme that emerged most frequently from the respondents interviewed, many of them sympathetic supporters of women's organizations themselves, is the need for some new thinking, some new language, and some new collaborations, coalitions, and strategies to take these concerns to a wider public. New thinking, new language, and new collective efforts also will help reframe the media images of women and children, especially images of poor women and children of color that have been strategically distorted by anti-immigrant, anti-affirmative action, and anti-welfare attacks.

Recommendations for Follow-up

What conclusions can be drawn from these analyses? To summarize, this chapter makes the case that much of the existing knowledge about women as donors is based on false gender stereotypes. Few differences between men and women donors seem to remain once other variables such as age, level of income, number of dependents, "age" of money, secure pension, and health are taken into account.

The research also shows that, although female-headed households do not have net worth comparable to similarly situated male-headed households, they nonetheless give and give generously to a variety of causes. Given the research available about women's philanthropy, the important questions are not about gender differences in giving behavior or even about gender differentials in capacities to give. The important questions are about what people give *to* and do *not* give to.

Clearly more refined analyses and strategies are needed for expanding resources for women's philanthropy, and for countering both "climate" issues and internalized restraints shown to affect giving to women's organizations. The following are suggestions for further work.

Research

- *Develop a comprehensive research project on women's wealth distribution and wealth management.* Few researchers focus on quantitative analyses of wealth and even fewer on issues of women and wealth. Even a cursory look at the available data, however, shows that further probing of existing data sets can yield information and analyses useful to other researchers as well as to practitioners. Statistical comparisons of existing data sets also would be a major resource to researchers working on these and related topics.[65]

- *Compile a "best practices" analysis of effective donor/organization relationships.* Further research needs to survey strategies and events that have worked to attract and build mutually beneficial relationships between women's organizations and donors, paying particular attention to (1) differences in demographics of donors—age, gender, levels of net assets, geographic location, etc.; (2) organizational data such as who within an organization creates and sustains the relationships; and (3) cost/benefit analyses that estimate how much actual time and funding an organization spends to develop and sustain the relationships. What kinds of benefits, monetary and non-monetary, accrue to organizations? What's a dollar value of volunteer time donated to the organization? What do donors gain from relationships that work?

- *Compile a "best practices" survey of organizations that organize and serve donors*, including the National Network of Grantmakers' Donor Organizers' Network, the Philanthropic Initiative, Next Generation, Third Wave Foundation, Rockefeller Foundation, Ms. Foundation for Women, Women's Funding Network, Resourceful Women, Funding Exchange, Tides Foundation, Chicago Community Trust, United for a Fair Economy's Responsible Wealth Project, and other groups that sponsor donor activism or serve needs of donors in other ways. Donor circles, for example, are emerging as innovative strategies for attracting and educating high-dollar donors. This is especially important for organizations like Rockefeller Foundation and the Philanthropic Initiative that are reaching out to the Boomers and Generation Xers who will inherit major wealth in the next millennium. An in-depth study could survey programs like these and compile "best practices": How are they structured? How do they attract participants? What role does mentoring play in the transmission of values? What does it take to make women (and men) think more creatively about their own philanthropy and link it to women's and girls' needs? What can be learned from these resources that might help counter some of the stereotypes about women donors?

- *Launch a comprehensive study of donors of color, both women and men:* What are their demographic profiles? Does their giving differ from "white" philanthropy and if so, how—especially in their support of social change organizations? What do they give to? What motivates them to give? How do they prefer to be asked? What keeps them connected to the organizations they fund? Are there differences in giving patterns among widows/widowers, never-married, married, divorced/ separated donors of color, differences among different racial/ethnic groups by gender?

- *Launch a comprehensive study of young donors*, both women and men: What are their demographic profiles? What are the philanthropic habits of their parents? Does their giving differ significantly from their parents? Or in the case of self-made wealth, how does their giving compare or differ from earlier generations of philanthropic entrepreneurs? What roles have donor activist groups and mentoring played in shaping young donors' philanthropy? What portion of young people with wealth are active donors? How do they experience class differently from preceding generations? How do their life styles reflect these differences? What do they expect from organizations they support? What types of connections and relationships have they developed with the organizations they support and do these connections differ from those of older donor generations?

- *Develop a survey and/or conduct focus groups and follow-up interviews with donors to women's colleges.* What other causes do they give to, what does/would it take to convert "traditional" donors to become donors to women's organizations?

- *Develop a survey and/or conduct focus groups and follow-up interviews with donors to women's organizations.* Study female and male donors to diverse women's organizations: What motivates them to give? How do they prefer to be asked? What keeps them connected to the organization? Are there differences in giving patterns among widows/widowers, never-married, married, divorced/separated donors? Are there differences among different racial/ethnic groups by gender? Additional research could yield interesting data on leadership, on successful efforts to institutionalize diversity, on the different fundraising pressures faced by local, statewide, and national organizations and on the advantages of linking both locally and nationally in larger fundraising and media cooperatives.

- *Develop a survey of gender variables in workplace giving.* Some evidence suggests that women more than men may contribute to workplace giving campaigns.[66] A state-by-state survey of members of the National Alliance for Choice in Giving, a coalition of local, statewide, and regional federations and funds participating in workplace payroll deduction campaigns, could add significantly to our knowledge of what appeals to women donors.

- *Develop a history and analysis of the impact of direct-mail and Web-based fundraising for both women's organizations and donors.* How did the first direct-mail initiatives and Web-based fundraising aimed at women donors evolve and how did the lists get built and used? How did use of direct-mail or Web-based fundraising affect the growth and development of the organizations using it? What strategies have been most successful in appealing to women donors over the years and have those strategies changed? What have been both the advantages and disadvantages to women's organizations using direct-mail fundraising and Web-based fundraising.

- *Develop a comprehensive research project on women's organizations.* Women's organizations historically have been institutional innovators, developing changes such as collaborative leadership models that have been on the forefront of institutionalizing diversity; flat, non-hierarchical organizational charts that stress team-building; recognition of family/work balance as good business sense; and track records of producing significant social service delivery, innovation, and change for over a century. Thoughtful research on women's organizations is just starting to emerge: cross-discipline, historical, theoretical, and applied.[67] A review of existing research and recommendations for further analysis would spark additional work on a key area of organizational innovation as well as assess what more research is needed to help strengthen women's organizations' stability and long-term institutionalization. A focus on resources is especially important. How many women's organizations, for example, have endowments or reserve funds, and how do their fiscal management practices compare with a sample of other similar organizations that are not women-specific?

- *Edit a video of clips from existing media campaigns aimed at changing public perception of gender bias,* then conduct focus groups to test new messages that change public opinion. What are the outcomes of previous or current media campaigns, such as those against domestic violence? What's worked or not worked to get messages out and change public opinion? Conduct a series of focus groups to measure what messages work to get at "what's in the air conditioning" and communicate realities of both the macro- and micro-inequities produced by gender bias and discrimination.

Implementation Strategies

- *Develop more pro-active projects that involve donors.* Nonprofit organizations need to get to know donors better, men as well as women, and find more ways to draw on donors' "associational capital" for the benefit of their organizations.

- *Sponsor programs and workshops that benefit donors*, such as financial asset management workshops modeled on existing resources offered by the Donor Organizers' Network, the Philanthropic Initiative, and others.

- *Ask for larger amounts of money, ask in person, and ask more often.* Even without more sophisticated development research, nonprofit organizations need to assume that current and potential women donors have the resources to contribute. They need to ask, ask often, and ask in person for generous gifts. Do not underestimate donors' capacities to give, and do not underestimate donors' interest in the organization and in its leaders.

- *Improve an organization's public image.* Take a hard look at how a nonprofit organization presents itself. Is the mission/vision clearly, crisply stated? Are audiences clearly defined? Does the organization brag enough? This seems obvious, but based on respondents' perspectives, most organizations could benefit from a public presentation makeover informed by donor feedback.

- *Develop a collaborative, national media campaign* linked to regional and local media campaigns that can begin to counter the "bad rap" suffered in the media by those most women's organizations serve, that can translate sophisticated, theoretical, research-based understanding of race/ethnicity, class, and gender issues to the wider public. What will it take to make the case in the national media? In regional/local media? Begin locally: What are the issues, the sound bites, the convincing messages in local communities that dramatize the existence of persistent bias in most women's lives? What are the images and messages that appeal to donors? Link local initiatives to each other and to a multi-year national media strategy for a broad coalition of women's organizations.

- *Experiment with collaborative fundraising strategies* that can draw on the strengths of a diverse number of organizations and give donors more incentive to contribute. Share recommendations to donors for other organizations that they might be interested in supporting. "Think yeast, not pie, if you want more dough."

- *Find ways to get more information about women's funds and women's organizations into the hands of trust officers and estate lawyers who advise the wealthy.*

ACKNOWLEDGMENTS

Portions of this chapter were published in *Women as Donors: Stereotypes, Common Sense, and Challenge*, vol. 1 of the Monograph Series *Women and Philanthropy: Old Stereotypes and New Challenges* (Battle Creek, Mich.: Kellogg Foundation, 1998); "Funding 'Norm' Doesn't

Fund 'Norma'," chapter in *The State of Philanthropy in America*, edited by Neil Carson, (Washington, D.C.: National Committee for Responsive Philanthropy, 2002); and "Philanthropy," article in *Routledge International Encyclopedia of Women's Studies: Global Women's Issues and Knowledge*, edited by Cheris Kramarae and Dale Spender (New York: Routledge, 2000).

NOTES

A note on sources and limitations to this research: As we have seen, reliable research on women and philanthropy is slim. To fill in gaps and analyze issues that ranged beyond the limits of existing documentation, 81 women and men were interviewed for this research in 1997: they included researchers; CEOs, senior executives, and program officers in "traditional" foundations; heads of nonprofit organizations, including Council on Foundations' affinity groups; current and former heads of women's funds; heads of women's organizations; women donors across the age spectrum; trustees; consultants and professional fundraisers and development directors. Twenty-eight percent of those interviewed were women and men of color. It is important to note that this sample was not drawn randomly. Because of the dearth of reliable research, the list of respondents necessarily included researchers whose opinions helped to shape my own interpretations about existing data, social climte issues, and the philanthropic and nonprofit sector in general. The list of respondents also was weighted to include people active in the women's funding movement and to include women and men in leadership positions in philanthropy, especially women and men of color. As with any anecdotal research, their observations should be read as food for thought. In most cases, respondents' perspectives are *opinions*, not facts, and some respondents may or may not have been acquainted with complete or up-to-date information.

1. Virginia A. Hodgkinson and Murray S. Weitzman, *Giving and Volunteering in the United States: Findings from a National Survey* (Washington, D.C.: Independent Sector, (1996), 49.

2. Ann E. Kaplan and M. Joanne Hayes, "What We Know about Women as Donors," in *Women as Donors, Women as Philanthropists*, ed. Abbie J. von Schlegell and Joan M. Fisher, New Directions for Philanthropic Fundraising, 11 (San Francisco: Jossey-Bass Publishers, 1993).

3. Ann Kaplan, telephone interview, August 15, 1997.

4. Kaplan and Hayes, "What We Know about Women as Donors," 11.

5. Chrisopher M. Toppe, Arthur D. Kirsch, and Jocabel Michel, *Giving and Volunteering in the United States: Findings from a National Survey* (Washington, D.C.: Independent Sector, 2001).

6. Ibid.

7. Paul G. Schervish, telephone interview, September 2, 1997.

8. John Havens, *Giving Behavior by Income and Gender: Do Men Give More?* (Boston: Social Welfare Research Institute, Boston College, 1994), 3, Schervish, telephone interview.

9. Emmett D. Carson, "The Contemporary Charitable Giving and Voluntarism of Black Women," in *Women and Philanthropy: Past, Present, Future* (working paper, New York: Center for the Study of Philanthropy at the City University of New York Graduate School and University Center, 1987).

10. Quoted in Kaplan and Hayes, "What We Know About Women as Donors," 13.

11. Melissa Brown, ed., *Giving USA 2004* (New York: AAFRC Trust for Philanthropy, 2004), 213–17.

12. Melvin Prince, "Women, Men, and Money Styles," *Journal of Economic Psychology* 14 (March 1993): 175, 181.

13. Albert Ade Okunade, Phanindra V. Wunnava, and Raymond Walsh, Jr., "Charitable Giving on Alumni: Micro-Data Evidence from a Large Public University," *The American Journal of Economics and Sociology* 53 (January 1994): 73–83.

14. Catherine C. Eckel and Philip J. Grossman, "Are Women Less Selfish than Men? Evidence from Dictator Experiments," *The Economic Journal* (1998).

15. In the last decade, there have been no research reports on the order of the Boston Diary study—research that actually *documents* giving, not just people's recollections of their giving. So the jury is still out on gender differences in giving and will be until we have more comprehensive, well-designed studies that take into account all the relevant variables that affect giving. In an article in the July 2004 issue of *Women's Philanthropy Institute News*, "Gender Differences in Giving: Going, Going, Gone?" *Chronicle of Philanthropy* reporter Holly Hall takes a retrospective look at some of the research and anecdotal writing on gender differences in giving. But even the targeted studies on alumni giving that Hall cites and other similar research still miss many complex variables that affect giving, not least among them relevant factors such as numbers of women in leadership and on boards, evidence of robust women's studies programs and women's research centers and institutes regarded as assets for attracting alumnae dollars. There is some anecdotal evidence that these and other giving opportunities addressing specific needs and concerns of women students, women faculty, and alumnae all may lead to more strategic giving from both women and men alums. But lacking in-depth, more nuanced data, we have to rely on anecdotal evidence—which can be thoughtful and persuasive, especially helpful in encouraging more women to get engaged in philanthropy, but does not constitute quantitative research.

16. Martha Britton Eller, Federal Taxation of Wealth Transfers 1992–1995," *Statistics of Income Bulletin* (Spring 1997), 12.

17. Barry W. Johnson, "Personal Wealth, 1992–1995," *Statistics of Income Bulletin* (Spring 1998): 70–95.

18. Barry Johnson and Jacob Mikow, "Federal Estate Tax Returns, 1998–2000," *Statistics of Income Bulletin* (Summer 2002), reprinted in *Giving USA 2003: The Annual Report on Philanthropy for the Year 2002*, 48th Annual Issue (New York: AAFRC Trust for Philanthropy, 2003), 83.

19. Susan A. Ostrander and Paul G. Schervish, "Giving and Getting: Philanthropy as Social Relation," in *Critical Issues in American Philanthropy: Strengthening Theory and Practice*, ed. J. Van Till and Associates (San Francisco: Jossey-Bass Publishers, 1990), Paul G. Schervish, "Major Donors, Major Motives: The People and Purposes Behind Major Gifts," in *Major Gifts*, ed. Dwight F. Burlingame and James M. Hidge III, New Directions for Philanthropic Fundraising (San Francisco: Jossey-Bass Publishers, 1997).

20. Schervish, "Major Donors, Major Motives," 1.

21. Ibid., 14.

22. Ostrander and Schervish, "Giving and Getting," quoted in Schervish, "Major Donors, Major Motives," 14.

23. Schervish, "Major Donors, Major Motives," 16.

24. For example, Teresa Odendahl, *Charity Begins at Home: Generosity and Self-Interest among the Philanthropic Elite* (New York: Basic Books, Inc., 1990); Susan A. Ostrander, *Women of the Upper Class* (Philadelphia: Temple University Press, 1984); and Francie Ostrower, *Why the Wealthy Give: The Culture of Elite Philanthropy* (Princeton: Princeton University Press, 1985).

25. Schervish, "Major Donors, Major Motives," 17, 18.

26. Dyan Sublett, "Women's Approach to Philanthropy: A Learning Model," in von Schlegell and Fisher, eds., *Women as Donors, Women as Philanthropists*.

27. Cheryl Hall-Russell and Robert H. Kasberg, *African-American Traditions of Giving and Serving: A Midwest Perspective* (Indianapolis: Indiana University Center on Philanthropy, 1997).

28. Hodgkinson and Weitzman, *Giving and Volunteering* (1996), 20.

29. John J. Havens and Paul G. Schervish, "A River Rises in Eden: The Bountiful Wellsprings of Giving and Volunteering," 1997 Independent Sector Spring Research Forum, p. 10.

30. Quoted in Susan A. Ostrander and Joan M. Fisher, "Women Giving Money/Women Raising Money: What Difference for Philanthropy?" in *Taking Fundraising Seriously: Cultures of Giving,* ed. Dwight Burlingame (San Francisco: Jossey-Bass Publishers, 1995), 11.

31. Ibid., 11–12.

32. U.S. Census Bureau, "Income Stable, Poverty Up, Numbers of Americans with and without Health Insurance Rise, Census Bureau Reports," press release, August 26, 2004.

33. Website www.pay-equity.org, citing U.S. Census Bureau report "Women," released in June 2004.

34. The Center on Philanthropy at Indiana University, *Giving USA 2001: The Annual Report on Philanthropy for the Year 2000* (New York: AAFRC Trust for Philanthropy, 2001), 47.

35. *Highlights of Women's Earnings in 2003,* U.S. Department of Labor, Bureau of Labor Statistics, Report 978, September 2004.

36. Center for Women's Business Research, *Top Facts about Women-Owned Businesses,* www.womensbusinessresearch.org, 2004.

37. Center for Women's Business Research, *Number of Minority Women-Owned Businesses Expected to Reach 1.2 Million in 2002,* www.womensbusinessresearch.org, 2001.

38. Center for Women's Business Research, *Top Facts about Women-Owned Businesses,* http://www.womensbusinessresearch.org, 2004.

39. Frank Stafford, telephone interview, March 11, 1998.

40. Arthur B. Kennickell, Martha Starr-McCluer, and Annika E. Sundén, "Family Finances in the U.S.: Recent Evidence from the Survey of Consumer Finances," *Federal Reserve Bulletin* 83 (January 1997): 1–24.

41. Barry W. Johnson, "Personal Wealth, 1998," *Statistics of Income Bulletin* (Winter 2002): 87–115.

42. Ibid., 88–89; Barry W. Johnson, "Personal Wealth, 1992–1995," *Statistics of Income Bulletin* (Spring 1998): 71–72, 77–78.

43. Nicki Newman Tanner and Peter Ramsey, "Raising Money for Women from Women: The Story of a Successful Campaign," in von Schlegell and Fisher, eds., *Women as Donors, Women as Philanthropists,* 117.

44. Jane Couch, telephone interview, August 27, 1997.

45. Okunade, Wunnava, and Walsh, "Charitable Giving on Alumni."

46. Tiffany Reed, e-mail correspondence, October 12, 2004.

47. Debra Furry, telephone interview, September 3, 1997.

48. Schervish, "Major Donors, Major Motives," 27.

49. The Philanthropic Initiative, *Wealth with Responsibility: 1996 Survey Results* (Boston: Bankers Trust Private Banking, 1996), 15–16.

50. Schervish, "Major Donors, Major Motives," 27.

51. Betsy Crone, telephone interview, August 25, 1997.

52. Karen D. Stone, Susan F. Rice, and Judith C. Angel, "Women, Money, and Political Clout," in von Schlegell and Fisher, eds., *Women as Donors, Women as Philanthropists,* 111.

53. Susan A. Hallgarth, ed., *A Directory of National Women's Organizations* (New York: The National Council for Research on Women, 1992).

54. *Encyclopedia of Associations* (Farmington Hills, Mich.: Gale Research, 1997).

55. Myra Marx Ferree and Patricia Yancy Martin, eds., *Feminist Organizations: Harvest of the New Women's Movement* (Philadelphia: Temple University Press, 1995).

56. Women's Funding Network, e-mail correspondence, October 12, 2004.

57. Judy Remington, *The Need to Thrive: Women's Organizations in the Twin Cities* (St. Paul: Minnesota Women's Press, 1991).

58. See, for instance, Ferree and Martin, *Feminist Organizations*; and Remington, *The Need to Thrive*.

59. See, for instance, reports issued by the National Committee on Responsive Philanthropy at www.ncrp.org.

60. National Council for Research on Women, "Immigration: Women and Girls, Where Do They Land? Who We Welcome and Why," *Issues Quarterly* 1, no. 3 (1995); "Affirmative Action: Beyond the Glass Ceiling and Sticky Floor," *Issues Quarterly* 1, no. 4 (1996); "Beyond Beijing: After the Promises of the UN Conference on Women. Who's Doing What to Turn Words into Action?" *Issues Quarterly* 2, no. 1 (1996).

61. National Committee on Responsive Philanthropy, *Axis of Ideology: Conservative Foundations and Public Policy* (Washington, D.C.: National Committee for Responsive Philanthropy, 2004); Sally Covington, *Moving a Public Policy Agenda: The Strategic Philanthropy of Conservative Foundations* (Washington, D.C.: National Committee for Responsive Philanthropy, 1997), 3. See also www.ncrp.org for more current updates.

62. Hodgkinson and Weitzman, *Giving and Volunteering* (1996), 72.

63. More detailed analyses of these issues are explored in Mary Ellen S. Capek and Molly Mead, *Effective Philanthropy: Organizational Success through Deep Diversity and Gender Equality* (Cambridge: MIT Press, 2005).

64. Lani Guinier, Michelle Fine, and Jane Balin, "Becoming Gentlemen: Women's Experience at One Ivy League Law School," *University of Pennsylvania Law Review* 143 (November 1994): 1–110.

65. For more detailed suggestions about research needed on wealth data, see Mary Ellen S. Capek, *Women as Donors: Stereotypes, Common Sense, and Challenges*, vol. 1 of the Monograph Series *Women and Philanthropy: Old Stereotypes and New Challenges* (Battle Creek, Mich.: Kellogg Foundation, 1998). Online at www.womenphil.org or www.wfnet.org.

66. Furry, telephone interview.

67. Ferree and Martin, *Feminist Organizations*.

WOMEN AS DONORS

Old Stereotypes, New Visions

JO GRUIDLY MOORE AND MARIANNE PHILBIN

Women own more than half the nation's investment wealth. They can be expected to accumulate even greater wealth as they increase their own earned income, live longer than men, and inherit much of the predicted $30 trillion intergenerational transfer of wealth in the coming decades. And yet, despite the resources that women control, despite the familiar stereotype of women as volunteers and givers, few people think of women first when they hear the word *philanthropist*.

The word—which is becoming less and less popular with philanthropists themselves—conjures up images of industrial tycoons and robber barons, cigar-smoking megalomaniacs who amass millions and give money away to increase their own power. If women come to mind at all, it is often women with white gloves and tiny hats, women of another century. One of the reasons modern-day philanthropists dislike the term is because it seems to belong to another era. In a study conducted by the New Ventures in Philanthropy project in Chicago in 2002, donors from many different backgrounds participating in focus groups repeatedly said that they preferred to talk about their charitable contributions in terms of "giving back" rather than "philanthropy."

Whether "giving back" or engaging in "philanthropy," times definitely have changed for women as donors, both in terms of how they perceive themselves, and how they are perceived by others. Until fairly recently, philanthropy was uncharted territory for large numbers of women. However, the social, economic, and political changes of the past twenty-five years have brought with them changes in fundraising and in giving. More and more women have entered philanthropy through their involvement with the nonprofit organizations and causes they've championed, through their activism and support of political candidates, and through their changing role in the workforce. The women's philanthropy movement has played a particularly important role, beginning in the early 1980s and growing from a handful of women-launched and women-focused foundations to nearly one hundred women's funds nationally and internationally.

While times have changed, challenges still remain. Despite how far we've come at the beginning of the twenty-first century, we can attest to the fact that a lot of erroneous assumptions still tend to be made about women and money: that women don't need it, or don't need programs of their own; that women don't make enough to give it away anyway; and that women don't or won't give it away even when they *do* have enough.

Giving by Women Versus Giving to Women

It is important to make a distinction between giving *by* women, and giving *to* women's programs. Women who give at substantial levels are not necessarily targeting their charitable giving to women's programs, and women's programs that are receiving support are not necessarily receiving support exclusively from women's foundations or women donors. It is equally important to note, in fact, that although individual giving by women is on the increase, giving by foundations to women's programs hasn't changed all that dramatically in the last decade or two. The vast majority of foundation dollars still go to "universal" programs, that is, programs that purport to serve all comers equally. The reality is that they don't, and can't. One size never fits all. Grants and programs aimed at serving the "general public" do not necessarily produce equal opportunities or equal outcomes.

The women's funding movement has worked hard to advocate for the use of a "gender lens" in proposal review, suggesting that donors and foundations need to open their eyes and look hard and in specific ways at how the agencies that they're considering funding address issues relative to women and girls, or even consider women and girls in their programming and decision making. Despite the work of the women's funding movement and the enormous changes that the existence of women's programs have made in diverse communities and in fields such as health and medicine, foundations, corporations, and individual donors still ask—if perhaps more sheepishly than before—"Why fund women?"

Understanding why gender-specific programs are important is not only key to creating more effective community programs, it is key to the development of women as philanthropists. Just as there are considerations specific to women in the programming nonprofits offer, there are considerations specific to women as donors, and both are worth exploring and understanding.

Are women donors different from male donors? Yes and no. Regardless of gender, for example, donors tend to respond positively to organizations that are responsive to them as individuals, that are innovative in their programming, that meet their missions, and that are well run as institutions. A key rule of fundraising, however, is to get to know your donors, and to learn as much as you can about what motivates and sustains them as individuals or groups of individuals. Over the years that we've spent fundraising with, from, and for women, we have seen certain patterns repeat themselves. Here's what we've learned about women as donors, with apologies for the generalities we are about to make.

Gender Is Only the Starting Point of Women's Philanthropy

More and more nonprofit organizations are attempting to reach out to women donors. Some look specifically at ways of seeking underwriting from women for programs that have a particular focus likely to be of greater interest to women. For every issue on the nation's agenda, and for many programs at many nonprofit organizations, there is a dimension specific to women. The more a nonprofit organization recognizes, articulates, and responds to that dimension, the more prepared they will be for a conversation with a prospective "woman donor" who they have reason to believe is interested in women's issues. (Not all women donors, of course, are interested in women's issues, or in programming for women and girls.)

As lead fundraisers for the Chicago Foundation for Women back in the 1980s, we learned very quickly that although some women intuitively understood the power that came from giving, and others intuitively understood the additional ways in which *their* giving could make history and foster social change when directed to programs for women, simply being a woman who happened to have resources provided no guarantee of interest or alignment with those concerns. Although we naturally had some reason to approach women for support of women's programs, gender alone was not a predictor of charitable intent, or interest in the aims and purposes of any given program or organization.

All donors are individuals. Some women are interested in gender-specific programs and some are not. Women are interested in directing their charitable dollars in different ways and in different directions, and for whatever reasons, some do not feel an affinity with the messages of the women's funding movement. In other words, neither gender nor wealth in and of themselves are predictors of what a donor will support.

Given that reality, we have found three elements to be defining characteristics of women's giving, regardless of what a woman donor may choose to support. Women give "best" when they recognize and realize:

- The opportunity for personal impact
- A sense of belonging, being part of a group
- A chance to forge change or support innovation

How do we help women donors achieve the goals noted above?

What Motivates Women to Give and What Would Motivate Them to Give More?

Although women have a higher percentage rate of giving to charity, their average gift size still comes in at a little more than half that of what men give. This raises a variety of questions: Are women ignored by fundraisers because women give less, or do women give less because they're ignored by fundraisers? Women have always made less money than men, and in terms of earned income, have therefore had less to give away. But have women also tended to give less in part simply because they are asked for less? Institutions that in the past have tended to overlook or marginalize women and their contributions have neither sought nor attracted women's dollars.

We must ask whether women have given less in part because they have not been motivated to give more. Do the institutions that approach women for gifts reflect women's interests and concerns in their programming? Are there women in leadership positions on staff and on the board of directors? Does the programming empower women? Are there relevant philanthropic models that appeal to women's preferences as donors? Until fairly recently, the answer was probably no.

It is also important to note, as the famous saying goes, that charity begins at home, and so do notions about what charity is and what kind of charitable behavior is appropriate. The hesitance to "give away" may be influenced in part by the fact that women have for so long been *the* "charitable resource" for their family and friends. Women are still looked to as the primary caregivers for the immediate and extended family, and the pressure to preserve family resources for family needs has been real. Statistics suggest, for example, that women spend eighteen years caring for children and another eighteen years caring for ill and aging relatives—all of which costs money—not only out of pocket but often in terms of earnings forgone, and those years are fraught with the stress of needing to be prepared for all contingencies.

Women's Giving Begins with their Own Assumptions

Women have also tended not to be "schooled" in the art of powerful giving as much as men have. They have had fewer philanthropic role models influencing them. In terms of gift size, women give out of their assumptions as to what's appropriate, and men give out of theirs. Sadly, it has been our experience that these are often two different sets of assumptions. Women working as passionate volunteer fundraisers still will get up in front of a group and ask for a "small contribution." Women passionate about an issue or organization still will give $50 when they could afford to give $500. Generally speaking, it has been our experience that they have not consciously considered $500 and rejected the notion—they often haven't even considered it, but gave almost unconsciously an amount that they equated with what a charitable contribution simply *is*, the levels at which perhaps their mothers gave, or at which other women in their social and economic circles give.

Women Are Motivated by the Examples of Other Women.

There are still not enough examples of women modeling powerful philanthropy and making sizable contributions. In fact, in the early 1980s, a few women's organizations with which we are familiar made conscious decisions *not* to single out women donors at high levels. There was pressure to treat all donors equally by listing annual donors in alphabetical order rather than by giving level. It was thought that women so valued relationships with other women friends that they wouldn't want to be identified—and separated out—as being able to afford a larger financial contribution than their friends. A subtle subtext regarding feminism and class also added a layer of discomfort with wealth and the display of wealth—the idea that one couldn't really be a true feminist if one had great wealth.

A major breakthrough in modeling women's philanthropy occurred for the Chicago Foundation in 1996 after we realized that we needed more individuals giving much higher annual contributions if we were eventually to launch a successful endowment campaign. We embarked on an effort to conduct a very visible campaign to acquire ten individuals or couples who would pledge $100,000 in annual gifts and fulfill those pledges by the year 2000. The campaign, entitled "A Million for the Millenium" was concluded quickly and we determined to give its success as much publicity as we could, even introducing the donors at the annual meeting luncheon with eighteen hundred people in attendance.

One year later, having embarked on our endowment campaign, we heard a woman give an enthusiastic "Yes!" to our request for $100,000, stating "I knew from the moment I saw those donors stand at the luncheon that I wanted to be part of that group! I thought you'd never ask!"

Women Need to Be Educated as Donors

Women, like all donors, need encouragement and education in order to be convinced to give to the cause or organization for which they're being solicited. It is naive to assume that a woman with financial resources will give to a women's project simply because she is a woman, or that she will give in a certain way, just because she is female. Nonprofits exist in a sophisticated and competitive marketplace, and the prospects they approach are exposed to, if not actually directly approached by, many other organizations and causes. Women who are solicited for charitable gifts, therefore, like all donors, need time to fully understand the cause or field, to get to know the organization, to feel comfortable with its leaders and managers, and to assess their own interests and preferences.

The process of getting to know an organization also affects giving levels. Women often don't consider their first gift their "real" gift. They will give the first time in an effort to get to know the organization. Once trust and confidence is established, and appropriate recognition offered, a larger gift often follows.

Group Affiliation and Leadership Is Important

Fundraising has always been organized around campaigns, because fundraisers know that being part of a group is motivating to donors, and provides important reassurance that all gifts are being maximized and leveraged by the existence of other gifts. This desire to "affiliate" is particularly prevalent among women donors

In a series of focus groups and surveys that the Chicago Foundation for Women undertook some years ago, for example, donors repeatedly commented that official membership in a group or organization was not of particular interest, but "affiliation" was, and affiliation was an important consideration in their decision to give financially to any organization.

What was meant by the term "affiliation" varied, and like so much where raising and donating money is concerned, each donor must be approached as an individual, on a case-by-case basis. For many of the women surveyed, affiliation did not mean active committee work or serving as a member of the board of directors. Some indicated that they felt affiliated by simply attending an annual luncheon, or being a part of a once-a-year program. The concept of affiliation also extends to affiliation with the network of supporters known to surround a particular organization. High-profile donors become highly associated with their causes. Donors who do not regularly appear as boldface names on the society pages also come to be known in their circles and communities as "the powerhouse" or a key insider at a particular charity. This creates the interesting phenomena of donor ownership, or social claim to a particular cause or organization.

On the nonprofit circuit, among women donors in particular, we'll often hear someone say, "Oh—that organization? Sure, I know that group: that's Sally Baker's organization." And the prospective donor to that group then ends up asking herself "Do I want to be a part of Sally Baker's group?" as much as she may ask herself "Do I care about building a new gym at the community center?"

Women Prefer to Fund Change

Women donors are often more interested in funding change than in preserving the status quo, more interested in using the money now rather than endowing it for use later. The women donors we've worked with who have taken the greatest joy in their giving have tended to be women who are excited by how their gifts can change the way things are, rather than preserve them. There are some obvious reasons for this: To encourage organizations to serve women and girls or the under-served more appropriately, traditional institutions may be in desperate need of the push that donors can provide. Women donors also tend to be highly attuned to the potential of personal impact. In preserving an institution or its way of doing business, donors may feel they are one of many. But taking the lead to change an institution brings a result that can been seen and felt and traced back to a donor's gift, sometimes in fairly dramatic ways. One Chicago area donor with both a sense of mission and a sense of humor, for example, donated money to her old law school specifically to underwrite the costs of putting a women's bathroom on the floor of the old law school where most classes where held—which until that point housed only a men's room. She also requested that a plaque be installed in the restroom, commemorating the contributions she and other women alumni made in order to have it installed. The desire to have personal impact often means that women are more likely than men to want to use some portion of accumulated wealth in their own lifetime, rather than preserve it, endow it, and pass it on to the next generation.

Solicitation and Cultivation — the Power of Friends and Volunteers

Regarding solicitation, in focus groups conducted a number of years ago by Chicago Foundation for Women, women rated a fundraising request made by a friend—as opposed to a staff professional—as the most effective solicitation method, and the circumstance under which they would be most

Figure 1. The Classic Cycle of Donor Relations

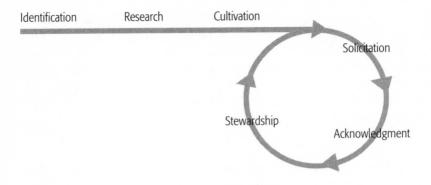

likely to give. Rated as the second most successful method was an appeal made by a volunteer who could speak with passion about the program and offer compelling stories about lives being changed.

As with all fundraising, the choice of contact person is key to the likelihood of a successful "ask." Cultivation of the prospective donor often includes cultivation and support of the contact person identified as the best "asker." In a series of donor interviews in 2002 conducted by students in Northwestern University's School of Continuing Studies, donors who were asked what motivated their initial giving to various programs almost all cited their curiosity about and respect for the involvement of a friend who was already giving or volunteering at that particular organization.

Although there are exceptions to every pattern, in our experience, the cultivation process for women donors can take anywhere from twelve to eighteen months. This is not only because charitable gifts tend to be carefully allocated, but also because women tend to be aware of the fact that in giving—and certainly in giving at a significant level—they are entering into a relationship. And beginning a new relationship requires thoughtful consideration.

In fact, during one discussion at a fundraising workshop we recently hosted, a woman noted that the classic cycle of donor relations parallels the steps women instinctively follow when reaching out to individuals with whom they're interested in becoming friends (see figure 1).

Personal Recognition Is Important

This is the most difficult area to generalize about—and as a result, one of the most important for nonprofit organizations to discuss directly with women donors and prospects. Some women want a lot of recognition. Some are petrified or appalled by the thought of it. Everyone's reasons are personal.

Although interest in public recognition varies considerably from donor to donor, all donors appreciate what we have come to think of as private or personal recognition. Women donors note the importance of thank-you letters, calls from board members or other volunteers or donors, acknowledgment from the friend that solicited them or introduced them to the organization. The institutional thank-you is required, of course, but often considered invisible, simply something the organization is required to do, like filing a tax form—and therefore relatively meaningless as compared to personal thank-you notes or other forms of acknowledgement.

In the roles we have played over the years as board members, staff leaders, and volunteers, we have seen issues of recognition surface more often than with solicitation. Many nonprofit organizations worry about missteps in the solicitation process, but it is in the recognition and acknowledgment phase that mistakes or misunderstandings more often occur. We have seen women discontinue giving to an organization more often because of an error or omission in gift recognition, than because of disenchantment with the organization itself. Needless to say, high on the list of irritations are always letters to women donors addressed to "Mr.," as well as thank-yous directed to male partners or husbands instead of the woman who initiated the contribution.

Other issues relative to women and recognition are born of the times in which we live. Although much has been done to encourage women philanthropists to model powerful giving and be visible as donors, issues such as privacy, security, and family safety remain real (and legitimate) concerns for some women donors, and obstacles to more public forms of acknowledgment.

Personal Development Is an Important Part of the Equation

Most nonprofits don't expect to find many "perfect donors." In the case of the Chicago Foundation for Women in the early 1980s, a perfect donor would have been someone who understood newly articulated and identified women's issues; who knew of the myriad, and for the most part small, groups locally trying to address women's issues; who understood the social milieu of the times in which women had just begun, in a sense, to learn how to earn money, let alone give money away . . . and who were willing to give and ask others to give.

There are barriers both internal and external to women reaching their potential as donors. In our experience, inviting women prospects and donors to be involved in creating opportunities and experiences that would help them to overcome those barriers builds the connections that women want. Providing them a voice in how their contributions are dispersed meets their desire for making a personal impact with their philanthropy and, when the issue an organization is addressing empowers women or affects systems change, it meets women's desire to fund change. The internal barriers are the toughest to address because to overcome them, a woman must address issues of money and power and how they played out in her family of origin; how money was valued in her home, school, and community, and the messages she took away as a child. And in some circumstances, a woman must confront how time, energy, and money are currently valued in her own marriage.

For many women born prior to the 1960s, money was something girls weren't supposed to worry about, and they were encouraged to focus their energies on learning to care for the physical, emotional, and psychological well-being of others. One needs an education to achieve a level of financial literacy and the wherewithal, comfort level, and confidence to manage wealth. Steered away from such an education, women often feel less than empowered to manage it, let alone give some of it away. Acting on the belief that "the personal is the political," many organizations involved in the women's philanthropy movement set about to educate women about the great disparity between women's and men's financial contributions, the debilitating effect this had on women's organizations and ultimately on women's lives. Women's foundations provided women with opportunities to explore the internal barriers that were holding them back from wielding their resources powerfully in the philanthropic arena, and educated women about the many issues facing women and girls.

The external barriers to women's participation in philanthropy prior to the early 1990s were many—women often were relegated to "auxiliary boards" of mainstream institutions where they were expected to raise money but had little or no input into how it would be spent. They often were ignored by the development and senior staff of nonprofits as their spouses were courted and cultivated—even when the bulk of the family's wealth originated from the woman. Needless to say, the women's philanthropy movement found a ready audience of women for its message and for the opportunity to be educated, trained, and handed all of the decision-making power in every aspect of a community foundation, including grantmaking.

The greatest of the external barriers perhaps has been the fact that so few women's projects and programs engaged in the very social change that motivates women donors had any visibility anywhere—even in the so-called "women's community." Women's funds have been working to overcome this last barrier by constantly seeking out and identifying projects and programs in diverse communities, showcasing them and providing donors firsthand experience of the programs' effectiveness. In our experience, providing donors with face-to-face dialogues with program staff and with the women and girls whose lives had been changed fueled women donors to increase their level of contribution greatly. Ultimately, many women donors have leveraged their giving by stepping into leadership roles, as role models and fundraisers, inspiring and challenging their friends and colleagues to join them in supporting important causes with significant contributions.

We viewed our work in the women's philanthropy movement as the "next phase of the feminist movement"—women wielding financial power to remove barriers and provide opportunities for women and girls so they could reach their full potential. What we hadn't realized when we began was that in moving along the road to becoming the "best donor" we could be, we would each undergo a personal transformation in which we moved closer to reaching our own full potential not only as donors, but as empowered women.

Final Reflections

For women, philanthropy, at its best and most effective, provides opportunities to make a personal impact through the nonprofits that women fund, in ways they couldn't possibly affect on their own. It provides a network of other donors who share similar values and concerns, and in the case of other women donors—to some degree colleagues who share similar journeys of transformation on their own roads to personal empowerment. Ultimately, philanthropy is a tool with which women can take the lead—wielding their financial power to forge the kind of changes they want for a just society—and be transformed into agents of change in the process.

Times have changed regarding women over the last thirty years. While women have changed the image that comes to mind when we think of a politician, a medical doctor, a lawyer, and a judge, nonprofit institutions are only now waking up to the fact that women are changing the image that comes to mind when one thinks of a philanthropist. In the past few years, with foundation funding shrinking along with the stock market and government cutbacks as well, the successful nonprofits of the future have begun to develop their individual donor programs, and are discovering that more than one-half of the prospects are women.

As Virginia Esposito, president of the National Center for Family Philanthropy noted recently, "Women's participation in philanthropy has changed just a bit since 1898 when Elizabeth Cady Stanton commented that: 'the hey-day of a woman's life is on the shady side of fifty, when the vital forces heretofore expended in other ways are garnered in the brain, when their thoughts and sentiments flow out in broader channels, when philanthropy takes the place of family selfishness, and when from the depths of poverty and suffering the wail of humanity grows as pathetic to their ears as once was the cry of their own children'" (*Eighty Years and*

DONOR TRENDS

Research involving interviews and focus groups with fifty-three donors was conducted in 2002 for Giving Greater Chicago, an initiative designed to support the development of new sources of philanthropic capital. Findings particularly relevant to women donors included:

- There is a general trend toward and a high degree of interest in more direct involvement in nonprofits on the part of donors.
- Donors, particularly those under fifty, are seeking organizations that satisfy their need for hands-on involvement. Donors of all ages are increasingly asserting more control over how their contributions can be used.
- There is often a lack of trust or a lack of understanding vis-à-vis nonprofits and how and why they operate the way they do. For example, donors frequently say that they want to see their giving go "directly" to "people in need" and may not see a connection between nonprofit organizational infrastructure and effective service.
- Donors note the difficulty of assessing the administrative versus program costs of a nonprofit organization.
- Donors give both time and money to the causes with which they associate or to which they are attached. The most common form of commitment is service on boards of directors. The closer the connection donors feel to a cause or an organization, the higher the amounts they tend to give.
- Donors climb an experience ladder. They tend to start out by giving to things directly related to their lives, and by being somewhat disorganized in their giving. With age and experience, they broaden their giving beyond themselves, gain more focus, and feel less need to be as directly involved.
- Donors who are regularly giving in substantial amounts to charitable organizations tend to have tight social networks, to give to organizations where people they know and trust are involved, and to expect reciprocity when soliciting their friends for their own favorite charities.

From Marcia Festen and Wendy Siegel, *Report of Focus Groups and Interviews on Charitable Giving* (Chicago: Greater Chicago Philanthropy Initiative, 2001).

More, 1898). "These thoughts and sentiments are certainly no longer confined to only women over fifty," Ms. Esposito continued. "We don't have to wait for our children to be grown—to be past our 'family selfishness' period—to embrace the potential of philanthropy to alleviate humanity's suffering. Far from it. The best interests of our families and our communities cannot only peacefully co-exist; they are mutually reinforcing."

Where money is concerned, women have been at a disadvantage for centuries. As the writer Letty Pogrebin has said, perhaps women don't give more because of an unconscious belief that "she may end up as the most worthy cause she knows." We guard our dollars because we never know when we might lose our jobs, perhaps because of sexual discrimination or harassment, or the glass ceiling. We never know when we might become afflicted with an illness that no one has bothered to research extensively, because it primarily affects women. We never know when we might be assaulted, no matter how careful we are walking home, or left by our partners and suddenly doing solo child care, or in need of any one of a thousand things, and not able to get help from social service agencies, government, the legal system, health care.

The great irony is that is it precisely what we fear most—*being left alone without resources*—that we most stand to change by becoming philanthropists attuned to women's needs and interests. The dollars we give as women, in the long run, may serve us much more than the dollars we save.

BACKBONE AND BITE
The Place of Volunteerism in Women's Giving

KATHERINE ACEY

In addition to the traditional concept of true commitment that means you
are willing to die for what you think is right, we will make equal space
for the womanly concept of commitment that means you are willing to
live for what you believe, and for the sake of whatever it is that you love.
June Jordan, Moving Towards Home: Selected Political Essays

My first experience with volunteerism occurred in eighth grade, when I was elected vice-president of my Catholic school class. Initially I was nominated for president, but my homeroom teacher hastily declined on my behalf. The year was 1963, and the presidency was reserved for boys, the vice-presidency for girls. Despite this inequity—or maybe because of it—I began to put my emerging values into action.

As class vice-president, I organized food and clothing drives and collected whatever lunch and candy money my classmates would give up for "those in the parish less fortunate" than we. I put money in the collection basket at church. I organized teens to participate in the March of Dimes campaign, and I volunteered in a day care center in a housing project. From early on, giving and contributing to the community has been an integral and routine part of my life.

I pursued my high school and college education at all-women institutions, where I was elected president of the student body in both schools. Perhaps this was my subconscious way of resolving that earlier rejection. Being young and not yet having experienced the benefits of the feminist movement, it would take me a number of years before I could name that eighth-grade experience as institutionalized sexism, and feel that I had the power to resist and to change those systems that kept women "in their place." While I was inspired in my early teens to volunteerism by efforts "to do good" rather than to do nothing, it was in my late teens that my activist framework began to be informed by my involvement in anti-war and civil rights organizing. Eventually, I found my way into the women's movement, through work in reproductive rights and sterilization abuse, as well as my involvement in anti-violence and international solidarity.

In today's world, women's foundations are a critical component in advancing and supporting human rights for women and girls. Central to the creation and continuation of women's funds are its volunteers. This chapter demonstrates how volunteers—who are overwhelmingly women—constitute the backbone of the women's funding movement. It is their time, money, skills, and most importantly, diverse lived experiences that inform and sustain our work and that give foundations the necessary bite to navigate the rich terrain of women's philanthropy.

This chapter shares the unique rewards and challenges faced by women's foundations in their efforts to build human capital through the meaningful utilization of volunteers. It examines how women construct boards, community grants panels, and other committees driven by, or dependent upon, volunteers. The chapter is reflective of my own more than four decades of volunteer activism in various arenas, and twenty-one years in the field of progressive philanthropy, the last sixteen as Executive Director of the Astraea Lesbian Foundation for Justice.[1]

Individualism and Solidarity

Women's foundations have strong roots in both community service and social movements. To better understand the emergence and growth of women's foundations and our reliance on volunteers, it is important to understand some of the cultural and philanthropic contexts that influence our choices and ways of operating.

Nonprofit organizations (of which women's foundation are a part) "give institutional expression to two seemingly contradictory principles . . . the principle of individualism—the notion that people should have the freedom to act on matters that concern them—and the principle of solidarity—the notion that people have responsibility not only to themselves but also to their fellow human beings and to the communities of which they are part. By fusing these two principles, nonprofit organizations reinforce both, establishing an arena of action through which individuals can take the initiative not simply to promote their own well-being but to advance the well-being of others as well."[2]

The Independent Sector, a coalition of nonprofit organizations, foundations and corporations, regularly publishes national (U.S.) survey data confirming these principles of individualism and solidarity. According to that data, in 2001, 44 percent of adults in the United States volunteered, equating to nine million full-time employees at a value of $289 billion. During the same period, charitable gifts to nonprofits totaled more than $200 billion. Research also has drawn a correlation between volunteering and giving. People are more likely to give or volunteer if asked; and those who see themselves as members or volunteers within an organization are more inclined to give to that group and to others. This data has not been lost on women's funds in terms of how we promote the giving of both time and money, which extends beyond our own organizations. Through our grants and philanthropic advocacy programs, we connect with a broader, global movement of women's organizations and groups that also encourage and engage their communities in volunteer activism and giving.

Volunteers as Valued Resources

Jewelle Gomez, writer, arts grantmaker, and former Astraea board member says, "I wish there was another word. 'Volunteer' as it comes to us sounds like a dilettantish way of passing time. But it's really one of the ways we've always defined community. When there's trouble, people who see themselves as connected show up. This is necessary for any community to survive and thrive. Without that sense of connection and commitment to show up, we are nothing. Activism is based on the same building blocks. Without a sense of commitment to each other, we're little more than a bunch of primordials huddled around a fire with a stick in our hands. It's a personal choice, but we must show up if we care about what happens in this generation and the next."

Universally, volunteers around the world provide an important service function in institutions ranging from hospitals and social services, to schools and religious organizations. In the civic, community, and advocacy arena, individual and collective action is an embodiment of the commitment to work for what one believes and loves. It is important to note that many organizations in the latter categories exist and flourish for which limited data is collected.

For centuries, women have organized themselves in the service of their families and communities. In the United States alone, women have founded institutions, started movements, and provided leadership for social causes for more than 250 years. "Before it was widely acceptable for women to work outside the home, many honed their organizational skills in associations they created. Activities ranged from political advocacy against slavery, for women's rights and the vote, for child labor laws, for peace and other health, safety, arts and cultural activities."[3] The abolitionist, suffrage, civil rights, women's, lesbian, gay, bisexual, transgender people (LGBT), and global human rights movements have been fueled by the resources, time, and dedication of "volunteer activists" and the leadership of women. While form and context vary broadly, women's activism, the creation of women's organizations, and movement building are rooted in every culture in the world. Women's foundations in the United States, Mexico, India, the Netherlands, Nepal, Ghana, and elsewhere are part of this continuum; they are a modern-day manifestation of the power of group action and initiative on the part of women around the globe to take control of our lives.

Sadly, institutional philanthropy historically has been unresponsive to the concerns of woman and girls and openly dismissive of lesbian organizations and the LGBT movement. Additionally, institutional philanthropy has been reticent for the most part in supporting social justice advocacy efforts. Despite witnessing a shift in attitude and behavior in recent years, "the indigenous philanthropy of culture-specific groups will continue to play a leadership role in addressing social justice issues. As these efforts show promise, they will influence the beliefs of the larger public and attract the support of institutional philanthropy. In this way, the indigenous philanthropy of culture specific groups is an essential element of efforts to address old and new problems of social inequality."[4]

Women's, LGBT, culture specific, and nationally networked local foundations like the Funding Exchange share core missions of promoting and supporting social justice advocacy at the local, national, and international level. Other shared characteristics include the reliance on "gifts" of time and money from members of those communities, giving rise to various institutions.

The Astraea Foundation for Justice and the Centrality of Volunteers

In 1977, a small group of women created a multi-racial, multi-class, feminist foundation in order to address the lack of funding for women—specifically lesbians and women of color. We believed that even the smallest of gestures, when combined, could be a catalyst for women's empowerment and for significant social change. A quarter of a century later, Astraea is regarded as a dynamic and forward-thinking global foundation, with a penchant for risk-taking shared with many of our sister funds.

While Astraea was forming and evolving, we knew of no groups other than the Ms. Foundation—the "grandmother" of the modern women's funding movement—that were engaged in similar discussions and activities. By 1985, when only a handful of women's foundations existed and gathered for our first joint meeting, many of us attended in our capacity as volunteers: board members, donor activists, community organizers. We were just beginning to realize the enormous potential of our nascent movement and the role we played. Recognizing this, some of us contributed more volunteer time to begin the process of formally building the Women's Funding Network.

Until 1987, Astraea existed solely on volunteer labor. The all-volunteer board gave and raised money, planned and held issue forums and cultural events, and did community outreach. Foundation volunteers made grants, wrote a newsletter and fundraising appeals, stuffed envelops, licked stamps (adhesive stamps had yet to be invented), and dutifully recorded gifts "manually." (Now, when there is a computer glitch, we long for those index cards.) We had a "mobile office," which means that we operated out of the trunks of various members' cars.

I was a volunteer board member at Astraea long before I became the first paid staff member. Today, with thirteen paid staff, a board, grants panels, advisory groups, events and other committees, our volunteer corps and our programs have quadrupled in size. This type of steady growth is indicative of many of the women's funds that existed in 1985 and those that have been created in subsequent years.

Most women's foundations and the groups we fund owe their creation to a core of volunteers who came together around a vision to address community needs or social inequities. As they organized themselves and others around their cause or issue, many volunteers "self funded," which some still do out of political choice or fiscal necessity. Even as many volunteer-led organizations transitioned from the "kitchen table" to boardrooms with paid staff, volunteers continued to play a pivotal role in the life of their organizations. This certainly has been true for Astraea, the organizations that we support with grants, and other women's foundations.

The Board of Directors and Community Funding Panel(s)

Volunteers are drawn to the missions and programs of women's funds, which emphasize democracy, diversity, leadership development, and the notion that women's issues—*their* issues—are central to a healthy, functioning society. In turn, our organizations are strengthened in the belief and practice that philanthropy belongs to the many, not just the few. The result is increased dollars, increased volunteers, and increased visibility and impact for community organizations and women's issues.

It is often the case in women's foundations that the *how* and *who* of our work is as valued as the *what*. The board of directors and community grants panels exemplify this belief and are two of the mainstays of volunteer involvement in the women's funds. They bring credibility and integrity to our missions, fundraising, and grant programs. According to fundraising expert Hank Rosso, "The trustees must bear the responsibility to define and interpret the mission and ensure that the organization will remain faithful to its mission. Board members should accept the charge that trusteeship concerns itself with the proper deployment of resources and with the accompanying action, the securing of resources."[5]

Board volunteers within women's foundations take very seriously their governance role and responsibility to and for their mission. Astraea's board spent an entire year (2002) focusing on strategic planning and revisiting/reframing its mission. Belief in the mission of women's funds is a primary attraction for volunteers and donors alike to engage. Astraea's "retooled" mission states:

> The Astraea Foundation for Justice works for social, racial, and economic justice in the U.S. and internationally. Our grantmaking and philanthropic advocacy programs help lesbians and allied communities challenge oppression and claim their rights.

There are variations in how each women's foundation constructs its board or grants panels (sometimes called grants allocation committees). However, all of them embody a spirit of participation, shared leadership, and the inclusion of different experiences and voices when setting priorities and making decisions. Partnering with staff, it is the active and diverse leadership of the board and panels that helps sustain our foundations and assure alignment with community needs and concerns.

Being a board member requires immense commitment to learning and in some cases *un*learning. It requires us to leave our comfort zones, whether they are about asking for money, struggling through issues of racism, heterosexism, and class differences, or debating which strategies to support. Astraea and the other women's foundations have not discarded some of the more "traditional" roles of trustees; that is, governance, fiscal oversight, strategic planning, and fundraising. We've merely changed and expanded those roles. We've created boardrooms of our own, where everyone brings something to the table and leaves with new knowledge, new skills, and stronger allies.

The roles of Astraea board volunteers mirror those of other women's foundations around the world. For example:

• We have realized 100 percent giving from our boards. Every member fundraises (some with the added cajoling of the development director and committee chair);

- The treasurer reports to the board and ensures that all her colleagues understand the budget and their responsibility for fiscal health;
- Board representatives on the community grants panels introduce funding issues and serve as liaisons between the two entities;
- Board members lead, with the senior staff, the strategic planning for the foundation;
- Board members sign contracts to underscore the seriousness of their role in the foundation;
- Board members represent the organization at conferences and speak publicly on behalf of the foundations and the issues faced by women in our communities;
- Board members make long-term commitments to the board (six years in the case of Astraea) and some transition to other work in the organization when their terms end. Many remain lifetime donor members.

The women's foundations recruit people both with board experience and those serving for the first time. We share a deep belief that our missions are best served by a broad representation of people and their accompanying commitment to leadership development and education on a number of levels. This type of training and volunteer leadership development strengthens our institutions and our movement immeasurably.

What Does a Board Meeting Look Like?

The basic principle of giving—whether time, skills, knowledge, or money—is universal. While expression of that principle may vary from group to group, or culture to culture, that expression contributes to the tradition and growth of volunteerism.

Still, bringing together a diverse group of women in common purpose must be intentional. It doesn't happen accidentally, although it may grow organically. It's not magical, although there are magical moments that help sustain us in the face of inevitable internal and external obstacles.

A typical Astraea board meeting is illustrative and demonstrates the interplay of the *how* and *who* (diversity in all of its manifestations) and the *what*, or task, at hand. A banker is seated next to a public interest lawyer, who is the treasurer the banker mentored when she held that position. Next to her is a financial consultant who had done military service. She is seated next to a secretary taking minutes who is also the executive director of a youth program that has taken a position against the war in Iraq. A graduate student in sports administration is seated next to a donor activist who spends most of her volunteer time working with other women with wealth around philanthropic activism. To her left is someone who organizes around racial and economic justice issues. She has just seconded the motion to accept the new investment policy that outlines social screens and risk management guidelines to insure that our $3 million endowment is properly managed. The semi-retired board chair, who helped found a local women's foundation, calls for the vote. The board numbers fifteen and growing, and ranges in age from twenty-four to sixty-four. Most of the women were born in the United States, but some are immigrants. Some have served on boards before while it is the first board experience for others. These women come from different racial, ethnic, and religious backgrounds; they are Chinese, Chicana, Anglo, African American, Arab, Jewish, and Christian.

The Community Funding Panel

Funding panels, grants allocation committees, and community advisory committees on grants each have a function different from the board's, but each is equally important in terms of the expertise and time it renders to women's foundations. These entities are diverse in many respects and are composed, in part, of women who have created some of the same groups we fund. They bring knowledge and experience on a range of issues (e.g., violence, reproductive health and rights, economic development and justice, aging, disability, education), as well as knowledge of various strategies that are employed by women's organizations (e.g., advocacy, policy analysis, community organizing, coalition building, media advocacy, and research).

Again, while there are variations among women's foundations, generally panel members meet with and interview potential grantees and come together to recommend grants. In the process of making decisions and distributing grants, volunteers learn about an array of issues and strategies that can be applied to their own areas of work, as they develop a wider lens around the common challenges and successes faced by women's organizations.

Young Girls and Women

Youth participation is another important factor influencing adult volunteering. Independent Sector surveys consistently find that adults who reported belonging to a youth group, being active in church volunteering, or participating in student government regularly show a much higher level of volunteering as adults than those who did not have these experiences as children.

INDEPENDENT SECTOR

This important finding is not lost on the women's funding movement. While women come to feminism and politics at different ages and life stages, women's funds realize how important it is to promote leadership among young women. This commitment is reflected in the composition of our boards and grants panels and other volunteer activity.

The youth-focused organizations that we fund must not merely serve; they must also include young people in meaningful organizational functions. Thus, youth serve as volunteers (including as board members), as staff, and as designers of their own projects. Young women and girls develop their leadership capabilities and skills not only through training, but through hands-on involvement. Some women's foundations have instituted programs where young women and girls are trained and then empowered with a pool of money to make grants to their own constituencies—an extraordinary and radical way to introduce them to the power of giving, and a highly effective experiential introduction to community involvement and philanthropic activism.

Building Bridges

Gary Delgado, Director of Applied Research and co-founder of the Center for Third World Organizing in Oakland, California, captures the essence of what underlies the *how, who,* and *what* that we are striving for in the women's funding movement.

> I've become clearer about the importance of having bridge people in leadership positions. By bridge people I mean people of color, people with disabilities, lesbian and gay people, and first generation immigrants—those who, because they don't exactly "fit" in this society, have been forced to carve out their own identities and their own unique perch from which they view the world. The ability of these groups of people to see across and through similarity and difference—to see sideways—and to integrate the knowledge of many cultures can be a valuable asset to developing new multidimensional organizations.[6]

There are many others who serve as bridge people and who add value to the "multidimensional" nature of women's foundations. Boards, grant panels, and events committees nurture and produce bridge people intentionally and consistently. This kind of intentional bridging of people, relationships, and issues is a special contribution that women's foundations make to the broad field of philanthropy and volunteer activism. Of course, staff provide key leadership in bridging people as well as various aspects of our work. But for most women's funds, the numbers of volunteers who serve will always exceed the number of staff. And many women's civic and activist organizations do not (yet) have staff; they must rely on volunteer leadership in their quest for a more equitable society.

Events and Other Opportunities

Women's foundations hold events—large and small—to raise money and visibility both for the foundation and for the grantee partners. They also sponsor workshops, forums, conferences and retreats that are not fundraisers but that provide a space for political discussion or exploration of an issue affecting women. The success of any event is heavily dependent on an engaged volunteer force, whether it is a house party of twenty women raising $1,000, or a large-scale awards breakfast drawing two thousand people and raising $100,000 dollars. Often, regardless of the kind of event, volunteers provide an avenue to partnering in different ways with other volunteers, staff, and grantees. Sometimes events are entirely volunteer-driven with minimal support from staff; other times the reverse is true. Either way, a positive and productive partnership between the two is required.

Events provide important opportunities for members of women's funds to participate in planning programs, conducting outreach to new communities and individuals within their circles of friends, fundraising, and supporting logistical details. Additionally, events are a good way to introduce people to a foundation, and a way to inspire them to become more active, either in the work of the foundation or with grantee organizations that they may be introduced to through a particular program. With women's funds raising anywhere from a few thousand to hundreds of thousands of dollars, volunteer committees can number in the hundreds and work for over a year to ensure an event's success. There is no question of the contribution such a workforce makes. Volunteers lead, coordinate others, and oversee multiple tasks, from handling logistics to securing a dynamic emcee or well-known speaker. Usually an event is barely over before the next one is being planned with the help of seasoned, and new, volunteers.

Not all women have the time or propensity to serve on a board, panel, or planning committee. For those women, there are other opportunities that benefit foundations while matching individual interests. Specialists in human resources help to refine personnel policies, financial planners serve on investment committees, CPAs review budgets and annual fiscal statements, expert advisors comment on grants dockets, and still others conduct workshops on any number of topics related to their own expertise. Whatever their role, volunteers enable women's foundations to exist, grow, and thrive.

Beth Ritchie, a professor, long-time activist, board member, and experienced advisor to various women's and other foundations, is a respected bridge builder who captures the sentiment of many women called to serve. She has served in numerous capacities and her comments further underscore the significance of relationship building. " For me, working as an activist in the anti-violence and anti-incarceration movements with women of color has been nothing short of a privilege. I have made my best friends here, found love here, felt like I was in the strongest community I could ever image here. To call it "volunteering" implies that I gave of myself. In fact, I found myself working to be a change agent helping to create social change. For me, to work for what I believe in has given meaning to my life. It's a political commitment as well as a personal blessing."[7]

Lessons Learned

Involving volunteers in the fundamental work of the women's funding movement brings many rewards and challenges. It is also highly instructive. Some of the key lessons we've learned are obvious and basic, although not always simple to implement. Here are the three most important lessons we've learned at Astraea:

- *Be prepared.* The importance of developing an organizational culture and systems that foster time-intensive commitment cannot be underestimated. Guidelines for recruitment, orientation, training, and recognition must be developed. All of this requires a tremendous organizational investment of time and human resources. The basic rule is that it takes resources to develop resources, and that is as true for volunteers as it is for funds.

- *Have clear expectations.* As with any good relationship, clear, negotiated expectations are essential. Volunteers are an unpaid labor force with other responsibilities as well. Expectations need to be reasonable and mutually understood and agreed upon. And volunteers need to be held accountable to these agreements, a major challenge for most organizations. Agreements may need to be renegotiated from time to time. Resist the idea that volunteers can be less accountable because they are "just volunteers." At the same time, have contingency plans if someone is unable to fulfill a commitment.

- *Role clarification is essential.* Clarity of roles is an essential ingredient to developing positive, productive relationships between staff and volunteers and among volunteer bodies such as the board. Such clarity is especially important during growth phases when an organization is transitioning from being totally or predominantly a volunteer organization to being a fully staffed entity. For example, the Astraea board functions very differently now than it did in the early years.

While board members occasionally write for the newsletter, content and production is coordinated by staff. Even when volunteers drive certain events, staff must convey the broader organizational policies around budget, diversity in programming, or other procedures. These three key lessons are as much about developing an organizational culture as they are about creating viable systems.

Conclusion

My journey since that day in eighth grade has been long and revelatory. By now, because of the efforts of many women activists, both paid and unpaid, I hope there are many more young girls serving as class presidents. Still, too many young girls go to bed hungry, or die from bombs dropped on their villages, or suffer rape on their way home from school. Their mothers work two jobs to make one salary. Their grandmothers can't afford necessary prescription medicine.

Anna Julia Cooper, a black educator and former slave, expressed my own feelings and that of other early feminists when she said, "The colored woman feels that women's cause is one and universal . . . sacred and inviolable. Not till race, color, sex, and condition are seen as accidents, and not the substance of life, not till the universal title of humanity of life, liberty, and the pursuit of happiness is conceded to be inalienable to all; not till then is woman's lesson taught and woman's case won . . . the acquirement of her 'rights' will mean the final triumph of all right over might, the supremacy of the moral forces of reason, and justice, and love in the government of the nations of earth."[8]

My personal volunteer activism and work within the women's funding movement, and more broadly, for social justice, has sustained me and provided me with knowledge and hope. And Astraea and other women's foundations have spent time building institutions carefully and thoughtfully, with support from thousands upon thousands of volunteers. Each institution is a vehicle for something bigger than itself. Our missions, when examined closely and collectively, speak to radical transformation and social change. Together as a women's funding movement, with the help of others, we can improve dramatically the material and social conditions of women. We might even dare to hope that one day we will achieve full human rights for all.

NOTES

1. Astraea was the Roman Goddess of Justice. In most ancient writings, Astraea is associated with natural law, matriarchal justice, and the personification of truth and justice. While this reference may seem particular to American culture, every country or region has traditions and values around community service and social responsibility that are influ-

enced in part by geography, religion, the role of government, family structures, and cultural norms. Even within the United States, with its wide diversity of people, numerous philanthropic practices unique to various subcultures historically have gone unacknowledged. Lisa Durán, "Caring for Each Other: Philanthropy in Communities of Color," *Grassroots Fundraising Journal* (September/October 2001): 4.

2. Lester M. Salamon, "The Resilient Sector: The State of Nonprofit America," in *The State of Nonprofit America,* ed. Salamon, 11 (Washington, D.C.: Brookings Institution Press, 2002).

3. Elizabeth T. Boris, "The Nonprofit Sector in the 1990's," in *Philanthropy and the Nonprofit Sector,* ed. Charles T. Clotfelter and Thomas Ehrlich, 12 (Bloomington: Indiana University Press, 1999).

4. The term "culture specific" is used to refer to groups of people who have in common immutable characteristics such as race, ethnicity, language, and gender, and a shared history due to these characteristics. Emmett D. Carson, "The Roles of Indigenous and Institutional Philanthropy, Advancing Social Justice," in *Philanthropy and the Nonprofit Sector,* 270–71.

5. Hank Rosso and Eugene R. Tempel, eds., *Hank Rosso's Acheiving Excellence in Fund Raising,* 2nd edition (San Francisco: Jossey-Bass, 2003), 17.

6. Gary Delgado, "The Last Stop Sign," in *Shelterforce Online,* National Housing Institute, at http://www.nhi.org/online/issues/102/stopsign.html.

7. Personal Communication with Betty Richie (n.d.).

8. Kim Klein, "Early History of Women in U.S. Philanthropy, Part 2: Black Women in Philanthropy: 1850–1950," *Grassroots Fundraising Journal* (October 1990): 3.

REFERENCES

Boris, Elizabeth T. "The Nonprofit Sector in the 1990's." In *Philanthropy and the Nonprofit Sector,* ed. Charles T. Clotfelter and Thomas Ehrlich. Bloomington: Indiana University Press, 1999.

Clotfelter, Charles T., and Thomas Ehrlich, eds. *Philanthropy and the Nonprofit Sector.* Bloomington: Indiana University Press, 1999.

Carson, Emmett D. "The Roles of Indigenous and Institutional Philanthropy, Advancing Social Justice." In Clotfelter and Ehrlich, *Philanthropy and the Nonprofit Sector.*

Delgado, Gary. "The Last Stop Sign." *Shelterforce Online.* National Housing Institute. http://www.nhi.org/online/issues/102/stopsign.html.

Durán, Lisa. "Caring for Each Other: Philanthropy in Communities of Color." *Grassroots Fundraising Journal* (September/October 2001).

Klein, Kim. "Early History of Women in U.S. Philanthropy, Part 2: Black Women in Philanthropy: 1850–1950," *Grassroots Fundraising Journal* (October 1990).

————. "Raising Money in All-Volunteer Organizations." *Grassroots Fundraising Journal* (September/October 2002).

National Network of Grantmakers. "Evaluation Guide." In *What is Good Grantmaking for Social Justice?* San Diego: National Network of Grantmakers, April 1993.

Rosso, Hank, and Eugene R. Tempel, eds. *Hank Rosso's Achieving Excellence in Fund Raising.* 2nd edition. San Francisco: Jossey-Bass, 2003.

Salamon, Lester M. ed. *The State of Nonprofit America.* Washington, D.C.: Brookings Institution Press, 2002.

Sen, Rinku. *Stir It Up: Lessons in Community Organizing and Advocacy.* Chardon Press Series, Kim Klein, ed. San Francisco: Jossey-Bass, 2003.

PARTNERS AND STEWARDS
Fostering Healthy Collaboration

KIMBERLY OTIS

Like many women who have become transformed by the "women's funding movement," I encountered the movement with much enthusiasm. In 1987, as the new development director for a New York City–based women's organization, Nontraditional Employment for Women (NEW), I was suddenly energized by the enormous potential of raising money by women, from women, and for women. The funding environment then was not necessarily friendly to women's organizations: It was the Reagan/Bush era of austerity and cutbacks for the nonprofit sector, so few foundations had funding priorities focused on women and girls. Nonetheless, I felt there was something extraordinary about growing an organization focused on women's economic self-sufficiency that could prove its success because of its track record, mission, and leadership.

After working for theoretically progressive, male-led nonprofit organizations in the 1980s, working in a female-run environment opened up a new world of mentoring, mutual support, and purpose for me. As opposed to feeling like I was working for the man who was the head of the organization where I was employed, working for a women's organization felt like I was working with a team for a good cause. It was not only a more nurturing environment, but a much more inspiring and motivating one. I felt suddenly that if women could pull together, the potential for real social change was enormous.

Through strong stewardship and partnerships, women are reinventing collaboration for social change in philanthropy in a myriad of ways. This chapter describes my experiences with various types of collaboration among women working in philanthropy, which have tended to emphasize the development of true partnership and careful stewardship in a field that is notorious for competition and unequal power relationships. Given the intrinsic power accorded to money in our society, and women's historical lack of access and control over money, the traditional power relationships between and among grantees and grantors are being reinvented through women's philanthropy. The chapter outlines how important it is to learn from the dozens of innovative collaborations in women's philanthropy that have developed since the late 1980s.

Collaboration and Growth

The theme of the 2003 Council on Foundations Annual Meeting in Dallas, Texas was "Working Together for the Common Good—What Have We Learned about Collaboration?" While the foundation community has done much to foster collaboration and partnerships, its attempts have also, not infrequently, failed. The lessons of why funder-driven partnerships— as opposed to bottom-up, more organic collaborations—have worked and not worked, are extremely important, especially in a climate of funder fatigue over the growth of nonprofits sharing similar missions and strategies. And in an economic downturn, formal mergers and restructurings are increasingly under consideration and development for many nonprofits.

Collaboration thus has become a huge field of interest for nonprofits, including working with the government and business sectors. Many new resources exist for explaining the different models of collaboration and strategic partnerships, outlining the lessons from experience and advantages and disadvantages of each model. The Leader to Leader Institute (formerly the Drucker Foundation) published a popular book in 2000 by James Austin of Harvard Business School, *The Collaboration Challenge: How Nonprofits and Businesses Succeed through Strategic Alliances*.[1] Dr. Elizabeth Boris, Director of the Urban Institute's Center on Nonprofits and Philanthropy, and senior fellow, C. Eugene Steuerle, published a more academic framework to analyze the renewed reliance on nonprofit organizations to provide government services in *Nonprofits and Government: Collaboration and Conflict*.[2] The Amherst Wilder Foundation has several good publications on collaboration in the nonprofit sector, including Karen Ray's *The Nimble Collaboration*, published in 2001.[3]

Dozens of other books, videos, reports, articles, and workbooks exist on nonprofit collaboration, which is on the rise in many forms. One of the better overviews for funders is *Beyond Collaboration: Strategic Restructuring of Nonprofit Organizations*, by David La Piana, and published by the James Irvine Foundation and BoardSource, (formerly the National Center for

Nonprofit Boards).[4] Certain principles are common to his work and much of the other literature, including the need for collaborating organizations to maintain and value:

- complementary missions;
- understanding motivations;
- achievable results;
- leadership for risk-taking and flexibility;
- clarifying expectations;
- a favorable political environment;
- keeping focused with benchmarks; and
- a clear delineation of roles.

These common features of good partnerships are much easier said, even written, than actually done. According to the LaPiana study, "Nonprofit organizations attempting to restructure through mergers, back-office consolidations, joint ventures, or fiscal sponsorships must overcome perceived threats to autonomy and board and staff interests, as well as potential culture clashes." Perhaps the most important linchpin of all of the above characteristics of successful collaboration is the last: a clear delineation of roles. While all of the other criteria may be met through good intentions and planning, often it is the lack of clarity about roles and responsibilities that can cause resentments about whether each party is carrying its fair share, and even cause the collaborative effort to fail and permanently damage relations between the partners. As such, mutually agreed-upon workplans need to detail roles and responsibilities clearly. Several examples of how that has worked in the women's funding movement are outlined in the pages that follow and the final section, "Lessons Learned."

Collaboration, Partnership, and Gender

Research is starting to show that male and female donors tend to have different motivations and respond differently to nonprofit requests. According to an article in the *New York Times*, women donors respond more to equality arguments, male givers more to costs.[5] As a corollary, traditional male models of collaboration are based on the need to pool resources to achieve economies of scale and heightened efficiency. On the other hand, women's philanthropy focuses more on collaborating to accomplish social change, perhaps because women's organizations have been so sorely underfunded, and thus have so much more to achieve. Nonprofits devoted to women and girls have for so long been making do with less. Thus, collaboration among women's groups in order to achieve efficiencies of scale is less motivational than collaborating in order to have a greater presence in media, the economy, and political and social institutions, thereby achieving greater social change.

Women's organizations are poised to become bigger players, or social change agents, through effective stewardship and collaboration. However, this conviction is sorely underdocumented in terms of scientific analysis based on solid research. Publications proliferate describing psychological motivations for female donors, and some do offer nuggets for contemplation. In her article, "Ten Things You Should Know about the Impact of Women on Philanthropy," Kay Sprinkel Grace lists as the number one consideration: "Women seek relationships, not recognition."[6] Sandra Shaw and Martha Taylor include collaboration as one of the "Six C's of Women's Philanthropy" in their book, *Reinventing Fundraising: Realizing the Potential of Women's Philanthropy*.[7] In addition to Create, Change, Connect, Commit, and Celebrate, the authors define collaboration as a hallmark of women's philanthropy, because:

- Women, through their giving, become collaborators with providers and recipients.
- Women prefer to work with others as part of a larger effort.
- Women feel that collaboration can avoid duplication, competition, and waste.

Thus, instead of condescending to grant applicants, forcing them to beg for funding and compete with other grantseekers, women in philanthropy see the grantmaking process as more collaborative with the goal of social change through effective partnerships. In contrast to the competitive, "backbiting" stereotypes of women being unable to work together, women's philanthropy is demonstrating that they can embody a more effective way of creating social change through philanthropy by joining forces, and understanding the stewardship entailed that is necessary. One leader of a grantee of the Girl's Best Friend Foundation in Illinois, Sisters Empowering Sisters, said it best: "It's about partnership, not a power trip."[8]

Stewardship is defined by *Webster's Collegiate Dictionary* as, "the careful and responsible management of something entrusted to one's care."[9] In practical terms in the nonprofit sector, stewardship means ensuring the good management of resources and paying attention to the interests of stakeholders. Typically, stewardship is used in reference to donor stewardship, which involves donor recognition in the recipient organization's printed and electronic communications, strong communication with the donor about how the gift is helping the organization in agreement with the terms of the donation, and connecting the donor to the charitable recipient in meaningful ways. However, in women's philanthropy, as Anne Mosle, president of the Washington Area Women's Foundation, puts it, "stewardship is about community." And in building community, establishing mutual trust has proven key to successful stewardship in women's philanthropy.

The Hunt Alternatives Fund — A Family Partnership

My foray into the grantmaking side of women's philanthropy began with a nine-year tenure as executive director of the Sister Fund, formerly the Hunt Alternatives Fund. Founded in 1981 by sisters Helen LaKelly Hunt and Swanee Hunt of Dallas, Texas, the Hunt Alternatives Fund was set up as a collaborative foundation. Helen and Swanee, along with founding executive director, Vincent McGee, established the the Hunt Alternatives Fund as a "pass-through" or "flow-through" private grantmaking foundation, as opposed to a traditionally endowed foundation. By setting up the foundation as a pass-through foundation, the Hunt sisters committed to making contributions to the Fund each year, which were then spent on grantmaking and program activities within each year.

The Hunt Alternatives Fund was a model of learning how to do social change philanthropy through a collaborative family foundation model. For over ten years, the Hunt Alternatives Fund supported grassroots efforts for social change in Swanee's hometown of Denver, as well as Helen's home in New York City. The similarities and differences they discovered in getting at the roots of poverty in the two communities were shared in making grants to such organizations as East Harlem Churches and Communities, Five Corners Community Center, and the Family Health Project. The benefits of the collaboration were substantial—both for the profound philanthropic learning among the two sisters and staffs and for the lessons learned from and between the grantees and communities in which they were funding.

As the grantmaking became more strategic, and Helen and Swanee gained more expertise in their philanthropic leadership, different approaches began to emerge. In New York City, a huge city with many competing social issues and other large philanthropic players, Helen felt more effective focusing on programs for women and girls, especially since less than 3 percent of all foundation dollars were then being invested in women's and girls' programs.[10] In Denver, the Hunt Alternatives Fund remained a real force for change in a range of community issues, including programs for women and girls, but also low-income community development, Native American programs, mental health agencies, and arts and cultural programs.

Because of the way that the Hunt Alternatives Fund was structured, it allowed for an unusually smooth transition into two foundations in early

WOMEN'S FOUNDATIONS AND VALUES-BASED STEWARDSHIP

At the Washington Area Women's Foundation, we are building a community of women and men who are concerned about the growing economic gap in our nation's capital and who believe that investing in women and girls is one of the most effective strategies for building strong families and communities.

Our vision is simple and clear: Creating a better life for women and girls results in a safe, strong, vibrant community. The Washington area community is embracing this vision. Over the past three years, our grantmaking and fundraising have tripled. We now have close to five thousand individuals who are investing in our vision with gifts ranging from $5 to $1 million. Many more have become stakeholders through donating countless volunteer hours.

As a relatively young public foundation operating in the rather choppy waters of Washington, D.C., we determined that our greatest asset would be our ability to engage women across race, ethnicity, age, profession, and neighborhood around a common goal of ensuring all women and girls in our local community a chance to reach their full potential. And we have. But there are always more to invite to join the circle.

The founders of the Washington Area Women's Foundation were bold and straightforward in their rallying call: Caring counts, action speaks, money talks. . . . Join the conversation. Gather information. Be strategic.

With every passing year, more women are heeding that call. We are making sure that when they do, the Washington Area Women's Foundation is there with information to guide them. As part of that effort, we conducted the Portrait Project, the first-ever analysis of how women and girls in our region fare on key economic and social indicators. We found that Washington, D.C. is much like an hourglass. On one end of the hourglass, we have tremendous financial, human, and intellectual resources, as Washington ranks first in women's earnings and education nationally. On the other end, we are confronted with extreme need—with one in three children living in poverty, as do more than one-third of women-headed households.

The Portrait Project clarified and strengthened our resolve to connect the world of resources and compassion to the world of unrealized dreams and potential. It also reit-

1993: the Sister Fund in New York and the Hunt Alternatives Fund in Denver, and later in Cambridge, Massachusetts. Typically, family foundations have split because of different funding principles, philosophies, or politics among family members. In this case, Helen and Swanee Hunt continued to share each other's principles of social change grantmaking and support for women and girls, but with different strategies because of

WOMEN'S FOUNDATIONS AND VALUES-BASED STEWARDSHIP (CONTINUED)

erated the importance of four key watchwords that guide our work: Trust, Communication, Collaboration, and Community.

- *Trust.* Relationships are primary and all else is secondary. Our donors and grantee organization, many of which are actually donors as well, are our priority stakeholders. Our relationship with both audiences extends past the "gift transaction." The ability to listen, respond, and act appropriately is a key component to building trust—in the institution, its leadership, and its mission.
- *Communication.* Clear and consistent communication is essential. Honest articulation of challenges is the first step to solving a problem. Donors appreciate this. With the balanced use of technology, newsletters, and convenings, we are able to connect donors with the most critical information and stories of lives and laws that are changed as a result of their collective philanthropy.
- *Collaboration.* Effective collaboration is not easy, but can yield powerful results. Flexibility, time, humility, and follow-up are required. Our success and impact are determined not only by an assessment of what we accomplished, but also by what we enabled or catalyzed others to do. Our ability to ensure that the most critical needs of women and girls are met is linked inextricably to our effectiveness in engaging leaders from the public, private, and philanthropic sectors to get involved. In order to be effective, we must understand and appreciate their values, goals, and objectives.
- *Community.* Women's funds are created on the power of the collective. The Washington Area Women's Foundation offers a multiplier effect for philanthropic investments and provides an opportunity to join a community of giving and learning. Each donor has her unique perspective and experience that connects her to us. Connecting each individual to our work is critical. As one wise woman said, "Women are like snowflakes. Individually, they melt. Collectively, we stop traffic."

Women are central not only to the future of our communities, but also to the future of philanthropy. We are a critical source of innovation, expertise, and resources. Despite the current economic climate, our experiences fuel our optimism about the future of women's role in both challenging and expanding the field of philanthropy. Women's foundations are increasingly influential stewards in our shared future.

Anne B. Mosle, President, Washington Area Women's Foundation

the different communities where they lived and their different experiences. Collaboration was a positive theme for the evolution of the Hunt Alternatives Fund from a formal partnership into an informal one—largely due to planning, innovation and mutual trust.

The Sister Fund — A Collaborative Endeavor

In November 1992, the last board meeting of the joint offices of the Hunt Alternatives Fund was held, and the Sister Fund was formed in early 1993. The Sister Fund's mission statement named four program area partners:

- Grassroots initiatives in New York City strengthening the lives of women and girls;
- the women's funding movement;
- national and international women's organizations; and
- our brothers joining us in this struggle, and with whom coalition is essential.

Working with these partners, the Sister Fund emphasized advocacy efforts, public education, and media initiatives, in the hope of leveraging its impact.

One of the major new developments to occur with the restructuring of the Hunt Alternatives Fund into the Sister Fund was a broadening of the decision making to a diverse board of directors to oversee all grants and programs, comprised of ten women leaders from all aspects of society and with wide-ranging expertise. Many people in the women's funding community and other philanthropic circles expressed amazement at Helen's "giving up power to a diverse board of directors." However, it soon became evident that she and the Sister Fund had gained power because of the access and credibility in communities of color and new issues that the diverse board members brought to the table. The Sister Fund became a notable leader in creating social change in the foundation community in New York, as well as nationally and internationally, largely because of the partnership with a diverse board of directors.

Nonetheless, especially at the beginning, working with the new board members was not always easy. The founding board of the Sister Fund was comprised of outspoken leaders in such wide-ranging areas as economic justice for low-income workers, education and politics, AIDS, lesbian and gay rights, and disability issues. As new board members of a new grant-making foundation, some directors felt that they needed to prove themselves. Board members advocated vigorously for their issues, and questioned how the work of the foundation got done. When I expressed frustration to Helen as board president, she gave me invaluable advice: My job was to empower the board. In other words, if I learned how to best steward board members strengths and talents effectively, they would be empowered and contribute to the work of the Sister Fund. If board members felt confident of their contributions to the organization, they would no longer feel that they had to prove themselves.

The board made decisions by different methods over the years—through voting on a one-to-ten scale, through consensus, and through honoring individual sponsorships of selected grantees. But most importantly, the board came to the table seeing the whole as greater than their individual leadership and causes combined. Respect for each woman as an individual was a highly held principle, which worked to strengthen the greater work of the Sister Fund. Because of the founder's and my shared belief in the moral imperative of diversity for social-change decision making, a strong majority of the board members were women of color.

Board members served three-year terms that were staggered, so new members joined the board of directors every year. For the first five years, the board had a broadly diverse composition of dynamic women, including Alice Cardona of the National Latinas Caucus, Mallika Dutt of the Ford Foundation, Idelisse Malave of the Ms. and Tides foundations, Tessie Naranjo of the Tewa people of New Mexico, Suki Ports of the Family Health Project, Harilyn Rousso of Disabilties Consulting Services, film-maker Catherine Gund (formerly Saalfield), Sheri Sandler of the Cooper Hewitt Museum, Linda Tarry of Project People Foundation, Leah Wise of the Southeast Regional Economic Justice Network, Ingrid Washinawatok of the Fund for the Four Directions, and writer Evelyn C. White. In 1998, new board members began to reflect more of a grounding in faith-based circles due to new directions at the Sister Fund. They included Annie Bovian of the Women's Advocate Ministry, Olivia Cousins of the Borough of Manhattan Community College, Barbara Dobkin of Ma'yan, Ada Maria Isasi-Diaz of Drew University, writer China Galland, and Karen Hessel of the National Council of Churches.

Program Partnerships of the Sister Fund

The collaborative nature of the infrastructure of the Sister Fund was also reflected in its programs. For instance, in 1996, the Sister Fund and the New York Regional Association of Grantmakers (NYRAG) hosted a meeting of faith-based funders as well as secular foundation representatives on the issue of welfare reform. Many of those in the room were amazed to see that they had allies whom they had not previously realized existed. Several of the faith-based funders never had identified themselves as part of the grantmaking community, and felt quite isolated in their work. Both the faith-based and secular women began to see new ways to collaborate, and to help their grantees approach new funding partners.

The Sister Fund consistently demonstrated the value of partnership not only through its program work, but also its grantmaking. One of its first collaborative projects was Iris House, the country's first comprehensive center for women "infected and affected by HIV/AIDS." Ruth Messinger, then president of the Borough of Manhattan, approached the foundation in 1992 to help fund a women and HIV/AIDS support group that had been meeting in her offices. With the instinct that this was becoming a bigger social issue than a support group could address fully, Helen encouraged the grassroots group's founders to think about a permanent safe space for women and HIV/AIDS. As the founding chair of the New York Women's Foundation (NYWF), she brought it to the table as the fiscal sponsor while a steering committee was formed.

Iris House was founded in honor of Iris de la Cruz, a local poet and inspiring AIDS activist who had recently died of the disease. I helped with developing proposals for the start-up organization, and Iris House succeeded in landing several start-up grants from the Aaron Diamond Foundation, the Sister Fund, and others. Most importantly, Iris House was awarded a large challenge grant from the Robert Wood Johnson (RWJ) Foundation's new Local Initiative Partnership Program, which encouraged even more collaboration with local foundations, political officials, and individual supporters. The New York Community Trust, the Liz Claiborne Foundation, and several other politicians and individual donors came on board who may not have participated without the significance and credibility of the RWJ challenge. Under the able leadership of Executive Director Marie St. Cyr, Iris House has expanded to a new home in Harlem and remains arguably the country's leading advocacy and support organization for women living with HIV/AIDS.

Another program initiative of the Sister Fund was the development and participation in donor circles—made up primarily of individuals and collaborative funds—comprised of foundation representatives, that pool resources around issues now so identified with the success of the "women's funding movement." One of the first was the Women's Voices donor circle developed by the Ms. Foundation for Women and the Center for Policy Alternatives in anticipation of the 1992 election. Several private foundation women donors, including Helen LaKelly Hunt of the Sister Fund, Mudge Shink of the Shaler Adams Foundation, and Twink Frey of the Nokomis Foundation, came together to fund and help lead a major polling and public education effort around the potential of the "women's vote." The donors met by conference call regularly with pollsters Celinda Lake, Linda Williams, and Linda Dival to hear about progress and respond to the needs of the project. Women's Voices became a major force for the women's vote and had a major impact on the 1992 elections—the "year of the woman." As one of the first donor circles, Women's Voices demonstrated that women could respond financially and effectively to a timely and important project if they were engaged and involved not only as donors, but also as supporters and leaders for the success of the project.

Other collaborative efforts between the Sister Fund and the Ms. Foundation were the Safety Circle and the Democracy Circle. Both were comprised primarily of individual donors, rather than private foundation representatives. The Safety and Democracy circles focused on policy issues surrounding domestic violence and the assault of right-wing groups on women. The staff of the Ms. Foundation, especially Grants Director Tani Takagi, soon realized how labor intensive the management of a donor circle could be, because of the personal sharing and peer learning that was involved, not to mention scheduling difficulties among the participants for meetings. Nonetheless, by developing a trusting relationship and stewardship among the donors, much was accomplished. By focusing as a group of funders on certain policy issues, grants were more strategic and focused on national policy impact. The Safety Circle addressed violence and abuse issues in a substantive, concrete manner, including providing legal support for high-profile cases such as Hedda Nussbaum's defense, or fighting the "false memory syndrome" hoax. The Democracy Circle continues to promote inclusive approaches to policy making as an alternative to the splintering effects of the right wing on American society.

The Sister Fund's initiative for the 1995 Fourth World Conference on Women in Beijing, China, and the parallel Non-Governmental Organization Forum (NGO) was the result of another successful collaboration with the Ms. Foundation for Women. With the help of consultant Stephanie Clohesy, the Sister Fund board decided that it had a unique niche in support of the conference, especially since so few other foundations were willing to play a major role. In part because of the large commitments already made by several major foundations for the United Nations Conference on Population and Development held in Cairo in 1994, and because of the financial failure of a grassroots effort to send women to Beijing, the need for resources and planning was enormous.

As a result, the Sister Fund devoted to the Beijing conference about half of its grantmaking budget, major staff and board involvement, and participation in the delegation that the Ms. Foundation organized. In addition to resources to ensure that grassroots women could attend who otherwise would not have been able, the Sister Fund organized panels and convened dialogues before and after the event. It was a difficult yet historic opportunity: Despite the visa problems and logistical nightmares, especially for women with disabilities, the conference was a huge success in bringing together the largest NGO gathering ever for a United Nations conference, with over thirty thousand women. The Ms. Foundation had a huge responsibility in bringing one of the most important delegations there, with dozens of diverse U.S. women. The Sister Fund's participation within that delegation, as opposed to sending a separate one, was a collaborative endeavor that supported both foundations, in addition to the grant support that the Sister Fund offered for media efforts around the conference.

Regranting and Endowing Intermediaries

Unlike many mainstream foundations, the Sister Fund believed strongly in the power of regranting in partnership with women's funds, which are public charities that raise funds and make grants for women and girls. Even today, some funders see such arrangements as adding an unnecessary level of bureaucracy to grantmaking, and many of these foundations believe that they know best how to make grants achieve their mission. However, the Sister Fund realized that partnering with sister foundations such as the Astraea Foundation or the Global Fund for Women meant that it could help reach communities of women that would not otherwise have been supported. The Sister Fund had a staff of three full-time professionals, who had neither the time nor expertise to make grants overseas, as the Global Fund for Women could, or to offer what organizations supporting lesbians around the country like the Astraea Foundation could. Moreover, by providing regranting funds to such organizations, the board of directors of the Sister Fund could support a much larger constituency of grantees with a single grant of $25,000, for example, to a women's foundation than a grant of $25,000 to one organization serving lesbians or women internationally. Through such regranting support, the Sister Fund became a major supporter of the women's funding movement, helping to strengthen individual women's foundations as they were in growth stages, to later be able to attract larger donors. Often gifts were made in honor of the founders of the women's fund, such as $150,000 granted to the Global Fund for Women's Honoring Women Fund in recognition of its founder Anne Firth Murray.

Joint Office Collaboration

Office collaborations have become increasingly popular among women's foundations and others in the progressive funding community. The Women's Building in San Francisco is a model for many others around the country. In 1994, the Astraea Foundation for Justice and the Sister Fund found that they were looking for new office space, and decided to partner in order to share the lease offerings and responsibilities. It was an ideal time for each foundation to consider such a partnership, since both were fairly stable and similar in terms of their missions, their identities were solid, and they were each striving for a greater presence in the community. Jointly, the two executive directors, Katherine Acey and myself, decided to work with a broker, aptly named Susan B. Anthony, who also had succeeded in finding a downtown office space for the New York Women's Foundation. We agreed upon an office space centrally located at Union Square, with the potential for each organization to grow, and we agreed to sign a ten-year lease. We jointly decided upon an architect, Francine Monaco, who designed the space with each of our different needs and tastes in mind. The large elliptical conference room, shared kitchen, and common areas allowed each foundation to be a convenor and host to strategic organizing and informational meetings of grantees, advocates, and other grantmakers. At the same time, individual offices permitted each organization to retain its independence and unique identity. For nearly ten years, this shared office environment has provided each foundation with a cost-effective way to benefit from the luxuries of a large conference room and reception area, as well as to learn from the work of each other and our partners in a welcoming, supportive, and respectful environment. Moreover, the joint space allowed for us to have a greater presence for women's philanthropy in New York, and many meetings and activities for social change benefited from the combined impact of our collaborative environment.

Finally, by leasing a space that allowed for growth, as co-tenants we decided to sublease as-yet-unused offices to partners in the nonprofit and foundation communities during the initial years. Asian American and Pacific Islanders in Philanthropy (AAPIP), the Latina Roundtable on Health and Reproductive Rights, and the Working Group on Funding for Lesbian and Gay Issues (later Funders for Lesbian and Gay Issues) became our first subtenants. In addition, offices were offered to help "incubate" new efforts, such as the Third Wave Foundation for young women fifteen to thirty years old, which was forming in the mid-1990s. One of the board members of the Sister Fund, and a former board member of Astraea, Catherine Gund, helped to make the partnership work extremely well. The Sister Fund provided more than the funding for the office space for Third Wave, including fundraising assistance, strategic planning advice, and office management. Other groups that found their first home in our collaborative environment included Project People Foundation, devoted to the women and girls of South Africa and founded by a Sister Fund board member, and the office for the Beijing Plus Five celebration in 2000, which was a coalition of dozens of women's organizations.

Women and Philanthropy

Along with the enormous growth in philanthropy and foundations over the past few decades, the field of philanthropic support organizations has also been growing and changing rapidly in recent years. Women and Philanthropy (W and P) was founded in 1977 as Women and Foundations/Corporate Philanthropy. At the time, only one other "affinity group," or funder network associated with the Council on Foundations, existed: the Association of Black Foundation Executives (ABFE). Today, there are thirty-nine affinity groups affiliated with the Council on Foundations, including the Disability Funders Network, Hispanics in Philanthropy, Grantmakers in Aging, and Funders for Lesbian and Gay Issues. There are dozens of other, often less-formal groupings of funders, and nearly thirty regional associations of grantmakers, such as the Donors Forum of Chicago and the New York Regional Association of Grantmakers. In fact, Grantmakers for Effective Organizations has researched more than three hundred funder networks in a recent report.[11]

Upon joining Women and Philanthropy as the new president and CEO in 2002, I was lucky to inherit a recently completed strategic plan that recognized and emphasized greater collaboration with the organization's natural and potential partners. The mission states:

> Women and Philanthropy provides leadership for foundations and philanthropists to create a more caring and just world through the full engagement of women and girls.

The new strategic plan for W and P emphasizes a structure that is about "centralized information and decentralized action." While the organization historically has provided illuminating research on issues of leadership and the status of women and girls, such as the Far From Done report series, W and P will continue to provide such data more through partnerships with other research centers. W and P is developing a comprehensive knowledge network, providing relevant information to a variety of audiences, through its revamped Web site: www.womenphil.org. It is also strengthening its advocacy work by joining the National Council of Women's Organizations, Women's EDGE, and other coalitions in Washington, D.C., thereby taking a stand on behalf of the membership on issues such as legislation in support of women's health or corporate discrimination against women. W and P is building an updated, interactive communications strategy to keep its members and partners informed and connected, and is seeking to build a sense of community within the philanthropic community for its members.

While much had been accomplished with over a quarter century of W and P's leadership in the field, its efforts are still very much needed. The Council on Foundations estimated that in 2003, women comprised approximately 70 percent of program officers and over 50 percent of executive directors.[12] Although women executives are mostly white women of privilege, and represent smaller foundations on average, the enormous rise of women's leadership in the field has not been matched by a proportionate increase in gender-conscious funding. According to the Foundation Center, funding for women and girls has increased from 0.5 percent of foundation funding in the 1970s to about 6 percent today, and is even falling off.[13] Moreover, because of the long commitment to women of color, it is important to look at the links between women's leadership in the field and funding for gender-focused programs, combined with the intersections with funding communities of color, immigrant women and girls, and other areas of diversity.

Many women remain isolated and disempowered in their relatively powerful positions, which is a problem that W and P is addressing through the development of peer-to-peer networks and caucuses focused on various cutting-edge issues and diverse communities, such as women of color board chairs or gender and education issues. By providing the opportunity for women leaders in philanthropy to share strategies, partner and support each other, greater gendered social change will result.

Women and Philanthropy is undertaking a major "theory of change" effort, which will examine basic assumptions about gender, diversity, and philanthropy. It will articulate the underlying beliefs and assumptions that guide our service delivery strategy and are believed to be critical for producing change and improvement in the lives of women and girls. Informing the theory of change process is a major theme: the need for philanthropy, including women's philanthropy, to look deeply at issues of intersectionality, as well as the connections between leadership and giving. Intersectionality refers to the interconnections and interactive relationships among issues and identities that are key to grantee and grantor successes. With few exceptions, the nonprofit and philanthropic communities have evolved as isolated entities that either focus on one population group, for instance Latinas in Northern California, or one issue, such as homelessness. Grantmakers and nonprofit leaders often speak of their frustration with having to develop and review proposals that reduce these complicated issues into tidy little packages that accommodate many funders' narrow conceptions of issues and identity groups. Philanthropic leaders speak of the tremendous imperative to find new ways to analyze complex issues and make grants that address the very real intersections among identities and issues.

Moreover, intersectionality means addressing the power relationships between grantees and grantors. In addressing the full context of a non-profit's agenda and mission, a grantee must be honest about how its strategy may not fit in a single pigeon hole of a grantmaker's program areas. In turn, grantmakers must be flexible to support grantees to address issues in a holistic manner. As such, intersectionality implies that grantees and grantors become engaged in a true partnership to address the full range of identities, issues, and collaborations involved in truly addressing social change.

Women and Philanthropy, as an "identity-based" affinity group, faces these challenges because of the many intersections among women and other identities and issues. Because women are over 50 percent of the world's population, are represented in almost every other identity group, and are affected by every issue supported by philanthropy, women are affected by every aspect of grantmaking. Women and Philanthropy has thus sought out partnerships with each and every affinity group, both issue-based and identity-based, since there is a gender perspective throughout all aspects of grantmaking (except perhaps animal rights funding). We are developing a Gender Impact Statement tool in partnership with many of these other funder networks and institutions. Already, as a Washington, D.C.–based affinity group, W and P is seen as a bridge-builder and collaborative leader among the other funding affinity groups of Council on Foundations and others.

Women and Philanthropy is also partnering with Jankowski Associates to produce a custom research product that is already proving to be helpful to women's foundations and our members in creating new relationships and stewardship strategies with new-wealth foundations. New foundation staff and trustees are being cultivated for membership and leadership in W and P, and as donors for local women's foundations and organizations, through collaboration. By focusing on new foundations, W and P and its partners are identifying potential alliances with new-wealth women and men among a group of foundations that work largely below the radar screen. This research creates a competitive advantage during a time of increased pressure to diversify funding streams.

Women and Philanthropy is using pilot case studies in collaboration with the Women's Foundation of Colorado, the Washington Area Women's Foundation, and the Minnesota Women's Foundation to determine effective stewardship strategies. We are also developing a toolkit for use in cultivating new-wealth foundations, providing our research partners with suggested resources, fact sheets, referral contact lists, board lists, and other tools for use in cultivating new-wealth foundations. Cultivation of these new-wealth foundations will be developed along a continuum, reaching new-wealth funders where they are, and providing different levels of en-gagement to bring them into the women's funding movement at a tailored pace. Since peer learning is such an effective means of cultivating these new foundations into the women's funding movement, Women and Phil-anthropy will coordinate the development of mentoring and supportive relationships between new grantmakers identified through the Jankowski reports and existing members of W and P who exemplify effective grant-making for gender and social change. This partnership will build on other collaborative efforts between W and P and the Women's Funding Net-work (WFN), including the New Wealth Women and Philanthropy Pro-gram, and joint plenary sessions that are now key offerings at annual conferences in conjunction with the Council on Foundations Annual Conference.

Women and Philanthropy has several natural partners, especially WFN. W and P housed WFN during its first five years when it was comprised of a growing handful of women's foundations. Originally called the National Network of Women's Funds, WFN has grown to include over ninety mem-bers around the country and internationally. While the two organizations have undergone significant changes over the years, W and P and WFN continue to share goals centered on increased funding of programs serving women and girls, through different memberships and strategies. W and P's more than 520 members come from the wide field of institutionalized phi-lanthropy, both emerging and mainstream, and advocates support for di-verse women's leadership and for more funding of programs for women and girls. Women and Philanthropy works almost entirely with institutional donors to encourage increased funding for women and girls. The Women's Funding Network works with its member funds for women and girls mainly to attract individual donors to encourage increased funding for women and girls. While each organization has clear priorities and target audi-ences, there are also areas of overlap between the two organizations. These overlap areas offer the two organizations meaningful opportunities to share resources and to work together to accomplish their missions.

Other logical partners for W and P include the Women Donors Network, Women's Philanthropy Institute at the Center on Philanthropy, Funders Network on Population, Reproductive Health and Rights, Grantmakers in Aging, Grantmakers for Education, and each of the identity-based affinity groups, including Asian American and Pacific Islanders in Philanthropy (AAPIP), Hispanics in Philanthropy, the Association of Black Founda-tion Executives, and Funders for Lesbian and Gay Issues. In fact, every issue and identity affects women and girls, and so every other affinity group of funders is a potential partner for Women and Philanthropy. Fortunately, such grantmaker associations have developed a practice of "swapping" memberships among key staff so that the work is informed and coordinated among affinity groups.

Lessons Learned

Partnership and stewardship are clearly hallmarks of the "women's funding movement." However, as stated earlier, collaboration in women's philanthropy is more often motivated by the desire for greater social change and impact, rather than interest in cost efficiencies or streamlined services. As demonstrated by the collaborations that helped launch successful efforts such as Iris House and the Third Wave Foundation, by offering more than funding, women's philanthropy makes social change happen through creative partnerships and careful stewardship. By working carefully to ensure mutually beneficial processes and structures, partnerships in the women's funding movement offer enormous potential for greater social change.

Despite all of the successes of the Sister Fund in strengthening women's foundations and the women's funding movement through regranting and endowment strategies, such partnerships were not always easy. The Sister Fund did not always receive full reports on its grants, since some of the women's foundations were more used to working with individual donors, rather than a foundation with more formal reporting requirements. In addition, the grantee organizations were sometimes at critical maturing stages in their development, with leadership transitions or "founder syndrome" issues, especially as the women's funding movement and individual funds reached the ability to scale up in the late 1990s. At times, the partner funds felt that working with the Sister Fund was more onerous than working with an individual donor, because of the multiple staff and board members representing the Sister Fund.

Working hard at clarifying expectations and ensuring a single point of contact for grantee organizations through the staff helped to ensure that these relationships worked. Although the Sister Fund had to push sometimes for the partner funds to fulfill grant obligations, it tried not to push too hard. At times, progress was achieving by retreating from the partnership for a period of time. Eventually, a consensus is often reached if a cooling off period is honored for all parties to determine the best course of action for future work together. In all, the regranting process is a learning one, for both funders.

Unfortunately, many foundations allow the power of grantmaking to foster a culture of unchecked power and organizational conviction that the foundation has nothing to learn from other funders. A regranting or endowment partnership is one of the best ways for such a culture to be put in check, and in fact to be enhanced by the reality of another's staff and board leadership, community standing, or grantmaking practices.

In terms of office collaboration, since many of the tenants in the office space were also grantees of the Sister Fund, especially the Astraea Foundation and Third Wave Foundation, it was important for the Sister Fund board and staff not to intrude on or question their work by taking advantage of the communal office space. We responded to assistance when asked, but refrained from making unsolicited suggestions or "invading" each other's space. The atmosphere remained highly professional and respectful, and taught mutual trust and respect among the co-tenants—primarily because we each saw first-hand how hard everyone else was working. Having the opportunity to stop by someone's office on occasion to ask for advice or a sounding board, was the most typical form of interaction. As so many non-profit managers know, peer learning is an invaluable gift.

As for Women and Philanthropy, given the proliferation of funder support networks, many foundation staff and trustees feel overwhelmed with the myriad of choices for membership and participation. Therefore, it is important that affinity groups define their niche carefully in order to attract members, and collaborate with other similar affinity groups on various projects to avoid duplication and competition. Although each affinity group realizes that it must compete with other groups for members from the foundation community, the number of foundations has been expanding so explosively, that room for growth remains among funder networks. However, in a climate of economic slowdown and austerity, such competition becomes more apparent as foundations pare down the number of professional development activities that they can support for staff and trustees. As a result, collaboration becomes even more important among funder support networks, in order to help foundation staff and trustees understand their grantmaking programs as holistically as possible. A new culture and era of collaboration, partnership, and stewardship is thus emerging for the future of Women and Philanthropy.

NOTES

1. James Austin, *The Collaboration Challenge: How Nonprofits and Businesses Succeed through Strategic Alliances* (The Leader to Leader Institute, 2000).

2. Dr. Elizabeth Boris and C. Eugene Steuerle, eds., *Nonprofits and Government: Collaboration and Conflict* (Washington, D.C.: The Urban Institute, 2002).

3. Karen Ray, *The Nimble Collaboration: Fine Tuning Your Collaboration for Lasting Success* (Amherst Wilder Foundation, 2002).

4. David La Piana, *Beyond Collaboration: Strategic Restructuring of Nonprofit Organizations* (James Irvine Foundation and BoardSource, 2002).

5. Daniel Altman, "He Crunches the Numbers for Clues to a Donor's Heart," *New York Times*, November 18, 2002.

6. Kay Sprinkel Grace, "Ten Things You Should Know about the Impact of Women and Philanthropy," *Contributions Magazine* (November/December 2000).

7. Sandra C. Shaw and Martha A. Taylor, *Reinventing Fundraising: Realizing the Potential of Women's Philanthropy* (San Francisco: Jossey-Bass Publishers, 1999).

8. Quoted in Neil F. Carlson, "Heir to Independence: The Girl's Best Friend Foundation," in *Women and Philanthropy*, 2003.

9. *Merriam Webster's Collegiate Dictionary*, 10th ed. (Springfield, Mass.: Merriam Webster Inc., 1993) 1154.

10. Angela Bonavoglia, "Getting It Done: From Commitment to Action on Funding for Women and Girls" (1992), in *Women and Philanthropy*.

11. Steven LaFrance, Andrew Robinson, Rick Green, and Nancy Latham, LaFrance Associates, LLC, *Funder Networks in Action: Understanding their Potential for Philanthropy, Data Highlights* (Washington, D.C.: Grantmakers for Effective Organizations, 2004). Also avaliable at http://geofunders.org/uploads/documents/live/networksresearch.pdf.

12. Council on Foundations, *2003 Grantmakers Salary and Benefits Report* (Washington, D.C.: Council on Foundation's Research Department, 2003), 14.

13. The Foundation Center, *Foundation Giving Trends: Update on Priorities*, Foundations Today Series 2004, 39–40.

VOICES OF YOUNG WOMEN

The Development of Girls' Funds

STEPHANIE YANG

The room is warm though outside I know it is snowing. Leaning back in my chair, I look around me and see faces that look nothing like mine. Still, an unbreakable thread binds us. We've been sitting at this table for hours. Our director quietly adds wood to the stove, letting us know that we still have work to do. I haven't spoken in a while, choosing to listen to what everyone else is saying. I know if I speak up, emotions may spill over, and I don't want to hurt anyone's feelings. But I also know that soon I will have to be part of what we're all trying to figure out. My opinion matters here. When the time is right to voice it, I will.

It's easier sometimes to gaze out the window at the snow, making everything invisible like a huge blanket shielding the ground from the sun. When I walk through freshly fallen snow, I notice how easily by my feet break through this cover, allowing the sun in and the small plants to stand tall. Even so, there are times I prefer the ground to remain covered, obscuring what is hidden and vibrant underneath.

Not long ago, I felt just like the ground, as though I were cloaked by a thick blanket of snow. Underneath my surface, I was passionate and active, but no one seemed to see that. What they saw instead was a quiet young woman, someone to smile at, or be wary of. Sometimes they said I was pretty. But mostly they ignored me, probably because I dress differently and my nose is pierced. I got decent grades in school, but no one took me seriously or asked for my opinion. I had begun to feel suffocated and I longed for the sun to come out to melt the snow.

Now I think about how much of the world is invisible, like me. There is so much I still need to discover, learn, and experience. Perhaps, with enough vision, I can begin to change the world.

I turn my attention back to the discussion: Should we fund a substance abuse program for young mothers or a mentoring program for immigrant youth? Both are important; how can we choose just one? When we began this morning, we had thirty proposals to consider, each one asking for about $5,000. The problem is that we only have $50,000 to grant, and I want to support everyone. I don't want to make compromises, but of course, I will have to in the end.

I recognize a common spark in everyones' eyes. We want so much to make an impact in our communities so that other young women can thrive and shake off their cloaks of invisibility. I want to take part in creating a world where no young mother has to give up her education because she has a child, where no young woman cries herself to sleep because her voice doesn't matter, and where no young woman who has been sexually abused is told simply to move on. We all want to make that kind of change, but can we do it with only $50,000?

We've been part of this program through a local women's fund for the past year, and it has been fun, and difficult. I've had to embrace my insecurities with this group. We've become like sisters, united by a common goal. Each time we are together, we become more confident to speak, to trust our instincts, to create solutions for our world. Even so, we recognize our individual differences. I see them when Parveen shrinks from conversations. I recognize the pain in Julie's voice as she shares pieces of her past. They are there in the way we each let down our guard and hope for acceptance. My sisters and the director recognize what lies beneath each of our blankets of snow. Together, we are becoming stronger, braver. In the warmth of this room, our protective layers are melting away.

For the past several months, we have grappled together over questions about our communities and how we can make an impact. I want to make the world safer for women everywhere. I see too many of my peers being verbally and physically abused by people they know. In this program, we talk about sexual assault and violence against women, and about many other issues. Malka asks why women still only earn 77 percent of what men do in a country claiming equality. Brandy admits to being confused as to why so many young women are getting pregnant

> "Before this program, I did not know what it really meant to be transgender or Muslim or non-white or homeless or whatever. I think now I really understand how important it is to recognize our differences and embrace them."
>
> —Sisterhood Fund Participant

and contracting STDs when so much information is available about safe sex and contraception. Rosa asks why young women still suffer from eating disorders, cutting, and drug abuse. These are just some of our questions. Most of us have been there in some way or another, so we share our own stories in a quest for answers. We understand each other, and together, we vow to change the world.

I feel lucky to be in this room. I know I am part of a small but growing group of young women across the country who can tell a foundation where it should spend its money. I know we can't change the entire world with $50,000, but we can begin, so I am an active participant.

Our $50,000 dollars is just a small piece of what other young women are contributing each year through youth philanthropy programs. In the past decade alone, more young women have been invited into the world of philanthropy as active players and decision makers than ever before. This is happening within foundations, in community-based organizations, and in schools. Young women are being given the tools to change things in our communities that will help to make our lives better. This occurs because we are actively engaging with each other to examine the dynamics of social and economic oppression. We want to make responsible and effective grants to community-based organizations that we care about.

A Historical Perspective

Historically, a divide has existed between those who make grants and those who receive them. Even in many progressive foundations, this is still the case. But slowly, foundations are inviting community members to participate in the grants review process and to lend a voice in decision making around funding allocations. Even so, distinctions are still evident around class and ethnicity between grantor and grantee, especially in the field of youth development funding, where distinctions also exist around age. The program officers reviewing proposals and making decisions often are not youth, and in many cases do not have access to the ever-changing reality that young people are learning to navigate on a daily basis. Hoping to address this need, many community foundations have made the commitment to include an authentic youth voice in their work by providing space for representative youth to make decisions about grants that affect local youth groups.

Engaging youth in a traditionally adult activity has been a challenge to many youth development agencies across the country. Social attitudes toward youth continue to question the relevance of youth opinions and to underplay the validity of the youth experience. Despite these roadblocks, many organizations are beginning to find, create, and nurture a youth-led voice in order to make more relevant funding decisions for youth-led and youth-serving organizations. Young people provide expertise and critical evaluation to proposals through a "youth lens" that helps in exploring strategies and interventions that can work.

It is deeply important that adults partner with youths in order to develop, guide, and foster youth philanthropy. Clearly, adults have a certain wisdom from years of personal and professional experience; at the same time, "youth reality" shifts daily, making communication between the two groups essential.

For example, in just ten years, the teen pregnancy rate has dropped nationally by 22 percent and Gay-Straight Alliance (GSA) groups are now becoming welcomed clubs on high-school campuses across the nation, while drug use has become a more widespread choice for teens across class and ethnic lines.[1] For decades, progressive philanthropic organizations have been working to solve the problems of a fast-paced society that plague our youth (e.g., teen pregnancy, substance abuse, foster care, child sexual assault, juvenile justice). However, in funding programs and strategies to affect young lives positively, youth themselves traditionally have remained outside of the dialogue and programmatic process.

In the mid-1980s, several visionary community foundations across the nation officially sparked a movement now known as "youth philanthropy." These foundations had been making grants to youth-serving organizations, yet traditionally had not included young people in decision making. Youth philanthropy is a process that engages youth in both fundraising and granting funds to community-based organizations and programs that work with their peers. Some youth philanthropy programs operate in similar fashion to older, more established programs, while others differ completely in methodology and structure. The unifying element is that youth are making decisions around money and priorities that have real and lasting impact on the communities in which they reside.

"Giving girls the money to fund projects is empowering. It makes them realize that we have faith in them as leaders and that their programs are significant. Once girls start seeing themselves in a different, more capable light, society may follow."
—Sisters Empowering Sisters participant

Early approaches to youth philanthropy involved the creation of youth boards that both raised and distributed their own funds. Some of these youth boards, eventually named Youth Advisory Councils (YACs) in many foundations, collaborated with adult boards, creating effective intergenerational partnerships. From this, new models emerged that have modified and built upon the initial strategies to engage a younger voice in philanthropy.

Today, over 250 youth philanthropy programs across the nation are providing opportunities for young adults to make fiscal decisions that affect their own lives and communities.[2] Some of these programs raise their own funds, others work from a set amount provided each year by the host foundation, and still others are endowed. Of these, a small number are gender-specific programs for young women operated out of women's funds and organizations specifically serving girls.

Women's funds across the nation have taken the lead within progressive philanthropy involving young women in grantmaking. They are strengthening the communities they serve while building a cadre of young women leaders capable of funding and implementing the kinds of social change programs they both seek. Involving young women in philanthropy helps develop leadership skills, decision-making capacity, and financial literacy among youth. In return, women's funds gain real insight into the lives of young women, the dreams and challenges they are facing, and the benefit of the knowledge each of the young women brings in finding lasting solutions to often devastating problems.

Today, young women and girls are faced with a culture of ambivalent expectations. While popular culture wants them to fit into a world of consumerism, self-criticism, and financial dependence, it also proclaims the benefits of self-confidence, individuality, and financial independence. Specifically around fiscal issues, very few venues exist where girls and young women can be involved in discussions about financial planning and security and philanthropy for positive social change.

Despite conflicting messages and the gaps in financial literacy, young women are acutely aware of their surroundings and when consulted can provide various ideas to address issues that impact their own lives and their communities. Young women recognize the strength inherent in their own leadership. By involving them in the philanthropic process, the effectiveness of funding increases. Young women are vital to developing philanthropic strategies for achieving both social and economic justice in their own arenas and beyond. Fostering leadership and critical thinking skills in young women promises a future peopled with active, committed women investing in their multiple environments. It also strengthens the

> "The program is where I can practice my voice. I not only learned about grantmaking, but I learned about who I was and what I am capable of."
> —Sisterhood Fund participant

work of every organization that hopes to integrate women into their activities.

Models for Success

Spearheading this strategy of engaging young women in philanthropy was the Michigan Women's Foundation. In 1995, the foundation implemented the first girls' grantmaking program, called Young Women for Change, making the first girl-led grant in 1996. This program brought together a diverse group of young women specifically to increase the economic and philanthropic knowledge, growth, and confidence of young women. The program now provides girls' grantmaking committees in two areas of the state: Kent County and the Metro Detroit area. The program has made nearly fifty grants since 1996, helping communities on issues such as improving financial literacy for girls, helping young women escape cycles of abuse and violence, and providing funds for scholarships for a girls' dance program.

Soon after the Michigan Women's Foundation initiative was launched, a number of other young women's funds emerged following similar missions and funding issues in their communities to promote social change and life improvement for young women and girls. Sisters Empowering Sisters was started by the Girl's Best Friend Foundation in Chicago, Young Sisters for Justice came through the Boston Women's Fund, The Sisterhood Fund was birthed by the Women's Foundation of California, and the Girls for Change program grew out of the Women's Foundation of Greater Kansas City. In varying modes, these programs train and place young women at the table as decision makers, and all of the programs ask young women to explore their ideas of leadership, to set goals, and to consider how each of them can create change, both in their own lives and for those around them. While the methodology and structure of these programs may vary, each one operates with the same goal of giving voice to young women and cultivating their leadership through training and participation. Together these programs are building a formidable network of young women leaders who are taking their place at decision-making tables throughout the country, and some instances, around the world.

In the early years, these programs were operating on their own, separate from each other. Each of the women's funds was learning and struggling alone without the direct benefit of a formal network to share information and strategies. Therefore, in an effort to build a supportive space for foundation staff and young women in these girls' grantmaking programs, the Girls as Grantmakers Network was established. In 2000, at an annual conference of the Women's Funding Network, the international association for women's funds, these five programs came together to determine what structure this network would have and how it might be supported. The network now meets regularly via conference calls and through an e-mail listserv to maintain support and encourage the cross-fertilization of ideas among programs. A *Girls as Grantmakers Tool Kit* was one product of this collaboration.[3] The Tool Kit is a comprehensive resource that details these five programs. It includes program guides, sample curricula, and videos. These materials provide the user with hands-on strategies for developing and implementing a successful young women's grantmaking component. As a result of this Tool Kit, more women's funds and community foundations are now equipped to host youth-led grantmaking groups. One such group is Girls in Charge at the Women's Foundation of Southern Arizona. Launched in the fall of 2001, this program works with junior high and high school age young women from Tucson, Arizona. The program is modeled after Young Women for Change and the Sisterhood Fund. Because of information sharing and dissemination of methodologies implemented by existing programs, many more foundations are now able to easily develop and nurture a youth space in their programs.

The Impact

We know now that young women's philanthropy programs affect many lives. The communities that these women call their own are diverse. Some belong to the African American community, others to the queer community, and still others to the immigrant community. Equally important, however, these programs benefit the young women who participate in them. The experience they gain includes developing transferable skills that apply to their future work as activists, volunteers, staff, and peer leaders. For example, prior to joining a girls' grantmaking program, Maggie Navarro wanted to change her community but had not held any positions of leadership. Within four years of participating in the Sisterhood Fund, Maggie became the first female executive director of a Barrios Unidos chapter in California. She was twenty-five at the time. Her work with young women in the juvenile justice system is changing the way that gang prevention programs approach the needs of young women and girls. Her leadership and commitment to social change are evident in the lives of the young women and girls she fights for every day.

Girls' grantmaking programs also are noticing an increased desire among recipients to attend post-secondary education, primarily four-year colleges. For those already in college, it is not uncommon to change majors once they become involved. Many enter social work, but DeAndra Johnson, a young single mother working full-time and carrying a full load in college, shifted her major from economics to biochemistry. Her growing awareness of women's health issues and the disparity in the treatment that young women receive, garnered from her involvement with the Sister Fund, prompted her to pursue a career in medicine. DeAndra, now working at Kaiser Permanente, has no doubt that she will be able to improve women's lives and well-being.

One effect of involving young women as decision makers in philanthropy is that the playing field for grant-seekers becomes a more level playing field. This peer-driven process ensures that agencies working with young women are reviewed by women who reflect their constituencies; that is, young women from those communities who can speak to the realities that illuminate the intricate nature of relevant issues. In addition, while many new organizations founded by young women may be overlooked by more traditional foundations because they lack a track record and, arguably, professional expertise, many of these programs have accessed funds as grant recipients of a girls' grantmaking program.

In all youth philanthropy programs, young women's voices have had a measurable impact on the way decisions are made, projects are evaluated, and young women's issues are addressed. This not only has strengthened the internal functions of the respective women's funds, it has increased directly the effectiveness of the grants made to young women and youth programs.

Girls' funds are also beginning to impact the work of other women's funds across the country. Since 2000, young women grantmakers have been attending the annual Women's Funding Network conference as participants, presenters, and speakers, engaging all conference attendees around issues of importance to young women. These representatives have led workshops that explore the development of successful youth-adult partnerships in philanthropy. The inclusion of these young women has opened a place within the women's funding community, ensuring that what younger women need is articulated by their peers.

In addition to sitting on grant review committees for foundations, many young women are finding their voice in other arenas, including serving on boards of directors. They are also becoming donors. Each of the programs profiled here have engaged program alumni in these ways, underscoring a commitment to young women and to building understanding between adults and youth. For example, Shira Frank, an activist within her own community in rural northern California, was able to expand her understanding of social justice as it relates to philanthropy through her participation in the Sisterhood Fund. She raised her voice on a variety of issues while learning about the dynamics of foundations and nonprofit organizational structure. As a result, Shira was invited to become a member of the board of directors of the Women's Foundation. As one of two board members under age twenty-five, Shira has been able to advocate further for young women and to educate others about the youth experience. She now sits on the board of Planned Parenthood in her hometown as well. In these roles, Shira contributes to her community in ways that are substantive and mutually respectful.

In some cases, the young women active in these programs become leaders within the women's fund with which they work. After completing two years in Young Women for Change in Michigan, Katie Bode-Lang joined the staff as a part-time program officer directing one of the girl's grantmaking committees. As a program participant, she had learned the skills of effective grantmaking. As a program officer, Katie was able to share her experiences with a new group of young women and at the same time directly inform the work of the foundation. Her involvement strengthened the program and helped her to develop further skills that she is now able to use in a new professional position. Her passion for social justice and community activism, nurtured through her experience with Young Women for Change, continues to be a key motivator in her life.

Another way that young women are affecting philanthropy is through working with programs that develop donors among youth, whether of wealth or not. Within some of the youth grantmaking programs, young women are learning how to sit on both sides of the table, making grants and seeking funds. The Sisterhood Fund requires each participant to donate and/or raise at least $50 each year. The goal is to educate young women that being a donor is not something reserved for the rich, but rather something that everyone can do.

On a larger scale, several organizations such as the Third Wave Foundation in New York and Resource Generation in Boston are developing the capacity of young women of wealth and youth who are part of family foundations to maximize their ability to be social activists through becoming a donor.

The Third Wave Foundation, a foundation for and by youth activists based in New York, seeks to build a lasting base for social activism through the empowerment of young women. The foundation's work is driven by young feminists, both female and male, committed to positive social change through grassroots philanthropy. In addition to making grants to women-led organizations and raising money through an extensive network of young, individual donors, the foundation co-hosts annual workshops for young people of wealth. These workshops help youth examine ways to give and how to develop criteria for that purpose. Growing a socially re-

"Instead of sending out messages of limitations to a woman's ability, society needs to send out messages that say, 'Women, you are equal and you can do anything you want."
—Sisters Empowering Sisters participant

sponsible group of young donors is an important piece of youth led social change.

Resource Generation, a Boston-based organization with a national scope, is another group that is organizing youth in this fashion and helping to build a base of young donors who are skilled in using their financial resources for social change. Through workshops and conferences, Resource Generation is helping to create an environment where young women of wealth are equipped to navigate traditional philanthropy and to make strategic gifts to organizations aligned with their social justice goals.

Engaging constituents in community-based organizations is not a new practice, but within philanthropy, it is often the reserve of more progressive foundations. Giving voice to affected communities and disenfranchised populations in this way increases the transparency of grant-making, and allows for the expertise of the community to inform the decision-making process. This process affords the foundation a better sense of what interventions, strategies, and realities they should consider as they address specific social issues. By involving young women in the decision-making process, whether through girls' grantmaking programs, by supporting young women as members of boards, or by developing their capacity as donors, a positive impact for all concerned is inevitable. Efforts like these have forged new models and made room for young women in philanthropy while ensuring that recipient organizations implement real solutions to the complex social problems of our time.

NOTES

1. Centers for Disease Control, National Center for Health Statistics Report, May 2002.

2. Youth Leadership Institute, "Changing the Face of Philanthropy," (James Irvin Foundation, 2002), 2.

3. The *Girls as Grantmakers Tool Kit* is available for purchase through the Women's Funding Network at their website, www.wfnet.org.

LESSONS LEARNED
Strategies for Success in Education and Endowment

TRACY GARY

As one of the beneficiaries of the civil rights and women's movements, I spent the 1970s trying to align my values, my investments, and my political and spiritual ideologies with the allocation of my inherited and earned income, and with something equally valuable, my time. Reflecting now on that personal journey to women's philanthropy, and on all that has happened, collectively, to help build the women's philanthropy movement, the experience feels "like a dream come true." As I often say, if someone had told me how much we could accomplish in building a movement based on shifting women's financial leadership in such a relatively short period of time, I would have said, "you've got to be dreaming." But I understand now many other women like me were on the same journey at the same time. Together, we have helped to launch a movement for nothing short of social revolution, and the full consequences of that movement have yet to be realized.

From Money Mentor to Donor Activist

As a young inheritor in my twenties with a degree in mythology from Sarah Lawrence College, I sought the promise of democracy during the post-rebellious 1960s. I had been blessed with parents who were diligent about my early philanthropic mentoring. They had assured me that while I would be inheriting money, it was ultimately more practical for me, and useful to the world, for me to earn a living. So I moved to San Francisco where a cousin, in town to study an organizational model for his own Boston-based Haymarket People Fund, introduced me to a new social change organization, the Vanguard Public Foundation. That was in 1973, the first year of the foundation, and after several months of volunteering, I was employed to help people find work in the nonprofit sector. I was thrilled to find other young inheritors at Vanguard, and to work in partnership with them growing and strengthening start-up nonprofit organizations and moving society to address the root cause of social problems, while engaging those who were most affected by those problems.

For the next seven years, I worked collaboratively in an experimental partnership that informed the basis of my belief in community-based philanthropy. In this model, donors, activists, and community leaders work together in a democratic process that values each varied contribution, perspective, and life experience equally. I continue to see this model as the wave of the future and the means to achieve a more viable democracy.

From 1973 to 1980, I also volunteered with Vanguard Public Foundation. Among other tasks, as a member of the grants committee, once a week I went with other donors and activists on over two hundred site visits. We met in lengthy sessions with diverse community leaders and visited projects that were advocating change and creating positive solutions for community problems involving the disenfranchised. I was in awe of the people whom I met during those years, and the conversations that I was privy to were amazing and inspiring. During those years, I contributed significant amounts of my money to Vanguard, while also increasing my personal knowledge of the areas we served throughout Northern California. I also learned about the power of collaboration. What l learned informed and catalyzed my own philanthropic endeavors. By the time I was thirty years old, I had donated half my inheritance, helped start five nonprofit women's organizations, and determined to give at least 60 percent of my money and time to women's and girls' serving agencies. This focus seemed to me to represent enlightened self-interest, as there were not enough women's resources and financial institutions empowering women. To my way of thinking, it was also totally engaging, creative and personally transformative work.

As someone who had been born into a family of financial privilege and who had been taught that mine was the dominant culture, my post-university education in the real politick was even more enlightening. It became clear to me that the wisdom capital, creative capital, and courage capital of the community activists whom I was working beside—the majority of whom were from different races, classes, and cultures than I—were as equally valuable resources as those of us who could put $5,000 on the table, but knew little about what solutions might be fitting. I quickly understood that listening carefully might be the best skill I could develop, but the larger challenge was learning not to dominate.

Between 1973 and 1980, while at Vanguard, I learned the basics of fundraising, grantmaking, and foundation administration, while also learning to grow what would become a model organization aimed at fostering positive social movement. The learning curve was both exhilarating and difficult. Political missteps were rampant. But I knew that I was called to do this work. So I decided to give away 90 percent of my inheritance by the time I was thirty-five. I had inherited over $1 million by then and I thought: I will live on the interest of my remaining capital and what I earn, and give a million dollars away. (Twenty years later, I have given away $2 million from earned and inherited assets and have never felt wealthier. My return on investment has been the women's and social change funding movements.)

It was a good plan, but I wanted a mentor. So I spent five years trying to find a woman donor who would fill that role. But every woman I went to between 1973 and 1978 told me that she was giving away her husband's money, or that she was too busy. I vowed then never to say "no" to the next generation of women donors. Finally, I happened upon Florette Pomeroy, one of only a few women philanthropic advisors at the time, who took me under her wing. I was elated to have someone who could help me navigate the land mines of fundraising and I learned much from my seventy-year-old friend and mentor about giving to, serving, and truly feeling part of my new community.

With time, my desire to integrate my own values and investments and to learn more about financial literacy grew. I also became fascinated to observe that while women donors outnumbered the men at Vanguard's grant-making or board discussions, it was almost always the men who dominated any mention of money, budgets, or investing. So in 1976, with fellow activist Betsy Weedon, I convened a group of women to see if we could discover for ourselves why women were holding back.

Through our discussions, the women at Vanguard realized that not only were we uncomfortable discussing money, we had also been acculturated, even at Vanguard, to let the men lead. We were emerging or ardent feminists. How could we possibly lead or be strong partners if we didn't feel confident about money, power, or influence in our own lives? To overcome that lack of confidence, we looked to lessons already learned. For example, at Vanguard, we felt that people of wealth needed to convene independently occasionally in order to raise our consciousness about privilege and about how money and position could be managed with the least amount of harm to ourselves. Women needed a similar forum.

Another barrier to women's giving was our lack of knowledge about our personal assets or net worth. We learned quickly that if a woman did not know how much she had, she would not have confidence about her assets lasting long enough for her to give more away. We finally realized that we needed to develop programs for women that would enable their own confidence, and competency, in financial literacy. We also wanted to create a space for discussions about some of the complexities of racism, sexism, and classism that were evident to us within foundations and spilling over into interactions with grantees. Ultimately, we were able to listen and learn from others in mixed groups, resulting in greater consciousness among all participants.

We also needed to learn how to better manage what money and influence we had, and how to "hold our own" in mixed groups. We needed encouragement about standing up for our values (such as being sure that investments were socially responsible or that advisors had similar world views to ours). Most of us were experiencing sexism from family or financial professionals and we supported each other in asking for what we needed. We found that by meeting as peers and coming out of isolation, and by mentoring and encouraging each other, we were more confident and more committed to making progress relating to what we still needed to learn, including how to be assertive. As we matured, we realized that women in other economic situations needed the same support.

At about this time, I was asked to serve on the board of the first battered women's shelter on the west coast, La Casa de las Madres. This invitation was followed by other requests to serve on the boards of a new university as well as the local public TV and radio stations. Each of these entities had budgets in the millions, and what I learned about creating development plans, donor acknowledgement systems, major gift fundraising, public relations, marketing, and budgeting, I shared with grassroots organizations and social change foundation colleagues. I also shared the concepts of multiculturalism and democratic decision making with each board I sat on, activating more mainstream leaders to re-evaluate their assumptions and perceptions. This cross-pollination was invaluable to everyone involved.

The Women's Funding Movement

The birth of the first locally based women's foundation came about when an older lesbian became concerned that when she died she would not have anywhere to leave her money. This founder suspected that there were other women similar to her and wanted us to do something for them. My feminist partners Roma Guy, Marya Grambs, and others with whom I had worked in 1977 to purchase and develop the Women's Building in San Francisco set about to address this problem with me. In 1979, at Roma's invitation, I made a $50,000 commitment to launch the Women's Foundation and pledged my support to help expand it. That foundation remains my place of greatest learning.

Soon I left my comfortable nonprofit philanthropic consulting practice to become Coordinator of Donor Services and Planning at the Women's Foundation. In addition to making a cash commitment over five years, I had volunteered as a founding staff person, working twenty to thirty hours a week for five years.

In its inaugural year, the Women's Foundation had the audacity to set the first year's budget at $300,000 so that we would be recognized as the country's first permanent, local women's foundation. We would operate on less than $100,000, give $100,000 in grants during the first year, and put the remaining $100,000 in a board-designated endowment.

My job was essentially to raise money from major donors—women and men willing to give $1,000 or more—and to help with strategic planning and educational programs for donors. As with the Women's Building, we were learning on the spot, but we had a clear vision about creating a dynamic, volunteer-driven model of social change.

During the first five years of the Women's Foundation, 1979 to 1984, over one hundred women volunteers joined us or were invited to serve on various committees. Their enthusiasm was amazing. They went to work as bees to a hive, working in one gigantic room on the top floor of the Women's Building, listening and learning and turning small change into gold to finance the seeding of the women's funding movement. A diverse board and staff complemented these volunteers' skills, diversity, and talents. Together our determination was unstoppable. The injustices that we had seen in the 1960s and the emerging and changing needs of women and families as women entered the workforce by the millions in the late 1970s, fueled our passionate convictions. We understood that women and girls had to be better resourced for the times, and that women's empowerment, skills, and leadership development were essential ingredients for shifting the male paradigm in the financial world. From the outset, we understood that the Women's Foundation would be an influential tool as well as a center for training and inspiration. We had few illusions that the monies we raised alone would lift women substantially, but we felt confident that we could create some wake and grow new leaders. We also knew that we were becoming politicized by what we were learning, and that we were sensitizing donors and others to the real circumstances of women's lives. Such constituency education ultimately resulted in greater citizen activism and stronger empathy among diverse populations.

The Lessons of Community-Based Philanthropy

We understood early that it was not only valuable to give grants and technical assistance to women's nonprofits, but it was also important to address existing inequities. In its first five years, for example, the Women's Foundation analyzed the local United Way and learned that in the early 1980s, eight times as much grant money from that collective charity was being distributed to agencies serving men and boys as to women and girls' serving agencies. Following our advocacy and recommendations, the United Way of San Francisco committed to redistributing over $1 million within two years to women and girls' after-school and worker-training programs, and not only to educate their staff and boards about the changing needs of women and girls, but also to share their insights with other United Ways. Our role as advocates and leaders in the community was just as important as building our endowment or making grants, and this victory in our first years paved the way for us to be vigilant about similar inequities as well as opportunities for lasting change.

Among the founders of the Women's Foundation, perhaps our most complex discussions were about how we could truly bridge the differences among class, race, and other potentially divisive issues. Who should the decision makers really be? Were we diverse enough to truly represent our constituents? Why weren't there more undereducated, poor, disabled, or disenfranchised women involved? How could we underwrite costs for childcare or transportation to be sure representative participants could join us and feel welcome?

In 1980, the Women's Foundation began offering financial education seminars aimed at all women with some level of financial resources. However, we soon realized that learning about money would be key for all Women's Foundation participants. At the same time, I was developing programs for women with inherited wealth and promoting a program called Managing Inherited Wealth. I wanted to convey that learning about money and philanthropy was as important to a woman's independence at the end of the twentieth century as driving a car was for our mothers at the middle of the century and voting was for our grandmothers at the beginning of the century.

By 1983, the Women's Foundation had refined its goals and had articulated six major objectives:

1. To create a dynamic, volunteer-based organization that would serve the empowerment of women and girls in Northern California through grantmaking and programs serving women and girls;
2. To create a foundation led by women and girls;
3. To commit to being representative of the full diversity of the women and girls that we aimed to serve, especially low-income women, girls, single mothers and their families, older women, women of color, and immigrant and refugee women;[1]
4. To offer financial education to women and girls in order to provide added tools for their empowerment and independence;

5. To form partnerships with other funders and to encourage the increased funding of women's and girls' nonprofit organizations by other funders;[2]
6. To create a model that would be replicable and to aid in the development of growing a movement of women's funds.

Since 1977, I have visited or given presentations at more than 70 percent of U.S.-based women's funds. What began as personal inquiry evolved into a quest to share what I've learned as a model of women's empowerment and the vision of a just and equitable *society*. This movement building has become my calling, and my professional life.

Lessons Learned

All of us engaged in women's philanthropy have learned much about starting a fund, building endowments, and garnering community support over the years of our work. Key lessons learned from 1977 to date include:

- *Don't rush!* Allow at least two years for "research and development" to determine the needs of the community and the available or potential resources (both human and financial capital). Maintain a comprehensive, coded mailing list, and engage prospective leaders and donors slowly and carefully.

- *Plan for diversity.* Begin with a planning group committed to diversity and be sure the communities you plan to serve are represented in the core decision-making and leadership circle. Plan to do ongoing work regarding race, class, and diversity issues so that all voices continue to be heard and respected.

- *Learn from others.* Attend the annual Women's Funding Network conference and other relevant forums and absorb as much as possible from the experience of other women's funds.

- *Set goals.* Be sure they are feasible, attainable, and credible. Aim high in terms of building an endowment. Develop useful tools such as an overall strategy and related work plans, monitoring and evaluation mechanisms, and financial tracking systems. Transparency and sharing are key values for success. Have a plan to diversify your donor base, and solicit "lead donors" at each contribution level before launching a public campaign. Identify and tap "key influencers" for an added and early impact.

- *Institutionalize.* Establish a volunteer program, committees, staffing, and board roles. Write job descriptions and articulate clearly objectives to be met.

- *Keep your eyes on the money*. Be sure to have financially savvy women on staff and on finance and fundraising committees.

- *Establish core donors*. Keep them involved to create the stability that is needed in the early days of establishing a women's fund.

- *Pay well*. Hire excellent staff early and compensate them accordingly. There is a direct correlation between successful women's funds and the amount of money raised.

- *Allocate time*. At least 40 percent of all organizational time, including all staff, board member, and volunteer time should be spent on fundraising. Women's funds are leadership development *and* fundraising or resource development programs; lead with development and the rest will follow.

- *Educate, educate, educate*. Establish a donor or community education program and implement it several times a year. Help prospective grantees with technical assistance for their own management and skill development.

- *Engage others*. Involve donors and grantees in your process. For community-based democratic organizations to work, they must be strong partners in community building. This means building relationships with other foundations, United Way, social change funds, corporations, and grassroots organizations.

- *Say thanks*. Determine how you will thank and support donors and volunteers. Then, do it.

Fulfilling the Dreams of Women and the Promise of Girls

When I look back now on the first years of the Women's Foundation, I realize with pride that we laid the cornerstone for what would become the women's funding movement in America. That so much of what we did has been replicated in such a relatively short amount of time is wonderful and gratifying. But the Women's Funding Network is only one resource for inspiring women's philanthropy. There are now many more models, some of which are highlighted in this book. Whatever the structure, women's philanthropic models are all working toward the same end: the empowerment of women in order to foster and sustain critical social change.

Now the time has come for the women's funding movement to help the next generation of women philanthropists and leaders to create their own organizations and set their own agendas. We must work intergenerationally, passing on leadership positions to younger activists and donors. We must become better at evaluating the impact of our work, communicating our strategies, and publicizing the outstanding contributions we are making as a movement established for social change. For without a doubt, the legacy of women's philanthropy will be the clear and indisputable evidence that this was indeed a significant and meaningful movement.

NOTES

1. We later added lesbians as a target population for grantmaking and programs.

2. In 1980, the Ford Foundation released a study revealing that the amount of money going to women's and girls' serving programs by all foundations and corporations was only 1 percent of all dollars given by foundations and corporate funders. Today it is only 6 percent, despite more than 120 U.S.-based women's foundations.

THE OTHER HAND

A Critical Look at Feminist Funding

MARSHA SHAPIRO ROSE

The authors in this volume, activists and practitioners in the women's funding movement, provide perspectives that serve as an invaluable resource for understanding the nature and function of women's funds. My outlook is somewhat different, as my primary connection to women's funds has been academic and scholarly.

From 1981 to 1990, I served as the foundations' coordinator for Michigan Technological University, located in Michigan's Upper Peninsula. My responsibilities included raising money for the university from private U.S. foundations. As part of my activities, I visited foundation leaders, primarily in Michigan. It was on one of those visits that I met Mary Jo Pulte, the founder and initial benefactor of the Michigan Women's Fund. Mary Jo told me how she had "come into a lot of money" as her estate was transferred to her authority and she explained that she wanted to do something special with the money. In her retelling, she described how one day she decided that she would use her new wealth to benefit the lives of women and girls. Thus, the Michigan Women's Fund was born.

In 1988, I was unfamiliar with the idea of a foundation dedicated solely to improving the lives of women and girls. As a feminist, I was elated at the possibility of such organizations. As a fundraiser, I sensed opportunities, particularly for scholarships for women students. As a sociologist, I was intrigued by the new organizational and social dimensions of these foundations.

Mary Jo Pulte was not alone in seeing a need for private money directed at women and girls. The Michigan Women's Fund was part of a growing movement to develop women's funds throughout the United States: By 1986, there were twenty-eight women's funds, and today the Women's

Funding Network boasts over ninety members with combined assets in excess of $200 million.

A Feminist Dilemma?

After leaving Michigan in 1990, I began a scholarly journey into the women's funding movement. Exploring a topic in which I had an academic as well as a personal interest easily can result in what I call a feminist dilemma—how to maintain an activist position and a simultaneously critical perspective. Feminist theory implies an activist position. Contrary to earlier sociology that strived for a value-free analysis, feminist theory dispenses with neutrality. At the risk of oversimplification, feminists contend that so-called value-free analyses were really a thinly veiled attempt to confirm the status quo and patriarchal hegemony. By describing social relationships in presumably "objective" terms, sociologists and other social scientists claimed to remove academic discourse from any hint of activism and elevated their work into the scientific realm. Feminist theorists, on the other hand, held no pretensions of objectivity.

A feminist dilemma does not occur when academics and others study overtly patriarchal organizations or relationships. Thus, feminists can research, for example, family dynamics, corporate hierarchy, and political disenfranchisement, and present a compelling critical analysis of these structures. However, the dilemma reappears when we, as feminist scholars, study feminist organizations, such as women's funds. How can we recognize the problems and limitations of feminist organizations without betraying our deeply rooted feminist beliefs?

Biographers often confront a similar dilemma. Sociologist Shulamit Reinharz, in her strong defense of feminist biographies, describes the pains and joys of writing about lives of women.[1] Given the relative paucity of biographies of women, Reinharz begins with the assumption that "writing biographies about women is thus inherently a form of protest" (Reinharz 1994, 37). In previous decades, for a scholar or journalist to pursue information about women's lives easily could result in academic and intellectual marginality. Only in the last decade or two, as the women's movement institutionalized women's studies programs at universities and as the number of women in academic ranks created a meaningful mass, has feminist biography established itself.

Feminist biography explores the lives of women through a gendered lens. Both the day-to-day activities and the professional contributions of women are interpreted with attention focused on the structural and personal mechanisms of oppression. These analyses are two dimensional: On the one hand, the biographer explains the subject's life within the historical and social context of her time. On the other hand, it is imperative that the biographer impose a gendered analysis, even if the subject did not.

Exploring feminist organizations has similar potential pitfalls, albeit more nuanced. Women's funds were created as a form of protest: Increasingly, women of wealth rejected the manipulations of the men who often controlled the women's assets; resentment over the lack of support for programs that benefited women and girls became more widespread; and a growing concern over the decline of federal dollars for social services precipitated the growth of women's funds during the 1980s (Rose 1994). Thus, the point of departure when writing about feminist organizations is different than that of biographies. Women's funds, for example, are explicitly feminist, whereas women's biographies, while providing a gendered analysis, are not necessarily feminist.

Biographies and analyses of feminist organizations share an additional peril: How does the researcher avoid falling into the black hole of admiration for her subject and therefore lose an important critical eye? As researchers, we select topics in which we have both an academic or scholarly interest as well as perhaps an intellectual curiosity. Having selected the subject, we mediate between the actor's presentation and reality through the gendered lens of feminist theory. Avoiding a feminist dilemma is exacerbated when the subject of our work is someone or something that we admire.

Opening a Critical Eye: The Kentucky Foundation for Women

I encountered a feminist dilemma when I worked through Sallie Bingham's papers. Sallie Bingham is a wealthy feminist who established the Kentucky Foundation for Women (KFW). Her papers are housed at Duke University in a majestic building with a plethora of eager staff to assist researchers. As I reviewed hundreds of documents, I wanted to start a Sallie Bingham Fan Club. Ms. Bingham, a prolific writer, speaker, and political activist, defied her family and asserted her agency, which often led to ostracism and criticism. How could one not become enamored of this strong woman who took $10 million of her wealth to create an organization that did not bear her name, but rather a foundation directed at benefiting women and girls? Her gift to the KFW was the largest single contribution to a woman's fund (Rose 2003).

The problems I confronted when writing about Sallie Bingham and social change are directly connected to the problems of critically analyzing feminist organizations. After all, Bingham was a model of feminist activism. Moreover, she "put her money where her mouth is." She donated many hours of her time and millions of dollars to help feminist and social change activism. Would I betray the sisterhood if I were to be critical of Bingham's work? Other biographers (e.g., Tifft and Jones 1991, 500) had criticized Bingham's intentions when she established a journal, *The American Voice*, dedicated to "feminism, liberalism, and egalitarianism" ("Ms. Bingham's New Voice").[2] Still others were critical of the way in which she handled her position at Bingham Enterprises, going so far as to refer to her (and her sister) as "the Black Sheep" (Kirkhorn 1979). In my interpretation of Bingham's work, I reached a different conclusion.

In 1986, Barry Bingham, Sr., the family patriarch, sold his vast media empire for $448 million. For nearly seventy years, the Bingham family had dominated Kentucky's media, owning the *Louisville Courier-Journal* and the *Louisville Times* and various radio and television stations throughout the state. At the time of the sale, popular opinion placed the blame for the dissolution of Bingham Enterprises squarely upon the behavior of Sallie Bingham.[3] For my purposes, the truth or falsehood of these claims is not as significant as the fact that the responses to Sallie Bingham's actions were one of outrage and resentment. Alternatively, the press could have directed their accusations and explanations of the break-up toward such issues as the hostile way in which Bingham's brother responded to her requests for changes in Bingham Enterprises, the manner in which her brother and father possibly mismanaged the company, or the changing economics of the communications industry. Directing the blame toward Sallie was an implicit anti-feminist position.

As I read more about the Bingham family and Sallie Bingham in particular, as a feminist, I wanted to redress what I saw as a legitimate grievance.[4] Similarly, I refused to interpret Sallie Bingham's behavior as that of a victim. As a scholar, however, I needed to maintain a critical eye. My solution to this feminist dilemma was to analyze Sallie Bingham's actions and those of the Kentucky Foundation for Women within a feminist and gendered framework.

The question that needed answering was: To what extent did Bingham and the KFW adhere to the feminist principles they espoused? In the case of the KFW, the organization developed three programs (a literary magazine, a grants program, and a retreat) and they successfully maintained feminist goals in each. Nevertheless, there were gaps, particularly in the early years of the foundation, where pragmatism replaced feminism. For example, a sizable number of authors for the literary magazine *The American Voice* held academic appointments or were previously published writers. The admirable goal of providing a forum for feminists who suffered rejection at other, more male-centered presses, had limited success. Moreover, confirming some of her critic's charges that the journal was self-serving, from 1991 through 1999, Bingham published ten articles of her own in the journal, more than any other author (Rose 2003).

One of Bingham's more hostile critics was Alex Jones, co-author of an authorized Bingham family biography. He reserved one of his nastiest comments regarding the second program of the KFW, grantmaking for the promotion of women artists and writers. During the first round of grant giving, the KFW gave $1 million each to the Women's Project and Ms. *Magazine*. Both organizations had ties to Sallie Bingham, but did not have a direct connection to Kentucky. When asked by a reporter to comment on these grants and KFW, Jones replied, "What we noted was that the Kentucky woman who seems to have benefited most from the Kentucky Foundation is Sallie" (Nance 1991, K2).

Jones's comment was erroneous. The Women's Project had staged two of Bingham's plays and Ms. *Magazine* had published a cover story on "Sallie Bingham: The Woman Who Overturned an Empire." However, both of these events took place prior to the organizations receiving the KFW grants. The more accurate assessment, aside from the noted exceptions, should have been that the women who benefited most from the Kentucky Foundation were the artists who have received over $5 million from the KFW and who otherwise could not have presented their work. In fact, I reconciled my feminist dilemma by acknowledging the positive outcomes of the Kentucky Foundation for Women, and recognizing that whatever transgressions may have occurred did not detract from the significant work of the foundation.

Teresa Odendahl in her analysis of the Women's Foundation of Colorado appeared to have struggled with another dilemma: What to do when a seemingly feminist organization is overtly anti-feminist.

Opening a Hostile Eye: The Women's Foundation of Colorado

In 1987, the Women's Foundation of Colorado was one of the first state-wide women's funds. Similar to other women's funds, the founders were responding to the paucity of grants that directly benefited women and girls. Swanee Hunt, daughter of oil magnate H. L. Hunt, and sister of noted feminist philanthropist Helen Hunt, along with other women of wealth, pledged $2 million for the foundation's endowment.

Less than three years after its inauguration, Teresa Odendahl published a scathing commentary on the foundation's leadership, goals, and direction. In both academic and other feminist circles, Odendahl, an anthropologist by training, is highly respected and admired for her work.[5] Odendahl's reflection on the Women's Foundation of Colorado came in large measure from her first-hand, although brief, experience as their executive director.

According to Odendahl, her interviews with members of the foundation's board were "more social than substantive." She reported that the interviewers appeared "interested in my table manners . . . and my sexual preference" (Odendahl 1990, 199). The tensions between Odendahl and key members of the foundation escalated during the next few months, culminating in a stand-off between Odendahl and the key benefactor of the foundation, Swanee Hunt. In the end, Odendahl resigned from the foundation and Hunt became its president.

At the 1992 National Network of Women's Funds Annual Conference in St. Petersburg, Florida, I sat next to Letty Bass from the Women's Foundation of Colorado. Having recently read Odendahl's condemnation of the foundation, I asked Bass for her reaction. She stated, understandably, that the members just wanted to get the situation behind them.

Nevertheless, Odendahl's critique of the foundation cannot be dismissed. Again, the question that must be addressed is: To what extent did the Women's Foundation of Colorado adhere to the feminist principles they espoused? According to Odendahl, at least during the earliest years of the foundation, the answer was a resounding "no." Diversity is a cornerstone of feminism and a necessary component for membership in the Women's Funding Network. However, for Odendahl, the foundation's commitment to diversity was superficial at best.

In her criticism of the Colorado Women's Foundation, Odendahl cites at least six areas of implicit anti-feminism behavior: (1) The initial composition of the foundation's board included no women of color; (2) When minority women were added to the board, they participated only on the Community Board, and not the Donor Board; (3) There was concern that one board member told Odendahl during her interview process "that she doubted whether [funding lesbian projects] was the kind of thing the foundation would get into" (Odendahl 1990, 200); (4) At the 1987 meeting of the National Network of Women's Funds (NNWF), the foundation's delegation did not meet the diversity requirement for participation; (5) A clear but unstated hierarchy of elite women dominating the foundation had emerged and was becoming increasingly apparent; (6) Finally, Odendahl cites Swanee Hunt's proclamation at the 1987 NNWF meeting that the "Women's Foundation of Colorado would not fund 'lesbian projects'" (Odendahl 1990, 202). Hunt made this statement even though, according to Odendahl, the policy had not been discussed at any board meetings.

Odendahl's hostile eye toward the Women's Foundation of Colorado clearly has merit. Nevertheless, the problems of the foundation were not unique. As some analysts have pointed out, feminist principles and philanthropy can be incompatible (Porterfield 1987; Ostrander 2004). Clas-

sism can interfere with benevolence.[6] Within the women's funding movement, there must be constant vigilance to ensure that feminist principles
of diversity and inclusivity are maintained (Rose 1994). However, women's
funds have two potentially conflicting interests: On the one hand, the
funds are a source of capital and on the other hand, the same funds must
raise money. Thus, are women's funds anti-feminist when they host fundraising events that cater to elite, wealthy patrons? Nearly all women's
funds need to have access to elite donors who contribute resources for the
foundations' programs. I contend that the incipient anti-feminism appears
not when they access resources. Rather, feminist principles are jeopardized
more easily in the allocation of those resources. The Boston Women's
Fund appeared to solve the dilemma.

Opening an Inclusive Eye: The Boston Women's Fund

From 1995 to 2000, Susan Ostrander studied the relationships between
the Boston Women's Fund (BWF) and its grantees (Ostrander 2004). The
theoretical issue with which Ostrander was concerned focused on the potential for anti-feminist structures emerging within explicitly feminist organizations. How is it that women's funds, and the Boston Women's Fund
in particular, avoid adopting masculine, hierarchical connections with
their grantees?

The year 2004 marked the twentieth anniversary of the founding of the
BWF and they planned a host of activities to commemorate the event.
The contrasts between the BWF and the Colorado Women's Foundation
were apparent from the outset in at least three ways: First, "BWF was created . . . by a multirace, multiclass group of women to generate and control money to support women-led community efforts toward social change"
(Ostrander 2004, 33); second, community activists in organizations similar to the grantees decide the grant-making process, not elite donors;
third, the majority of the board of directors overseeing the BWF are
women of color (Ostrander 2004).

But most revealing, perhaps, is the way in which the BWF dealt with
the issue of a dramatic increase in the number of grant proposals that did
not conform to the foundation's guidelines. Most of the proposals came
from organizations that met the foundation's criteria of diversity, clear
goals, sufficient operating budgets, and their focus on programs directed at
women and girls. The two areas where potential grantees were increasingly falling short rested on their insufficient social change agenda and the
lack of constituency control.

Given this incompatibility between the foundation's interests and those
of its targeted audience, three options were available: (1) Continue the

current situation and reject proposals that do not conform to the guidelines. The problems with this option are obvious. The foundation's grants committee rejected 65 percent of proposals during 1995–1996. Maintaining the status quo negates the foundation's mandate to serve the low-income women in the greater Boston area. (2) Instruct their targeted organizations to redirect their proposals to conform to the foundation's interests. This strategy is often employed by more traditional philanthropic organizations as well as many women's funds. For example, many foundations provides workshops for potential grantees on the preparation of proposals that conform to the foundation's guidelines. (3) Change the foundation's criteria and goals in consultation with the grantees. Only the last option reinforces feminist philanthropy, and best describes the direction for the BWF. After much discussion, the Boston Women's Fund altered their priorities and responded to "grantee-expressed needs" (Ostrander 2004, 41).[7]

Discussion

The three women's funds discussed in this chapter share an overriding commitment to helping women and girls. Each foundation began with strong feminist guidelines and each foundation was in the vanguard of the women's funding movement. However, it would be insufficient to claim that the foundations vary only by geographic emphases. Rather, the Kentucky Foundation for Women, Women's Foundation of Colorado, and Boston Women's Fund are quite dissimilar: In Kentucky, the foundation began with a single endowment and focuses on the arts throughout the state. In Colorado, the foundation had its roots among a group of very elite women and directs most of the its grants toward helping women obtain economic self-sufficiency in all regions of Colorado. In Boston, a diverse group of women established the foundation and, initially at least, supported women's organizations that facilitated social change in the Boston area.

In order to best understand these and other similar organizations, we must use a critical and constructive lens. In each instance, we must ask the key question: To what extent did the foundation adhere to the feminist principles they espoused? Answering this query makes possible a reasoned analysis of the organization. We would be examining the women's funds from a feminist perspective, without losing our critical eyes. In other words, we would be avoiding a feminist dilemma.

NOTES

1. Reinharz describes five painful properties: (1) the inability to locate information; (2) the emphasis often placed upon the private, rather than the public lives of women; (3) the anguish of uncovering "another woman's oppression"; (4) the willingness of women

to change their names, either through marriage or the use of pseudonyms; (5) acknowledging and dealing with the writer's anger toward oppressors. For Reinharz, the joyful properties of writing biography outweigh the pains. These joys include: (1) the recognition that the writer has uncovered a meaningful subject; (2) the creation of an understanding and supporting relationship with another woman; and (3) the "opportunity for personal growth" (Reinharz 1994: 43–72).

2. *Louisville, Kentucky Observer* [ca. 1985], unprocessed May 1998, Bingham Papers (author unknown).

3. Some examples include "After a Woman Is Scorned, a Publishing Family Cashes Out" (Nielson 1987); nearly all the obituaries of Barry Bingham, Sr., (Sallie's father) alluded to her role in "destroying" Bingham Enterprises (Nance 1991).

4. For Sallie Bingham's side of the story, see her autobiography, *Passion and Prejudice: A Family Memoir.*

5. Dr. Odendahl has published widely on the nonprofit sector. Her works include *Charity Begins at Home: Generosity and Self-Interest among the Philanthropic Elite; America's Wealthy and the Future of Foundations;* and *Women in Foundations: Career Patterns of Women and Men, Women and Power in the Nonprofit Sector.*

6. The social work of elite women during the early twentieth century is an oft-cited example of the imposition of elite standards upon working and lower-class immigrants.

7. Ostrander lists three other, although similar, options: (1) The foundation could "provide special seed monies to organizations to bring them into line with the redistributive methods of community organizating that BWF wanted most to fund; (2) They could give larger, and fewer, grants to those organizations that met its current criteria; (3) The foundation could provide technical assistance to grantees to help them prepare proposals for the work "that BWF wanted most to support." (2004: 38).

REFERENCES

Bingham, Sallie. 1989. *Passion and Prejudice: A Family Memoir.* New York: Applause Books.

Hall, Peter Dobkin. 1989. "The Empty Tomb: The Making of Dynastic Identity." In *Lives in Trust: The Fortunes of Dynastic Families in Late Twentieth-Century America,* ed. George E. Marcus and Peter Dobkin Hall. Boulder, Colo.: Westview.

Kirkhorn, Michael. 1979. "The Bingham Black Sheep." *Louisville Today:* 36–41. Subject Files Series, box 2, newspaper Clippings, 1952–1980 folder, Sallie Bingham Papers, Rare Book, Manuscript, and Special Collections Library, Duke University.

Knight, Louise W. 1992. "Jane Addams's Views on the Responsibilities of Wealth." In ed., Dwight F. Burlingame. *The Responsibilities of Wealth,* Bloomington: Indiana University Press.

Nance, Kevin. 1991. "Villainess Image Beginning to Fade." *Lexington Herald-Leader,* April 14, 1991.

Nielsen, John. 1987. "After a Woman is Scorned, a Publishing Family Cashes Out." *Fortune* 115 (January 5): 93.

Odendahl, Teresa. 1990. *Charity Begins at Home: Generosity and Self-Interest among the Philanthropic Elite.* New York: Basic Books.

Ostrander, Susan A. 2004. "Moderating Contradictions of Feminist Philanthropy: Women's Community Organizations and the Boston Women's Fund, 1995 to 2000." *Gender and Society* 18, no. 1 (February): 29–46.

Porterfield, Amanda. 1997. "Philanthropy and Feminism: Tensions and Congruences." Paper delivered at the ARNOVA Annual Conference, December.

Reinharz, Shulamit. 1994. "Feminist Biograpy: The Pains, the oys, the Dilemmas." In *Exploring Identity and Gender: The Narrative Study of Lives,* ed. Amia Liebich and Rughellen Josselson. Thousand Oaks, Calif.: Sage.

Rose, Marsha Shapiro. 1994. "Philanthropy in a Different Voice: The Women's Funds." *Nonprofit and Voluntary Sector Quarterly* 23, no. 3 (Fall): 227–42.

Rose, Marsha S. 2003. "Southern Feminism and Social Change: Sallie Bingham and the Kentucky Foundation for Women." In *The New Deal and Beyond: Social Welfare in the South since 1930,* ed. Elna Green. Athens, Ga.: University of Georgia Press.

Tifft, Susan E., and Alex S. Jones. 1991. *The Patriarch: The Rise and Fall of the Bingham Dinasty.* New York: Summit.

❧ PART II ❧

WOMEN AND SOCIAL CHANGE

Part II explores the special relationship between women and social change and examines the contributions of women's philanthropic leadership within the social context of the wider world. It shines a light on resourceful women "from cradle to grave" and looks at philanthropy through the lens of gender, concluding with a discussion of how women's philanthropy might evolve in a technology-driven future.

WOMEN'S BIGGEST CONTRIBUTION

A View of Social Change

CHRISTINE H. GRUMM, DEBORAH L. PUNTENNEY,
AND EMILY KATZ KISHAWI

Over the past thirty years, philanthropic institutions in the United States and around the globe increasingly have invested their resources in ways that they anticipate will lead to powerful and positive change in the lives of women and girls (Capek 2001). The women's funding movement has grown in response to a variety of social, political, and institutional injustices that leave women and girls at a disadvantage in terms of achieving their full potential. Funders within this movement have supported all kinds of activities directed at ameliorating these injustices, including direct services, education, and advocacy. Worthwhile investment strategies and practices have been developed over time by individual institutions and shared among other foundations and funds with the same interests in and commitments to building a more just and equitable society.

Like the grassroots women's organizations that change the world at the local level, the women's funding movement has achieved its strength and influence in part as the result of moving from a deficiency or needs-based model to a paradigm that emphasizes the undertapped potential of women and girls to contribute to social change. Funders within the movement have partnered with the organizations they support to make their vision of what can be a reality, establishing themselves as society's true builders and change-makers. Women are widely recognized and acknowledged as leaders in the creation of global well-being, as evidenced by a recent statement by Kofi Annan, Secretary General of the United Nations.

When women are fully involved, the benefits can be seen immediately: their children are better educated; they are healthier and better fed; they are better able to protect themselves against AIDS and other diseases; their families' income and economy improve. And what is true of families is true of communities—ultimately, indeed—of whole countries. (2002)

Participants in the women's funding movement joined together in the mid-1980s to form the Women's Funding Network (WFN), a member organization that focuses its energies on social change that positively affects the lives of women and girls. During the last several years, Network members have been engaged in ongoing discussion about the need to consolidate systematically their knowledge and expertise. Doing so is necessary in order for member funds to demonstrate the significance of their social change investments and their influence on the broader field of philanthropy, both important aspects of planning future investment and fundraising strategies. WFN members know that their investments have had significant impact because they can look back at the history of their efforts and the outcomes they produced. But in spite of visible changes in the landscape of women's lives and the social contexts they inhabit, the tools and processes for identifying and measuring the changes as they unfold remain less than fully developed. As part of its commitment to increasing resources directed to women and girls' issues, WFN invested in a multi-year research and development effort that produced an evaluation tool called *Making the Case: A Learning and Measurement Tool for Social Change*.

This chapter describes how the women's funding movement has contributed to profound institutional change at many levels and in many categories, and how it has helped construct new ways of thinking about the possibilities for change. The Women's Funding Network's work on the *Making the Case* tool is described, and examples from its member funds' work illustrate the kinds of positive outcomes the tool is expected to capture. A brief literature review on social change sets the stage, then examples are provided from the work of the women's funding movement to support the contention that women's contributions to social change affect not only women and girls, but the well-being of entire communities. Several sections reflect key areas in which investments by WFN member funds have had an important impact. Finally, some of the many challenges faced by women change-makers are explored.

A Brief History of the Women's Funding Movement

As the women's funding movement began to take form, the Ms. Foundation for Women, Astraea Lesbian Foundation for Justice and the Women's Foundation of California all played central roles in defining its shape and direction. In addition to the targeted grantmaking and capacity-building work in which these funds engaged, they also worked to build momentum for the establishment of local women's funds in communities around the United States and around the world. By the mid-1980s, the movement had expanded sufficiently to invite the development of an entity through which member funds could relate to one another and enhance their communications, collaboration, and strategic activities. Called the Women's Funding Network (WFN), this entity is now a central part of the women's funding movement. The Women's Funding Network includes more than one hundred women and girls' funds and over twenty-three supporting organizations, and works to change society by improving the status of women and girls locally, nationally, and internationally, and to strengthen and empower its member funds. The WFN represents the essential architecture around which many of the existing women's funds originally were built, and, since its inception in 1985, WFN has been the central organizing mechanism for women's funds in the United States and Canada and—in partnership with Mama Cash and the Global Fund for Women—around the world, making this a truly global phenomenon. During this period, WFN's members have raised more than $400 million and granted more than $200 million toward making the full participation of women and girls possible and recognizing their key contribution to creating strong, equitable, and sustainable communities and societies.

For WFN, the importance of the contribution made by women in philanthropy is much broader than their expanding presence at the philanthropic table. Over the past thirty years, the rapid increase in the number of women participating in philanthropic decision making failed to increase significantly the investments of institutional philanthropy going directly to women and girls. On the other hand, the women's funding movement as a particular stream within philanthropy has been much more targeted in its investments. Those involved in the more specific movement have always emphasized intentional social change, making a difference in the lives of women and girls, and contributing to a better world. The Women's Funding Network has established itself as the collective voice of this movement and the vehicle through which the creative energies of its members are articulated.

Members of the women's funding movement are guided by four principles of social change philanthropy that reflect several important characteristics of efforts to build a better world:

- *Democratize.* Participants in the movement share problems and solutions; to create an effective movement for change, everyone must be able to find a place at the table.

- *Decentralize*. Decision-making power is distributed to multiple locations at the most impacted local level.
- *Diversify*. Ensure that critical and too-often-silenced voices are heard; make certain a range of voices are contributing to every discussion.
- *Demystify*. Fundraising and grantmaking processes are open and transparent so it is clear how money is raised and disbursed.

Making the Case — A Research and Development Project

The Making the Case research was designed to improve WFN members' ability (a) to articulate how social change investments will help create the structure, culture, knowledge, and influence that will shift the world in desirable directions, and (b) to track effectively how these investments and activities are related to outcomes at various levels. These goals originally were articulated by the Center for Effective Philanthropy as necessary steps for the maturing movement (2002).

In addition to exploring how change is understood and measured in the broader universe, the research developed and tested a model for understanding and measuring the impact of philanthropic investments and activities that benefit women and girls. The findings of three rounds of interactive instrument design and testing among organizations within and outside the Network enabled WFN to present its members with a tool that incorporates its members own understandings of social change and how it happens. Conceptualized as a series of "shifts," the outcomes of social change investments will be captured through measuring:

- *Shifts in definition/reframing*. The issue is viewed differently in the community or the larger society as a result of the work;
- *Shifts in individual/community behavior*. Behaviors in the community or larger society are different as a result of the work;
- *Shifts in critical mass/engagement*. Critical mass is developing, people in the community or larger society are more engaged as a result of the work;
- *Shifts in institutions/policy*. An organizational, local, regional, state, or federal policy or practice has changed as a result of the work; and
- *Maintaining past gains/holding the line*. Earlier progress on the issue has been maintained, in the face of opposition, as a result of the work.

The model takes into account the contexts in which organizations undertake their work (Internal Motivations and External Connections), and how their approach contributes to the change they produce (Taking External Action and Building Internal Knowledge). The recently released evaluation measurement tool allows members of the Women's Funding Network (and soon other organizations) to both capture and learn from their experiences in social change investment. Making the Case will enable WFN members and their grantee partners to track and understand their achievements in ways that will enable them to develop more effective future strategies and attract new donors to the movement. Findings from the data collected to date demonstrate that while the activities of individual organizations may seem to have a relatively small impact, when viewed in combination, the outcomes are significant. Additionally, when simple tools are available for systematically tracking the work being supported and the specific outcomes associated with those efforts, it becomes easier for those supporting social change philanthropy to claim the impact of their investments.

Understanding Social Change

People mean all sorts of different things when they refer to social change, sometimes meaning "making a difference," sometimes meaning "systemic change." For the purposes of the Women's Funding Network work, social change means that life is different and better for women and girls and that women and girls are central actors in the definition and process of that change in communities. Social change philanthropy specifically invites people to invest not simply in addressing social *problems*, but in long-term strategies to address the *causes* of those problems. The literature on social change is broad and presents a complex set of perspectives about what it is and how it occurs. This brief review is not exhaustive, but attempts to make sense of change in a way that will resonate for philanthropic institutions and others working toward social change that positively affects women and girls.

What is Social Change?

One of the reasons that social change is difficult to measure is that it occurs at different levels within society. For example, structural change is different than cultural change, although the two are interconnected. Change in social structure is change that happens within society's institutions—the government, the economy, the workplace, the family, for example—and change within these institutions represents the kind of large-scale change that is often a major goal of philanthropic investments. Change in culture is change that happens in the way people do things, in the symbolic and expressive behaviors they engage in both within and outside institutional contexts. While some scholars argue that structure creates culture, a more dynamic view suggests that culture both reflects and affects social structure (Rubin 1996). Women's philanthropic institutions invest in both kinds of change in order to achieve their goals.

The outward appearance of change depends on the distinct lens through which it is viewed. From a macro perspective, change sometimes is seen as something that happens to people, something they have to deal with, accept, and adapt to. For example, the late twentieth century saw the movement of certain kinds of jobs from within U.S. borders to other countries. For many, change of this magnitude appears to be the result of historical forces, as a reality that individuals can do little about. And the corollary change that happened in those other countries—increased labor abuses and compromise of workers' rights in some instances—can be almost completely invisible to people struggling to adapt to the loss of their own job (Basu 1995). From a micro perspective, the impact of this kind of change can be comprehended by examining how individual lives are advantaged or disadvantaged as a result of shifting labor markets (Rubin 1996). For individuals, understanding what happens in people's lives when an employer abandons a neighborhood is much easier than comprehending the meaning of the macro-level statistics about the global movement of jobs. For social change philanthropists, making the connection between the macro and micro levels of change is crucial because it is often the gray area toward which their investments are targeted.

How Does Social Change Happen?

There is no question that macro-level change is critical in terms of increasing justice for women and girls, but scholars disagree about the order in which the "inputs" must occur in order to achieve the desired outcome. From one perspective, "Laws are made to function as locomotives pulling social change in a desired direction" (Kaul 1991). This view suggests that the primary goal of social change investment should be to affect public policy directly, to begin by actually changing laws that would then drive change at other levels of society. But history provides other lessons. Change also emerges out of efforts at the community level, and change that occurs among smaller groups of people clearly also drives what happens legislatively (Bruyn and Rayman 1979; Elshtain 2002; Naples 1998). Many aspects of the broader women's movement and the more specific efforts within it effectively illustrate this possibility (e.g., Gordon 1994; Sapiro 1990; Skocpol 1992).

There are many lenses through which to think about social change and how it happens. Western perspectives characterize social change as something that the community can organize around, influence, and guide (Bynum 1992; Franz and Stewart 1994). Other cultures consider change as an external, natural, and inevitable force to which people respond but over which they have little direct control (Maruyuma 1983). Adding to the complexity of the question are the variety of cultural interpretations and perspectives that demonstrate that what is meaningful and appropriate change in one setting may be undesirable in another (Teske and Tétreault 2000; Thomas 2000). What constitutes appropriate change is also a contested arena within societies, communities, and even social movements, with conservatives, liberals, progressives, and radicals competing for the power to establish their own definitions of appropriate conditions, opportunities, and policies (Ryan 1992).

Within this complexity, the proactive effort of any particular group to influence the direction of social change becomes one among many competing influences. History demonstrates that social change occurs in different ways on different occasions in different places (McCarthy 2001). Because social change is the result of myriad, sometimes unconnected actions and because it is not necessarily an immediate or direct result of any given effort to create it, it can be difficult for any group to claim a direct causal link between a particular set of actions or investments and a broad social change outcome (Center for Effective Philanthropy 2002). The action or investment may not only be separated by years from a concrete measurable outcome at the macro level, but the issue itself often changes as the process of effecting social change proceeds (Buechler 1997; Schechter 1982). One theory suggests that social change is a question of balance and that while philanthropists and activists may work on an issue for lengthy periods with little concrete evidence of success, a tipping point may come when the efforts have produced enough issue salience in the form of smaller-scale change that the issue develops an impetus of its own and progresses with less struggle to the macro-level change desired (Gladwell 2000). Large-scale social change can be a grindingly slow process in which success is achieved only in small increments on convoluted pathways subject to all kinds of positive and negative influences over time (Buechler 1997). It also can happen abruptly, in relationship to a change in political leadership, for example, or to a natural catastrophic event that alters the human environment. And because change is dynamic rather than static, it is rarely complete: Success for one interest group inevitably represents failure for another, resulting in ever-changing landscapes of pushing and pulling at social issues.

Women as Builders; Women as Agents for Change

For participants in the women's funding movement, there is no question that conditions in the world are viewed as potentially responsive to proactive efforts to change them, that is, that human actors can influence their reality. The reason philanthropists make strategic investments at a variety of levels is because they believe they can affect the course of change. The long tradition of women investing in the creation of a better world confirms that investors believe in social justice and are willing to invest resources in ways they believe will result in positive social change (Capek 2001). Women around the world have invested financial and other resources in ways that make sense in their particular local situation, but also have attempted to maintain a sense of the global consequences of local action (McCarthy 2001).

The thirty-year history of the modern women's funding movement provides stark evidence of the extent of the impact of women's insistence on being central actors in the definition and creation of social justice. Related movements also have produced profound impacts on American society. During the Progressive Era, women fought for the protections of Mother's Pensions, for the right to vote, and later for protections under the Social Security Act (Gordon 1994; Skocpol 1992). After mid-century, women organized and participated in numerous movements, including the shelter and anti-violence movements, the welfare rights movement, and the civil rights movement (Morken and Selle 1994; Schechter 1982). Toward the end of the century, U.S. women had succeeded in dramatically increasing the number of women in Congress, expanded the role of women in supporting the rights of groups with less access to the centers of power such as lesbians, immigrants, and the disabled (Rubin 1996), and joined forces with women around the world in the international movement for human security. Within these movements, women not only invested in creating change, but did so from within frameworks that reflected their own ways of interacting, being inclusive, and getting the work done (Gittell, Ortega-Bustamente, and Steffy 1999).

Participants in the women's funding movement have established goals that represent the virtual transformation of the social, political, and institutional domains. These goals include the development of social structures that enable women and girls to achieve their full potential, and investments aim both to ameliorate current problems and to build better systems for the future (Covington 1997; Feree and Martin 1995). Teske and Tetreault (2000) argue that a feminist vision of the future depends on how people relate to one another, and the extent to which the understanding of power is related to the collectivity of effective action (power with rather than power over). They use a "hopeful metaphor . . . The Butterfly Effect" (116) to describe how small changes in context ultimately can change the world.

The following examples illustrate some of the many achievements associated with the deliberate strategic investments of members of this movement. We have divided the examples into the categories "Women Building Solutions," "Women Building Long-Term Change," and "Women Building a New Philanthropy." The examples in each category illustrate the idea that women are working from the local to the global level.

Women Building Solutions

One important aspect of the history of the women's funding movement is the success it has achieved in bringing relevant issues to public consciousness and in building the structural frameworks necessary to keep these issues visible and to expand public funding streams for their support. In 2004, war and an international economy in disarray compete for the public's attention, making it likely that the violence and poverty still affecting women and girls will seem relatively less important. In spite of these realities, women's and girls' energy and ideas have never been more central to creating world solutions. Their commitment to creating a global community that provides the umbrella of human security to every person is key to resolving present-day issues. For women's and girls' funds, the idea of a global community represents the framework for relating to the world. Members of the Women's Funding Network build global community when they make grants to engage women and girls in changing the world by supporting economic justice, freedom from violence, direct service, and advocacy. Human safety and security, by necessity, have been a major focus of women and girls the world over. Women look for security in freedom from violence—in their homes, on the streets, in their communities, in their countries, and across borders. The Women's Funding Network seeks economic security for women and girls who still fight for access to jobs and equal pay. The Network pursues security by supporting the building of a world that provides access to quality health care across the life span; it supports safe communities by advocating for a cleaner, healthier environment.

Freedom from Violence

Support from women's and girls' funds is one of the reasons why violence against women is no longer a closeted crime in many places. WFN member funds have achieved systemic change through their ongoing focus on these issues: Communities have been strengthened by member funds' efforts to change personal behavior, societal norms, law enforcement, and legislation at every level of government. WFN member funds have invested in the courage of women and girls in the face of violence and have propelled the issue from the shadows into the minds of the public and into the hallways of capitols and seats of government and business. Grants from women's and girls' foundations have funded the anti-violence programs, shelters, and advocacy necessary to break the cycle of violence. They have also funded programs that train police departments and hospital emergency room staffs in the informed and appropriate responses to the special needs of rape and domestic violence survivors. They have heightened community awareness and provide support for counseling, legal referral, and crisis services to women who have experienced harassment or domestic violence. In addition, women's and girls' foundations focus their grant-making on increasing access to these services for immigrant and refugee women, who traditionally are underserved and often among the most vulnerable.

The Chicago Foundation for Women's Funding Initiative to End Violence against Women and Girls riveted attention in its community on overlooked issues and resulted in increased funding from government sources to support domestic violence and rape crisis programs. This started a chain of effects, the first of which was that the courts changed the way they handled the cases of women in domestic violence lawsuits. Through educational efforts, community attitudes began to shift in ways that supported the strategies of survivors. Finally, the foundation was able to see an attitudinal change in police handling of cases involving violence against women and girls.

When the Washington Area Women's Foundation strategically released a detailed portrait of the capital region's women and girls, it helped the foundation raise over $2.5 million to address some of the study's findings—some of which included the importance of addressing women's safety. The groundbreaking 2003 report, A Portrait of Women and Girls in the Washington Metropolitan Area revealed a twenty-first-century "tale of two cities": an area where women enjoy the highest rates of employment and earnings in the country, but where 57 percent of the families living in poverty are women-headed households, rising to an even more alarming 70 percent in the District of Columbia. The study also points out that no issue strikes at the heart of a woman's ability to participate fully in society more than her physical safety—with vulnerability to violence and lack of personal safety emerging as two of the strongest themes in community forums where women had the opportunity to talk about their lives.

Personal and public safety is one of the objectives of the Women and Families Financial Independence Initiative—a multi-year initiative in response to the study, to help the area's low-income, women-headed families build long-term economic security and self-reliance.

Sex Trafficking

As the concept of freedom from violence has engaged the attention of government bodies at the local and global levels, women's funds have been at the forefront of educating these entities about the scope of the problem, as well as supporting the leaders in producing solutions. For example, the Atlanta Women's Foundation funded a citywide initiative in 2001 to stop child prostitution. They created a task force, convened a summit, and successfully lobbied the legislature to pass a bill making the prostitution of children a felony. The attention they received for this effort resulted in a major donor approaching the foundation and offering to support a shelter for exploited children. The Atlanta Women's Foundation leveraged community outrage to engage the Office of the U.S. Attorney, which criminally prosecuted pimps involved in the sexual exploitation of children under federal racketeering laws.

Responding to the advocacy efforts of women's organizations, and with early support from women and girls' foundations including Mama Cash and the Global Fund for Women, the United Nations has undertaken to address sex trafficking. The UN established a special *rappateur* on violence against women as a result of women around the world working diligently to generate attention for the issue. Sanctions against sex trafficking within and across borders comprise one aspect of the UN's work. The UN has taken an important step forward in coordinating an international response to trafficking by adopting a package of instruments against various forms of transnational organized crime, including the UN Convention against Transnational Organized Crime and the Protocol to Prevent, Suppress and Punish Trafficking in Persons, especially Women and Children. Both the Convention and Protocol obtained the ratifications needed and were entered into force in December 2003 (United Nations Office on Drugs and Crime 2003). No longer relegated to the sidelines, the right to freedom from violence for women and girls is now enforced through law by the international body whose charge is, in part, to solve international economic, social, cultural, and humanitarian problems and to promote respect for human rights and fundamental freedoms.

Economic Security

A key goal of many women's and girls' foundations is to help achieve economic justice for women by supporting a broad range of activities, such as training in nontraditional jobs, legislation to increase access to capital, and advocacy for pay equity. These funds know that when women and girls thrive economically communities are stronger. As a result, they support programs that promote economic self-sufficiency for low-income women and provide financial management education for girls, including learning programs for teen women on the language, culture, and networks necessary for business ownership. These funds also expand economic opportunities by creating solutions to the lack of childcare services and advocating that employers adapt to the needs of working mothers.

The Ms. Foundation for Women invests in economic security for women and their families, and strategically supports its grantees in coupling training and loan programs with advocacy and policy objectives. One area of focus for the Ms. Foundation has been building women's small business skills, an important move toward stability since the recession of the mid-1980s. Women supported through these programs now understand better how to position themselves in the market niches that can survive a sagging economy. Ms. Foundation staff believe that in light of the current recession, it is more important than ever for low-income women to be able to sustain themselves economically and advocate for systemic change. Putting this belief into action, the Ms. Foundation funds the Childspace Cooperative Development. This organization trains childcare industry providers and at the same time works to influence policy that affects childcare workers and the broader community of parents and children they serve.

Internationally, Tewa, the Nepal Women's Foundation, provides small grants to help advance women's economic opportunities through micro-enterprise programs and helping secure economic rights for Nepalese women and girls. Tewa makes economic empowerment grants, for example, to support women in nontraditional trades including training to become electrical repair technicians and off-season vegetable farming. Tewa's grants for micro-credit and income-generating activities have resulted in earnings and savings that women use to send their daughters to school and to improve the nutritional quality of their meals. All Tewa's grantmaking focuses on the overall objective of supporting empowerment for women who can then make choices in their own lives, over their economic status, their bodies, and their education. Importantly, 65 percent of the foundation's grantmaking resources come from local fundraising efforts among women and men, who usually contribute 10 rupees (25 cents USD) at a time. This process of inviting every woman to the philanthropic table has enabled Tewa to organize them, to give voice to their collective will, and to strengthen their collective pool of resources in powerful ways.

Women Building Long-Term Change

Women's funds not only have positioned themselves to define relevant issues and deliver critical services, they have assumed leadership roles within a larger context in terms of their capacity to respond in times of community crisis and take action on a broad array of challenges. Recognition within the larger society of their ability to make these contributions is growing, and extends well beyond the community of other women's funds.

In the immediate aftermath of the events of September 11, 2001, women's funds in the region of New York and Washington, D.C., focused attention and resources on women and communities directly affected by the events but who remained outside the view of more mainstream response efforts. They responded with increased fundraising, grantmaking, and instrumental support in a variety of emergency contexts. The New York Women's Foundation (NYWF) quickly raised more than half a million dollars from donors on a continuum from a young girl who shared her bake-sale earnings to the Beastie Boys, whose concert generated $75,000 for the foundation. The NYWF moved rapidly to begin its grantmaking, capitalizing on connections to its grantees to hear first-hand from the people directly affected but unable to access the millions of dollars being directed to more visible survivors of the attacks.

Across the Hudson, the Women's Fund of New Jersey increased its support to grantees such as the New Jersey Coalition against Sexual Assault, whose expertise in dealing with post-traumatic stress was mobilized in hotlines for individuals affected by the attacks.

In more day-to-day realities, women funds also have demonstrated their capacity for central roles in broad initiatives that affect the public at large. Recently, the California Endowment funded a countywide outreach and education initiative intended to reduce cervical cancer in the Los Angeles area. The ability of the Los Angeles Women's Foundation (recently merged with the Women's Foundation, now known as the Women's Foundation of California) to pinpoint personal, intensive, and tailored programs within the county prompted the Endowment to award the group a major grants for outreach and education. Because the foundation already had established connections with such groups serving all kinds of women, they were uniquely positioned to respond and present themselves as the most effective mechanism for achieving the Endowment's goals.

Leveraging widespread community connections and a network of health *promatoras*, the Women's Foundation of California produced remarkable results. The foundation gave away $960,000 in direct grants to twenty-two women's organizations who spent a year and a half informing women about cervical cancer, and making appointments for screenings. The *promatoras* provided education for more than 102,000 women in multiple languages including several Asian languages and Spanish. Over 17,000 women, many from marginalized communities, were referred to cancer screening appointments resulting in 16,000 screenings. At the end of the project, the tests of more than 2,400 women were reported abnormal and over 700 women were receiving follow-up care.

Women Building a New Philanthropy

Since 1985, the Women's Funding Network (WFN) has worked to create a global community and strengthen human security. WFN members have reinvented philanthropy by inviting those traditionally viewed as the "recipients" of others' charitable giving to assume their places as valued participants in the philanthropic process. Thirty years ago, women were more likely to support charitable causes by doing volunteer work than by making a monetary donation. Family money was more often in the husband's name and women rarely controlled family resources sufficiently to have decision-making power over major gifts. Beginning in the 1970s, women increasingly took charge of their own money and began to make independent decisions about their philanthropic investments. Gradually, they pulled together to create foundations for the support of women's and girls' programs that were not being funded adequately through more traditional means. As women's participation in all spheres of social, economic, and political activity grew, so too did their philanthropic capacity and expertise. By the late 1970s, four women's and girls' funds had pioneered a new model for women philanthropists to support social change from a unique perspective. This burgeoning activity took shape under the premise that every women has the potential to be a philanthropist.

These funds launched the growth of what would eventually become the Women's Funding Network. Members of the Network believe that the way to make the global community stronger over the long term is to ensure that a broad spectrum of people are brought into the process of creating change, including defining what is needed, planning how money is raised, and deciding how grant resources are allocated. The traditional donor/grantee relationship is changed every time a diverse group of women sit together at the table of social change philanthropy. Women's and girls' funds operate with a feminist consciousness of diversity, inclusiveness, and empowered choices and demonstrate that women are often at the center of accomplishing much-needed social change in communities.

Part of this philosophy is a commitment to cross-class philanthropy, in which donors and grantee partners sit in the same room at the same table making decisions together. The relationship between donor and grantee can be a delicate balance. Donors want assurance that their money will make a difference; grantees resist having to jump through donor-defined hoops in order to get their work off the ground. Women's funds have been on the leading edge of forging unusual donor-grantee partnerships, breaking down conventional barriers that might separate the fuel of the women's funding movement from its engine. By strengthening ties among donors, funds, grantees, and the women and girls whose lives each group is working for, women's funds topple traditional power dynamics to build long-term connections and systemic change.

Women's funds also help to bridge the gap by extending a hand to promising organizations and programs even when they are unable to take them on as grantees. Sometimes that means rewriting the book on the traditional grant application process. For instance, each year, the Women's Fund of Greater Memphis (WFGM) stretches its dollars as far as it can, but not all the deserving organizations that apply for grants get funded. Rather than close the door with a polite letter of rejection, WFGM teams up with these applicants to leverage their connections as funders and brainstorm other funding sources. This unofficial policy has led WFGM to draw upon its knowledge of the funding niches in Tennessee and bring these potential donors into the circle. WFGM invites applicants not awarded funds to its annual grants reception so they can mingle and make connections with other funders. And when WFGM simply did not have room in their budget for the West Tennessee Area Health Education Center to train Hispanic women as certified nurses, it reworked the proposal and shopped it to a local insurance company that provided $25,000 to fund the initiative.

Challenges to Achieving Long-Term Change

Members of the Women's Funding Network and other participants in the women's funding movement face many challenges to achieving the kinds of success they envision. These challenges are both local and global, internal and external, and comprise the topic for discussion and action among members of the movement when they come together. Some of the latest thinking in the Network centers on the intersection of multiple parts that make up women's identities. These include women in targeted communities, women of differing economic backgrounds, women with disabilities, lesbians, bisexual and transgender women; in short, women who come to the table with their oppressions and privileges all rolled into one identity.

The Challenge of Money

Money challenges come in different shapes and sizes, but in spite of the increasing expertise of women's funds at generating resources, there never appears to be enough. The dramatic changes over time that have occurred in state and national funding streams for programs and services that positively affect the lives of women and girls attest to the success of the women's funding movement in directing resources more appropriately. But the fact remains that dollars that directly affect the lives of women and girls are often those that are cut first when economic times get difficult, and the task for the Women's Funding Network can sometimes consist of trying to hold onto previous advancements, rather than mobilizing its capacity for bringing in new dollars. Members of the Women's Funding Network are moving into the new century with strategies in place for overcoming the challenge of money. Member funds are growing and the assets currently in place in those funds can be leveraged for the future. In just five years, the collective assets of member funds have grown from $119 million to over $250 million, as more funds have emerged and existing funds have increased their resources. Women are donating more money than ever before, and new opportunities have emerged for tapping into the growing financial resources—including dollars earned in the new economy and dollars transferring from one generation to another—controlled by women. New strategies have been developed for convincing women with financial assets to leave a legacy for women and girls through planned-giving programs. And women's funds have gained expertise in positioning themselves and delivering messages about who and what they represent that should help to ensure ongoing investment toward the work they do.

The Challenge of Integration

For members of the Women's Funding Network, trying to take a local, national, and global approach to increasing the well-being of women and girls can be a difficult task in the context of a world in which most political and economic actors fail to value an integrated approach to development. The primarily market-based approaches of highly developed countries can take precedence over the human security approaches favored by more globally conscious individuals and organizations, and the needs of women, girls, and other groups can be marginalized in this kind of economic perspective. Women's and girls' funds around the world, however, have achieved a degree of resilience to this reality over time that has enabled them to develop strategies for weathering this challenge and emerging in better times prepared for ongoing progress.

The Challenge of Diversity

In a global context in which specialization and segmentation are the guiding principles, it can be a challenge to maintain principles of inclusion and diversity. While WFN member organizations are committed to these principles and fully able to operationalize them when working with one another and with grantee organizations, maintaining them when interacting with the larger world is sometimes difficult. The inclusion of diverse voices in decision-making activities can slow things down, a fact that is troublesome to some. The critique, which tends to be one of inefficiency, is overcome by women's and girls' funds through their stance that equality is as important as efficiency, and that the two principles need not be in conflict. For WFN members, it is inefficient to leave out the voices and valuable contributions of every community member, even if it means that progress is somewhat slower than it might have been had a segmented approach been taken.

The Challenge of Being Heard

The central premise of women's and girls' foundations is that women and girls, those closest to many of the most pressing social issues, are also central to the solutions. Providing sustainable funding is one way to ensure that those solutions are enacted. Achieving widespread recognition for this work, however, represents an ongoing challenge.

While members of the women's funding movement take these challenges seriously, they also see them as opportunities for refining their thinking and redirecting their work. And, true to form, they believe that the most effective way to address these challenges is to come together to talk about them and tap into the expertise existing within the diverse and talented group they represent. Sometimes the best ideas come from great conversations. This is the guiding principle behind WFN's "Social Change Conversations," which sparked Network-wide dialogues on key issues concerning the future of the women's funding movement. Reflecting on social change and what the women's funding movement is doing to move a change agenda forward, participants in these conversations have contributed productive ideas in response to the challenges they face. Through the conversations, WFN members have shared ideas on how they can learn from the experiences of intersecting social movements, identities, and interests in order to achieve long-term change. They have explored issues such as the need to identify new constituencies for inclusion in reconfigured social movements; the intersection of race, religion, class, age, and sexual orientation; and the role women entrepreneurs and men can and must play in terms of future progress toward a world that is a better place for women and girls. Conversation participants have contributed their insights and ideas for taking the women's funding movement agenda forward by approaching its challenges as though they were opportunities. These include:

- the opportunity to move beyond immediate circles of current partners in order to build broader alliances;

- the opportunity to contextualize the framing of issues impacting women and girls for the specific audience in question;
- the opportunity to engage at the level of transformation, which can be more powerful than change, which can represent simply trading one thing for another;
- the opportunity to maintain the global view in spite of the compartmentalization that is required by the current systems of power;
- the opportunity to work with men for positive social change represents a challenge, but true change will not occur without it;
- the opportunity to lift our voices and achieve prominence in the public eye;
- the opportunity to engage new donors through a meaningful understanding of their philanthropic attitudes, motivations, and dreams.

In its thirty-year history, the Women's Funding Network has moved its members' collective agenda for improving the lives of women and girls forward all over the world. Using an asset-based approach, the Network works to build a strong global movement for human security. The impact of its work is measurable. The Network is amassing capital and strength to break the last glass ceiling: women's ability to exert their own visions for change through philanthropy. Women's funds have been instrumental in supporting fundamental changes in the workplace, exposing and challenging institutionalized violence against women and girls, and directing public funds to issues that directly impact them. In 2004, the Women's Funding Network continues to grow, demonstrating a widespread belief that United Nations Secretary General Kofi Annan was correct: When women and girls fare better, communities, countries, and the entire world are better off.

REFERENCES

Annan, Kofi. 2002. Opening Remarks to Panel on the Observance of International Women's Day. http://www.un.org/events/women/2002/sg.htm.

Basu, Amrita. 1995. *The Challenge of Local Feminisms: Women's Movements in Global Perspective*. Boulder, Colo.: Westview Press.

Bruyn, Severyn T., and Paula M. Rayman, 1979. *Nonviolent Action and Social Change*. New York: Irvington Publishers.

Buechler, Steven M. 1997. "New Social Movement Theories." In *Social Movements: Issues and Perspectives*, ed. Steven M. Buechler and F. Kurt Cylke, Jr. Mountain View, Calif.: Mayfield Publishing Company.

Bynum, Victoria E. 1992. *Unruly Women*. Chapel Hill: University of North Carolina Press.

Capek, Mary Ellen S. 2001. "The Women's Funding Movement: Accomplishments and Challenges." In *Women and Philanthropy: Old Stereotypes and New Challenges*. Volume three of monograph series. Battle Creek, Mich.: W. K. Kellogg Foundation.

Center for Effective Philanthropy. 2002. *Toward a Common Language*. Boston: The Center for Effective Philanthropy.

Covington, Sally. 1997. *Moving a Public Policy Agenda: The Strategic Philanthropy of Conservative Foundations*. Washington, D.C.: National Committee for Responsive Philanthropy.

Elshtain, Jean B. 2002. *Jane Addams and the Dream of American Democracy*. New York: Basic Books.

Franz, Carol E., and Abigail J. Stewart, 1994. *Women Creating Lives: Identities, Resilience, and Resistance*. Boulder, Colo.: Westview Press.

Ferree, Myra Marx, and Patricia Y. Marten. 1995. *Feminist Organizations: Harvest of the New Women's Movement*. Philadelphia: Temple University Press.

Gittell, Marilyn, Isolda Ortega-Bustamente, and Tracy Steffy. 1999. *Women Creating Social Capital and Social Change: A Study of Women-Led Community Development Organizations*. Silver Springs, Md.: McAuley Institute.

Gladwell, Malcolm. 2000. *The Tipping Point: How Little Things Can Make a Big Difference*. Boston: Little Brown.

Gordon, Linda. 1994. *Pitied but Not Entitled*. New York: The Free Press.

Kaul, H. 1991. "Who Cares? Gender, Inequality, and Care Leave in the Nordic Countries." *Acta Sociologica* 34: 115–25.

Maruyama, Magoroh. 1983. "Cross-Cultural Perspectives on Social and Community Change." In ed. Edward Seidman *Handbook of Social Intervention*. Beverly Hills, Calif.: Sage.

McCarthy, Kathleen D., Ed. 2001. *Women, Philanthropy, and Civil Society*. Bloomington: Indiana University Press.

Morken, Kristin, and Per Selle. 1994. "The Women's Shelter Movement." In *Women and Social Change*, ed. Feliece Perlmutter. Washington, D.C.: NASW Press.

Naples, Nancy. 1998. *Grassroots Warriors: Activist Mothering, Community Work, and the War on Poverty*. New York: Routledge.

Rubin, Beth A. 1996. *Shifts in the Social Contract: Understanding Change in American Society*. Thousand Oaks, Calif.: Pine Forge Press.

Ryan, Barbara. 1992. *Feminism and the Women's Movement: Dynamics of Change in Social Movement Ideology and Activism*. New York: Routledge.

Sapiro, Virginia. 1990. "The Gender Basis of American Social Policy." In *Women, the State, and Welfare*, ed. Linda Gordon. Madison: University of Wisconsin Press.

Schechter, Susan. 1982. *Women and Male Violence: The Visions and Struggles of the Battered Women's Movement*. Boston: South End Press.

Skocpol, Theda. 1992. *Protecting Soldiers and Mothers: The Political Origins of Social Policy in the United States*. Cambridge: Harvard University Press.

Teske, Robin L., and Mary Ann Tétreault, eds. 2000. *Conscious Acts and the Politics of Social Change*. Columbia: University of South Carolina Press.

Thomas, Caroline. 2000. *Global Governance, Development, and Human Security: The Challenge of Poverty and Inequality*. London: Pluto Press.

United Nations Office on Drugs and Crime. 2003. Signatories to the UN Convention Against Transnational Crime and its Protocols. http://www.unodc.org/unodc/en/traffickinghumanbeings.html.

THE FORD FOUNDATION
A Model of Support for Women's Rights

BARBARA Y. PHILLIPS

June 2001. Lora Jo Foo, lawyer and activist; Peggy Saika, President of Asian American Pacific Islanders in Philanthropy (AAPIP); and Jai Lee Wong, board member of AAPIP, are engaging twenty other women activists and scholars from Asian American communities in critiquing Lora Jo's report, an historic first study documenting the social justice agenda of Asian American women. Discussing the realities of violence, health, welfare reform, trafficking, sweatshops, sexual orientation, and immigration, the women enforce a high standard of truth-telling while also being attentive and sensitive to the challenge of remaining respectful toward communities in which they are deeply imbedded and which they love. The report is published by the Ford Foundation in 2002 and becomes an integral factor in the subsequent partnership of the Foundation with Asian American Pacific Islanders in Philanthropy to strengthen the Asian American women's movement, to open conversations about gender within Asian American communities, and to share the insights of these women with other funders, the broader civil rights community, policy makers, and others.

May 2002. Robert L. Demmons, former Chief of the San Francisco Fire Department, and Denise Hulett, civil rights attorney, are concerned that opportunities for women and minorities remain constricted in many metropolitan fire departments. Of the approximately three hundred thousand firefighters in the United States, fewer than six thousand (2 percent) are women. The fire service exhibits more resistance to the employment of women than any other public employee profession. Demmons and Hulett are working to understand the barriers to greater participation in this field. With respect to one of the well-documented obstacles—hiring and promotion examination processes—they are applying the Noah Principle advocated by Johnetta Betsch Cole and Beverly Guy-Sheftall in their book, *Gender Talk: The Struggle for Women's Equality in African American Communities:* "There will be no more credit for predicting the rain. *It's time to build the ark*" (emphasis in original). With the help and participation of men and women in fire service committed to professionalism and fairness, together with psychometric experts, this ark is a set of hiring and promotion examination processes that are job-related and do not perpetuate the historic, unfair advantaging of white males.

December 2002. L. C. Dorsey of the Mississippi Delta and Shirley Sherrod of southwest Georgia, together with six other black women from rural Mississippi, Alabama, and Georgia, are absorbed in conversation with Manisha Gupte and other Indian women, learning about the unique organizational structure and multi-strategies of MASUM—Mahila Sarvangeen Utkarsh Mandal—a women's rights organization with a staff of seventy, 75 percent of whom are minority caste, lower class, Muslim, and disabled. They are in the village of Malshiras in Maharashtra, several hours' drive into the mountains from the city of Pune in India. The hosts are Pramada Menon and Geetanjali Misra of Creating Resources for Empowerment in Action (CREA), an organization of Indian women working toward gender equity with a focus on issues of sexuality, reproductive health, violence against women, economic justice, and women's rights. Women from the rural South are in India for two weeks engaging in exploration and learning to fuel their own movement for economic and social justice known as the Southern Rural Black Women's Initiative for Economic and Social Justice.

Ongoing. Anne Ladky of Women Employed (WE) in Chicago is a leading national advocate for women's economic advancement. She works with a dynamic staff to make life better for working women, especially the millions who earn low ages, by analyzing issues, educating policy makers, and building support to improve opportunities and incomes. The organization develops its agenda by listening to women and engaging them in defining and advocating for solutions. With strategic know-how built over three decades, Women Employed advocates for fair working conditions and higher pay, access to good training and education, and strong enforcement of fair employment laws. Currently, in addition to its advocacy goals, a top priority is to make career-building information and tools directly available to women in low-wage jobs. Women Employed is pioneering the development of on-line resources like "Career Coach," a new on-line career exploration and planning program (at www.womenemployed.org) that includes assessment tools, profiles of hundreds of career-path jobs and people who hold them, and personalized planning help. WE's "Upgrade Your Future" campaign is introducing thousands of women to well-paying careers in information and technology and connecting them to resources for training, education, and financial aid.

These vignettes of individuals, the communities with which they work, the strategies deployed, and the goals to which the work aspires tell the lived reality of a learning foundation. This chapter offers a summary version of the rich and complex history of that foundation's commitment to the struggle for women's rights and social justice. While that commitment has been global, this chapter emphasizes work in the United States consistent with the geographic focus of this volume and because another chapter is devoted specifically to the international aspects of philanthropy. The chapter will provide a brief description of the Ford Foundation as an institution, explore the foundation's values and approach to engagement in the field of women's rights including a brief discussion of the global women's movement, and conclude with thoughts about current challenges facing the advancement of social justice for women in the United States

The Institution

The Ford Foundation is a resource for innovative people and institutions. Our goals are to strengthen democratic values, reduce poverty and injustice, promote international cooperation, and advance human achievement. A fundamental challenge facing every society is to create political, economic, and social systems that promote peace, human welfare, and the sustainability of the environment on which life depends. We believe that the best way to meet this challenge is to encourage initiatives by those living and working closest to where problems are located; to promote collaboration among the nonprofit, government, and business sectors; and to ensure participation by men and women from diverse communities and at all levels of society. Founded in 1936, the foundation operated as a local philanthropy in the state of Michigan until 1950, when it expanded to become a national and international foundation. An independent, nonprofit, nongovernmental organization since its inception, the foundation has provided some $12 billion in grants and loans. These funds derive from an investment portfolio that began with gifts and bequests of Ford Motor Company stock by Henry and Edsel Ford. The foundation no longer owns Ford Motor Company stock, and its diversified portfolio is managed to provide a perpetual source of support for the foundation's programs and operations.

The trustees of the Ford Foundation set policy and delegate authority to the president and senior staff for the foundation's grantmaking and operations. Program officers in the United States, Africa, the Middle East, Asia, Latin America, and Russia explore opportunities to pursue the foundation's goals, formulate strategies, and recommend proposals for funding within three major program areas.

The Asset Building and Community Development program seeks to improve the lives of the poor and disadvantaged by helping them to build assets—social, financial, educational, and environmental. Engaging the fields of development finance and economic security, and workforce development, its Economic Development unit focuses on helping low-income people to build financial assets through increased access to employment opportunities, credit, opportunities to save, and homeownership. Engaging the fields of environment and development and community development, its Community and Resource Development unit supports work on community development and the environment to give low-income communities greater ownership and control of key community institutions and resources.

The Peace and Social Justice program seeks to promote access to justice and the full range of human rights for all members of society; secure the rule of law and the narrowing of inequality by fostering effective, open, and accountable governmental institutions; and strengthen civil society by broadening the participation of individuals and civic groups, including philanthropic organizations. The Human Rights unit supports groups working on human rights in the United States and around the world. Grants focus on the rights of women, migrants, refugees, marginalized racial and ethnic groups, and international human rights efforts. The unit also funds work on reproductive and sexual rights, HIV/AIDS, and the movement for reproductive health. The Governance and Civil Society unit supports efforts to improve government performance, policy making, and accountability, and builds public awareness of budget and tax issues. Priorities include conflict prevention and the governance of international security and economic policy. Through work on civil society, including global institutions, it seeks to increase participation in public affairs beyond the act of voting. The unit also works to strengthen civil society organizations while stimulating the practice of philanthropy.

The Knowledge, Creativity, and Freedom program engages the fields of education and scholarship; religion, society, and culture; sexuality and reproductive health. Its Education, Sexuality, Religion unit supports education research and reform in grades K–12 and in university systems; graduate fellowships, social science training, university curriculum development, and research in the social sciences and humanities and in area and international studies, with particular emphasis on gender, identity, and pluralism. Work on religion focuses on clarifying and strengthening the social values in the traditions that can contribute to building just and healthy pluralistic societies. Work on sexuality focuses on deepening public understanding of the relationship between sexuality, human fulfillment, and identity and the policy implications of this new knowledge. Engaging fields of media, arts, and culture, its Media, Arts, and Culture unit supports the development of media, information, and technology resources to advance social change and human achievement and understanding. Grant-making includes both infrastructural and access issues and independent production, with a focus on print, film, radio, and Web-based media. In the arena of arts and culture, the unit fosters new artistic talent, strengthens arts institutions, attends to cultural knowledge and resources, and encourages contributions of artists and arts and culture organizations to the quality of civic life. It also assists projects that advance understanding of cultural identity and community.

In the Beginning

During 1979 and 1980, the Board of Trustees pondered a stark and bold description of the significance of sex discrimination that remains salient to today's work:

> Sex discrimination is a universal problem. Everywhere girls' and women's basic rights and opportunities are circumscribed and societies are deprived of their skills. Sex discrimination is a major factor in poverty and a costly constraint on productivity. It pervades all institutions with strong reinforcement from culture and custom. Wherever and however it exists, it is unjust.

This description accompanied an information paper emerging from the advocacy of men and women staff members presenting an empirical data-based analysis of sex discrimination and its consequences and making the case for expanding future programming. It is significant that the Ford Foundation conceptualized the objectives of the women's programs to be improvement of women's status and circumstances and reduction of sex discrimination. Because of this conceptualization, the foundation's existing work in population was not considered part of the women's program because it had commenced with an emphasis upon national development goals rather than improvement in women's lives. When the population programming shifted to place women's concerns at its center, it became included within the conceptualization of the women's program. This consciousness of centering women's concerns and women's rights was and remains a defining characteristic of the foundation's work in this field.

Of course, the foundation's work with women's movements did not begin with this conversation of 1979–1980. Significant work began in the early 1970s, initially focusing upon poverty and economic roles. The work soon expanded to sex discrimination in law and social practice, access to education and employment, and to health and family issues including reproductive choice and changing assumptions about proper gender roles. However, the impact of the 1979–1980 conversation was considerable. The foundation expanded the existing Women's Program from $8.4 million to more than $19 million for the 1980–1981 biennium to integrate concern about women's issues in every area of the foundation's work, both in the United States and overseas. In October 1979, the Women's Program accounted for 5 percent of the foundation's program spending. At the end of fiscal year 1980, the percentage had grown to 11 percent. Franklin Thomas, then-president of the Ford Foundation, established a foundation-wide working group in 1980 chaired by Susan Berresford, current president of the Foundation, and a Women's Program Office to coordinate the expanded work in this field.

Leadership from the top made a difference. At one grant-review meeting, when someone raised an issue about women, a colleague responded by saying, "Well, that's taken care of in the women's program." "No," Franklin Thomas interrupted. "We're *all* responsible for this." The message was clear: Grantmaking officers would be expected to consider gender and to ask whether it was an important factor in the problems each program addressed.

Years of Expansion and Evolution

Work expanded in the areas of education, income and employment, childcare and family relationships, health and nutrition, and general advocacy programs with the assumption that it is of primary, but not exclusive, importance to focus on low-income women. The foundation partnered with both governments and nongovernmental, nonprofit organizations, but most of the work was and continues to be with NGOs. Through sizable, long-term commitments, the foundation enabled a number of national and local organizations to challenge discrimination and to build a body of law, policy, and practice to protect women's opportunities.

In education, grants supported the development of knowledge about women through the establishment of women's studies in universities and other research institutions and the development of gender-sensitive curricula. With respect to employment, grants supported research on women's work and constraints on their advancement. Among other employment challenges, research identified problems of women who work in typically female occupations and are deterred from entering traditionally male occupations. Other funding expanded economic opportunities and improved conditions of work by developing and testing model programs, supporting self-help initiatives by women workers, and supporting legal action to combat sex discrimination on the job. Grants assisted female workers to form their own organizations, to publicize problems of these workers, and to monitor government enforcement of sex-equity legislation. Female domestic workers were supported in their efforts to establish or stabilize self-help organizations to improve conditions of domestic employment. Support for legal action to enhance the rights of women workers included support for organizations engaged in enforcing existing laws through litigation, research, advocacy, monitoring, and public education techniques. Other grants sought to improve opportunities for women by enhancing women's leadership and policymaking capacity such as support to projects that help women move into school superintendent positions and other educational leadership and pubic policy positions.

In childcare and family relations, grants were made to strengthen relationships in families. For example, to help mitigate conflict and violence within families, particularly conflict resulting from family members' efforts to change established patterns, support was provided in the South Bronx, East Harlem, and Worcester, Massachusetts, to help women in low-income, highly disrupted families cope with family violence and stress. Other projects focused on assisting parents, community agencies, and governments design, implement, and study childcare systems that parents want and can afford.

In health and nutrition, the foundation explored the interrelationships among women's health, nutrition, and contraceptive practices. The focus was primarily on increasing access to abortion and increasing knowledge about abortion services. Support was provided to projects designed to protect the availability of safe and legal abortion services by experimenting with provision of direct services, documenting the needs for services, or studying the issues in the abortion debate. The projects supported also were intended to reduce the divisiveness of the issue.

Two strategies were supported with respect to general advocacy programs. First, funds were used to support feminist policy analysis in new and existing organizations. For example, analyses of government policies in such areas as social security, child care, health care, employment and credit, and agricultural development were undertaken to identify the sex-differentiated consequences of alternative policy courses. Second, support was provided to projects facilitating communication among feminist leaders.

Internally, the foundation further institutionalized its commitment by establishing the Women's Program Forum in 1985. This association of grantmakers and other staff members contributed to the foundation by convening fora on critical issues and engaging in collaborative grant-making initiatives with special reserve funds to advance the women's agenda. Efforts have included supporting the participation of women in the Fourth World Conference on Women in 1995, the UN General Assembly five-year Review in 2000 of actions resulting from that World Conference, and the UN World Conference against Racism, Xenophobia, and Other Intolerances in 2001. This collaboration allowed women's rights activities, both domestic and international, to be supported in different field initiatives throughout the foundation. With a recent name change to the Global Forum on Women and Social Change, staff continues the evolutionary work of determining the role, goals, and strategies that are most appropriate to this entity as it continues to advance the foundation's thinking about women's rights and equality.

The Global Women's Movement

During the 1990s, major international conferences in Vienna, Cairo, and Beijing dramatically reshaped the discourse of women's concerns. The Ford Foundation made significant grants supporting the participation of women from around the world, particularly with respect to the Fourth UN Conference on Women held in Beijing in 1995. The Beijing conference dramatically reframed the global women's rights movement as grounded in human rights. Subsequent work has included fostering partnerships to strengthen institutions engaging in research, intellectual analysis and development of theoretical frameworks, and the development of policy and programmatic recommendations and advocacy tools necessary to hold governments accountable. In addition to supporting women's organizations around the world through its overseas offices, support has been provided to women's organizations in the United States for research, training women in other countries on the international human rights mechanisms, working within the UN system, and advocacy skills in general. The main focus of support has included promoting activities based on the Beijing framework, training on the use of UN conventions, and research into specific women's rights issues. The U.S.-based organizations were intended to help women recognize cultural practices and national laws that violate their human rights, give women the tools they needed to hold their governments accountable, and provide general back-up support to country-level women's NGOs.

Women's organizations no longer have to rely upon U.S.-based organizations for this expertise. While continuing to support some U.S.-based organizations who have evolved in their mission and development of appropriate partnerships with women in developing countries, the Ford Foundation is expanding its partnering with women in developing countries so that they have the resources not only to speak for themselves, but also to lead in international, regional, and local arenas.

One of the more powerful frameworks emerging from women of the global south shifts the women's rights paradigm from the United States' emphasis upon "redress of grievances" to "building democracy." This framework for advancing women's rights as essential to building and strengthening democracy resonates strongly with women of color and poor women in the United States who experience alienation from and disempowerment within democratic institutions because of race or ethnicity and class subordination. This new paradigm carries the potential for new and deeper understandings of social justice and equality among women as well as the larger society

We Have Traveled a Distance

The results of women's movements around the globe include transforming the debate on women's issues and achieving significant advancements. In many countries, laws now prohibit sex discrimination in employment, education, consumer credit, and home mortgage lending. Traditionally male-oriented occupations now experience women competing for jobs. A woman's right to abortion was secured in many countries, yet remains highly contested, and still illegal in others. Violence against women has risen to become a global concern. In the United States, advocacy of the movement opposing violence against women won a response that includes federal programs and funding to state and local governments as well as to nonprofit organizations to provide prevention and intervention services. Another major gain was new access for workers to time off without pay for childbirth or serious illness provided by the federal Family Medical Leave Act, and the women's movement is beginning to make gains at the state level with legislation providing for paid family leave from work. Recently, California passed the country's first state Family Medical Leave Act incorporating monetary compensation, thereby expanding exponentially the number of families who would experience some change in their lives.

An example of the impact of the work supported by the foundation over time and with respect to a particular field is work that began with population programs and now engages issues related to human rights, reproductive health, human sexuality, gender identities, and relationships. The population programs begun in the 1950s supported the study of demography, contraception research, and family-planning services. By the 1970s, the foundation recognized that the need to reflect the growing aspirations of men and women, new gender roles, and protecting human rights were a better foundation for reducing poverty and promoting development. As a result, the foundation worked to translate the then-new concept of reproductive health into community services and advocacy for men and women while broadening women's and girls' participation in education, earning, and decision making. In response to the HIV/AIDS crisis unfolding in the 1980s, the foundation began engaging with pioneering community groups working to prevent the disease, provide care for its victims, and reduce the stigma associated with it in many places. Most recently, in the 1990s, the foundation added a new program on human sexuality, seeking to build new knowledge about sexuality and healthy human development, to promote related changes in youth services and family support programs, and to clarify basic rights to safety and services for gays, lesbians, and others who do not conform to traditional gender identities.

The impact of this learning upon the foundation has been substantial. Most significantly, we see more clearly the complex interrelationship of the fields with which the foundation engages. Work on reproductive and sexual rights, HIV/AIDS and the movement for reproductive health is located within the Peace and Social Justice program. Grants to advance knowledge about sexual development in order to inform public opinion and public policy are located in the Knowledge, Creativity, and Freedom program. And grants in the Asset Building and Community Development program focus on youth development, including responsible sexual behavior. No longer within one office of the foundation, this configuration makes visible and reinforces linkages with other fields.

This evolution speaks to our conviction that issues related to reproductive health, human sexuality, gender identities, and relationships involve serious moral matters of public as well as private significance. The foundation's engagement reflects its belief that exploration, discussion, and respectful debate will help build understanding and foster social change. As Susan Berresford, president of the foundation, has said, "foundation support [for this work] can help people around the world create welcoming and supportive communities that reduce human suffering and damage, and it can help us understand changing cultural norms as they are reshaped by social movements and fresh ideas. It is work in which we think the Ford Foundation's role can be distinctive and path breaking."

We have, indeed, learned a great deal from our partners since the days of "population control."

Miles To Go

Over the next ten years, three key challenges must be addressed if women are to achieve social justice in the United States. First, legal advocacy has yet to provide a strong platform for economic, social, and cultural rights for women. Second, despite the advancement of formal equality in law, economic and social inequality remains the reality of women's every day lives. Third, women of color, low-income women, and other underrepresented groups of women continue to lack opportunities to participate meaningfully in institutions built by movements for social justice as well as in general society. Each of these challenges is discussed below.

First, the existing tools of legal advocacy have yet to build a strong platform for economic, social, and cultural rights for women. There have been considerable gains in the legal recognition of women's rights; but the agenda is far from complete. Significant progress has been made in the repositioning of women's rights as part of human rights discourse, but realization of those rights remains more an aspiration than a reality. While there have been victories and significant change in the status of women, the continuing subordination of women, particularly women of color and poor women, has expanded our understanding of social injustice and inequity. Progressive international instruments, court victories, and legislative mandates require translation, implementation, enforcement, and seemingly perpetual vigilance against rearguard attacks to effect change in the lives of real people. As those victories are won, deeper sources of inequality are revealed and require thoughtful, meaningful legal strategies in partnership with community.

Occupational segregation, unequal pay, sexual harassment, unpaid family leave, inadequate child care, and discrimination in employment and educational opportunities are among the continuing obstacles to women's equality and social justice that require legal advocacy both to defend gains made and to advance the agenda. A particular challenge is the implications of a 1995 Supreme Court decision, *United States v. Lopez,* that limits the power of the national government and enhances the autonomy of the states to the detriment of mechanisms and standards previously relied upon to protect civil rights. There is a critical need to develop a sound jurisprudential underpinning for continued federal protection of civil rights.

The Personal Responsibility and Work Reconciliation Act of 1996

(Welfare Reform) effectively ended sixty years of entitlement to federal public assistance. Its enactment resulted, in part, from significant failure of the women's movement to advance a transformative agenda at the intersection of race, gender, and class. The consequences to poor women and, disproportionately, women of color are severe. We remain challenged to defend and advance the rights of poor and minority women and to expand the responsiveness of our legal system, policies, and practices to the convergence of race, gender, class, sexual orientation, and other socially significant factors.

Violence against women—arising at home, on the street, in the workplace, in prisons, as well as during war—remains a major challenge from perspectives of health and human rights. It occurs through sexual and domestic assaults as well as actions of the police and others exercising directly the power of the state; it arises from the resurgence of fundamentalism, increasing militarism, the impact of market forces, trafficking of persons, public policies, and consequences of racism and other forms of subordination. While passage in 1994 of the federal Violence Against Women Act was a milestone victory for advocates, it is not a magic antidote to violence and in implementation has heightened concerns about reliance upon the criminal legal system. The critical challenge facing gender-based violence movements is to develop and broaden the understanding of strategies and interventions that effectively address violence in diverse conditions and situations. Among other matters, we need to consider holding governments accountable for supporting the human rights of women to be free from violence, including providing communities with resources to explore effective interventions and services that would keep decision-making power within the community and supporting a broader agenda that invests in education, employment, housing, and other basic needs.

Recognition of and the right to exercise a broad range of reproductive rights remains a challenge. Efforts to advance reproductive rights confront oppositional social and cultural norms as well as a misconception that reproductive rights encompass only protection of the legal right to abortion. While the right to choose whether or not to have an abortion remains protected in the United States, a variety of state laws and efforts at the federal level make that right illusory for many women. Further, significant obstacles remain to the exercise of a broad range of reproductive rights, particularly by women of color and poor women. Current major challenges include (1) policies and practices that infringe upon the reproductive autonomy and right to safe pregnancy of women of color and poor women, (2) the construction of "fetal rights" through policies and legal precedents, (3) HIV policies punishing pregnant women, and (4) drug policies specifically criminalizing pregnant women and mothers—all intertwining race politics, hostility to reproductive rights, and gender-based assumptions.

We are challenged to craft new legal theories with innovative companion remedial proposals to confront structural inequality, and to develop strategic law-related plans responsive to the deep and continued significance of race, class, sexual orientation, and other particularities as they intersect with gender. We are challenged to build upon the human rights framework as well as our knowledge of appropriate lawyering for social change, which includes understanding partnership with an organized constituency speaking on its own behalf and comprehensive problem solving.

Second, despite the advancement of formal equality in law, economic and social inequality remains the reality of women's everyday lives. The success of foundation-supported efforts contributes to the continual evolution of a deeper understanding of the sources of inequality and potentially effective tools of advocacy. In fact, women have been at the forefront of economic, social, and cultural rights and engaged in dispelling the dichotomy between the public and private spheres. Still, there continues to be a real need to ensure the consideration of gender in conceptualizing and enforcing economic and social rights.

The global economy is having profound effects upon women's incomes, job opportunities and quality of life around the world. In the United States and elsewhere, educationally and economically disadvantaged women are quickly becoming part of an underclass of workers—working increasing hours with fewer benefits in a growing sector of low-income service work. Current changes in the workplace, therefore, necessitate a shift in focus, particularly when considering priorities for educational and public policy interventions. Ways must be found not only to ensure economic parity for women as a group, but to distinguish between the needs of low-income and higher-paid professional women. We need greater discernment with respect to the concerns of women in the global south affected detrimentally by structural adjustment programs. In the global north, we need to understand the concerns of women who are negatively affected by policy shifts such as welfare reform in the United States.

The new economy is also accentuating racial differences among women. Women of color and white women enter the work force from different points of privilege. While white professional women still experience discrimination, studies show remedies that result in significant advancement for white women do not necessarily serve that same function for women of color. Women also continue to face obstacles in entering blue-collar jobs that are available in the post-industrial world. Professions as diverse as construction, transportation, fire fighting, and policing offer a living wage, unionized benefits, and opportunities for advancement, but remain closed to women.

Third, women of color, low-income women, and other diverse communities of women continue to face impaired opportunities to participate meaningfully in women's movements for social justice as well as in the general society. There remains a need to cultivate a more diverse leadership cohort for the feminist movement.

The power of the women's movement is diminished because of the lack of full and equal participation by women marginalized by significant social factors such as race, class, and sexual orientation. The consequences of the absence of full participation by the multiple communities of women are considerable and include a narrowing of vision, analyses, and strategic thinking that is detrimental to advancing social justice. Most significantly, the work that would emerge from addressing the structural and systemic barriers that constrict the lives of the most subordinated women would transform our society for all women. Social justice does not trickle down, it results from the eradication of fundamental obstructions and the systems sustaining inequality together with nuanced attention to social realities. Transformative work cannot occur as long as women of color and low-income women provide the narratives, but do not lead and participate meaningfully in the setting of agendas, priorities, analysis, and policy recommendations.

While social justice for women remains an unfulfilled ideal, the Ford Foundation is inspired by and feels privileged to support the women and men who bring vision, courage, and commitment to this work in the United States and globally. While seeing the miles to go, we recognize the importance of also recognizing and celebrating the accomplishments— the changes in laws and social realities that have moved societies closer to achieving the universal aspiration for human dignity and fulfillment. Girls are going to school in record numbers and staying longer. Notions of gender that deprive societies of women's contributions to and leadership in civic, political, economic, and intellectual endeavors are being transformed. The workplace and the family are benefiting from recognition of the dignity of women. We now understand that violence in the home is part of a continuum of violence that extends to war and we understand the state's obligations for both. We have learned across all the fields in which the foundation works that effective philanthropy—whether related to health, eradication of poverty, governance and political participation, knowledge creation and education, peace and security—requires taking gender into account.

GIVING GLOBALLY

International Perspectives

PATTI CHANG AND KAVITA RAMDAS

n almost every nation in the world, women and children constitute
the populations most lacking adequate food, shelter, and protection
from violence. Basic human rights are denied to millions of women
worldwide on the basis of entrenched and systematic gender discrimination. Women are poorer, less educated, and more vulnerable to disease.
Yet women perform more than two-thirds of the world's labor, raise the
world's children, and care for the elderly and the infirm. The challenges
women face daily are daunting, yet women are also at the forefront of some
of the most exciting breakthroughs in social, political, and economic development. Women-led grassroots and community-based organizations
are pioneering creative and effective solutions to some of the world's most
pressing problems. They are rebuilding societies torn apart by conflict, infusing poor societies with entrepreneurial energy, and forging new responses to the spread of the HIV/AIDS pandemic. It is estimated that
some 70 percent to 80 percent of local community-based or nongovernmental organizations (NGOs) are groups of women coming together to
address issues as diverse as reforestation, pollution and water conservation,
violence, economic development, and access to education.

Yet despite the incredible dynamism of such efforts, most women's organizations are excluded from access to the most basic of resources—money.
Almost a decade after women's rights were declared human rights at the
1995 United Nations Fourth World Conference on Women in Beijing,
women's groups remain underresourced and outside the focus and scope of
most international aid or donor programs as well as private philanthropic
giving in both the United States and Europe.

This chapter explores why most donors resist investing in women. We
provide insight into the rich and varied landscape of the global women's

movement and argue that it deserves both the recognition and the resources of mainstream philanthropy.

Perceived Challenges to International Giving for Women

For a donor to fund abroad, she must be willing to leave the safer shoals of familiarity to explore the deeper ocean of uncertainty. She must understand that there is a connection between funding a woman abroad, and herself. She must be willing to hurdle the many obstacles of provincialism, nationalism, and racism that often get in the way.

Reasons for not funding women's projects and programs internationally range from donors only wanting to support their own neighborhoods/community/region/state/nation, to the desire to preclude the difficulties of evaluating funded programs. Issues of accountability, mistrust of governments, misuse of funds, and feeling overwhelmed also contribute to resistance.

Many people have a desire to see results quickly, to help those whom they know, and to make their immediate environment a better place to live. It becomes far more elusive to fund the primary school, clean the community park, or volunteer at the local hospital. The ability to touch, feel, and see the direct results of labor or philanthropy creates a more immediate sense of satisfaction. Funding locally also has been described as patriotic. Volunteerism in the United States often has been perceived as the "all-American" thing to do.

There are further doubts as to whether money sent overseas is being used appropriately: "How do you know that the money that you send is truly going to women and girls, and not into someone's pocket?" "There's a lot of corruption in those (typically brown or undemocratic) countries." "Won't the government take all of the money?" "How will we know that these programs are actually making a difference?" "There are so many people who need help, isn't it just a drop in the bucket, or throwing good money after bad, or having it end up in a black hole?"

These thoughts and concerns often underpin people's thinking so that when funding is made internationally, it is generally limited in scope to projects involving "brick and mortar." Results are far more visible when a school for girls or a women's clinic is constructed than when quality healthcare or transportation is funded.

When a small group of American women who were born in China decided to fund a project in the villages of China in 2000, they formed the Dragon Fund and their personal efforts went to building greenhouses, buying computers, constructing a four-story women's training center, and providing one thousand scholarships to fourth-grade girls. These young scholars are being carefully tracked by this group of American women who believe that unless they are able to account for each one of these students, and ensure other donors that each cent given is going directly to these girls, they may not be viewed as credible by other donors. The standards these women have placed on themselves for ensuring success, and on the teachers in China, are incredibly high.

These high standards, however, have not deterred this group. They continue to direct funds overseas to an area of great need and are making a critical difference for these communities. Speaking of the thousand girls enrolled in school through the Dragon Fund, the director of the program said, "These girls will have at least nine years of education. We are confident that they will surpass the majority of their peers and bring hope for a better future to their families and communities in rural China." Other funders are now doing the same, many of them motivated by the tremendous work being undertaken by women-led and women-focused groups around the world. Who are the organizations, both inside and outside of the United States, that are transforming the lives of women and girls around the world?

What Are Women Doing? An Overview of the Global Women's Movement

For almost thirty years, a silent revolution has been transforming lives from rural villages in India to urban slums in Brazil. The leaders of this revolution do not wear uniforms, they do not have titles, they lead no armies, they do not appear on television. Their faces are not in celebrity publications, but they are familiar to each of us: They are the ordinary women who do extraordinary things every day of their lives to feed their families, educate their children, strengthen communities, and provide hope for others.

- In China, women like these started the first domestic violence hotline when the Chinese government claimed domestic violence was a "western phenomenon." Today, the Maple Women's Counseling Center has been replicated in seventeen major cities across China.
- In Brazil, the women's movement was a catalyst in the successful effort to remove a military dictator and replace it with democratic governance.
- In Uganda, a grassroots women's campaign wrestled the HIV/AIDS pandemic to its knees by changing how women and men thought about and acted on issues of sexuality and power.

Hundreds of thousands of citizen activists around the world are at the vanguard of social change and peace and justice movements. Women make up the majority of these activists; they are inspired to act to protect and improve the lives of those who matter most to them—their children, their families, and their communities. They work to address gaps in basic services, filling the needs of poor communities by running soup kitchens, homeless shelters, battered women shelters, legal aid cells, local schools, or after-school programs. In low-income rural areas, women have initiated projects to preserve forests, protect environmental resources, and clean toxic wastes that poison water and soil in their communities. In urban areas, women have taken on some of the world's most challenging problems, including poverty and HIV/AIDS and other sexually transmitted diseases.

Women's groups work on a wide range of issues that strengthen and advance societies. They seek to affect political systems and political participation; they build women's ability to contribute actively to economies; they reform and strengthen cultural institutions and traditions so that they are inclusive of both girls and boys. In 16 years of existence, the Global Fund for Women has heard from over 5,000 groups in 190 countries. Despite limited resources, the Global Fund has funded over 2,200 of these groups and awarded over $30 million in grants to further their agendas of peace and social justice. Some examples of the breadth of issues that women are working on include:

- *Economic justice.* Phulki/Bangladesh aims "to spark the development of the socio-economic condition of disadvantaged people, particularly promoting the rights of women and children." Its objectives include: (1) to provide capacity building to female garment workers through adult education; (2) to raise garment workers' awareness on social and health issues; (3) to teach workers about their rights, including legal rights. Activities have included creating a series of factory-based crèche facilities for the children of garment workers and operating four night shelters for street children.

- *Trafficking in women.* Since 1996, Global Alliance Against Traffic in Women (GAATW) in Thailand has worked to: "(1) combat trafficking in women; (2) expand the network of organizations working on trafficking issues; (3) safeguard and promote the human rights of women who migrate and who are trafficked; and (4) raise awareness around these issues through workshops, publications, and the media." The group also advocates for migrant women workers in the sex industry, domestic work, and as mail-order brides. The group's main efforts focus on research, advocacy, and training. Some specific activities include organizing forums and training workshops, direct intervention (translation, legal aid, fundraising) to migrant and trafficked women, and videos, newsletters, and research assessments about trafficking in Asia.

- *Environmental protection.* Oral Ataniyazova is a Global Fund Advisor working in Uzbekistan at the Center for Reproductive Health and Environment (Perzent). Perzent is active in different areas of improving the health situation and the environment in the Aral Sea disaster region. In 2000, Oral won the prestigious Goldman Prize, often referred to as the "Nobel Prize for the environment" for her ongoing contributions to an isolated society that is impoverished and suffers from disease and neglect.

- *Ending harmful practices.* The Foundation for Research on Women's Health, Productivity and the Environment works to eradicate female genital mutilation of girls in Gambia and to help improve the health status of women and children. It also explores ways to preserve the natural environment and to improve the economic power of women. Activities include creating a new passage rights curriculum with the cooperation of "local circumcisers," coordinating programs on women's health and skills development, and offering income-generating activities.

- *Increasing access to education.* Retired and active female teachers founded the Association des Femmes Educatrices du Mali (AFEM) in 1991 to promote women's and girls' literacy and human rights. Its 400-strong nationwide membership in Bamako, Mali, and four regional branches now includes teachers and other women interested in education. AFEM provides literacy classes, assists women's development projects, organizes and gives technical assistance to women's groups, and performs evaluation and research on education and women's rights issues. The organization works with rural, periurban, and migrant women and girls.

- *Pro-lesbian rights.* Founded in 1997, Kontra is one of three lesbian groups in Croatia. It aims to awaken lesbians and strengthen the lesbian scene in society by organizing meetings, lectures, workshops, training, video screenings, and parties.

- *Peace building.* Bat Shalom works to foster human rights and social justice in Israel through protests, humanitarian assistance, and electronic bulletins. It also calls for an end to the occupation of Palestine and reaches out to Palestinian women to promote peace.

- *Disability rights.* Foro de Mujeres por los Derechos Humanos de las Personas con Discapacidad (The Women's Rights for Persons with Disabilities Forum) is the women's division of El Foro, a Costa Rican organization for reflecting and acting on the defense and promotion of human rights for people with disabilities. Founded in 2000 in conjunction with "From Policy to Practice," El Foro is leading the Costa Rican disability rights movement in its multi-pronged effort to achieve human and civil rights for people with disabilities. Using media campaigns, rallies, and training workshops, the women of El Foro are at the forefront of public education.

Yet, despite the key role that women play in communities around the globe, women's organizations tend to be significantly underresourced, lacking access to much-needed financial support.

In the United States, a number of organizations are working on these same issues, making the connection between what happens locally and what happens globally. They, too, are underresourced and face barriers to accessing necessary financial support.

- *Economic justice*. Sweatshop Watch, based in Los Angeles, is a coalition of labor, community, civil rights, immigrant rights, women's, religious, and student organizations, and individuals, committed to eliminating the exploitation that occurs in sweatshops. The coalition serves low-wage workers, with a focus on garment workers in California, as well as nationally and globally. Their Corporate Accountability Campaign aims to hold retailers and garment manufacturers accountable for the conditions of workers who sew their clothes. Their Globalization Project aims to mitigate the negative consequences of globalization on garment workers by analyzing current and future trade policies and economic trends and their impacts on garment workers; by strategizing to maintain garment production jobs; by transitioning garment workers who are displaced into living-wage jobs with security; and by developing a strong global network of garment workers and their advocates.

- *Trafficking in women*. CAST, the Coalition to Abolish Slavery and Trafficking, assists persons trafficked for the purpose of forced labor and slavery-like practices and works toward ending all instances of such human rights violations. CAST provides social services to survivors of trafficking in the Los Angeles area. CAST also provides policy advocacy focusing on the human rights of trafficked persons, public education, and community organizing to promote the dignity and freedom of trafficked persons while creating awareness of the problem.

- *Environmental protection*. The Center on Race, Poverty and the Environment provides assistance to women in the rural community of Alpaugh, California, to research solutions to their drinking water problems associated with dangerously high levels of arsenic and to implement those solutions. Their approach of organizing, and providing technical and legal assistance to grassroots groups, attacks head-on the disproportionate burden of pollution and environmental hazards borne by poor people and, particularly, minority communities in rural California.

- *Ending harmful practices*. The Center for Gender and Refugee Studies (CGRS) at the University of California, Hastings College of Law, provides legal expertise and resources to attorneys representing women asylum-seekers fleeing gender-related harm, at both the practice and policy levels, and seeks to track decisions in these cases. CGRS also works to coordinate legal and public policy advocacy efforts through domestic and international networking, and engages in public education efforts in order to educate decision makers and the public and to contribute to the formulation of national and international policy and practice. CGRS is headed by Karen Musalo, the lead attorney in the landmark Fauziya Kasinga case, which granted asylum to a young woman from Togo trying to escape genital mutilation.

- *Pro-lesbian rights.* NCLR (National Legal Resource Center) is based in San Francisco, with a primary commitment to advancing the rights and safety of lesbians and their families through a program of litigation, public policy advocacy, free legal advice and counseling, and public education. Their mission is to create a world in which every lesbian can live fully, free from discrimination. Through impact litigation, public policy advocacy, public education, and direct legal services, they advance the legal and human rights of lesbians, gay men, and bisexual and transgender individuals across the United States.

- *Bi-national U.S./Mexico border work.* Clinicians at Fronteras Unidas Pro-Salud in Tijuana have established a precedent-setting maquiladora or factory health-provider training, despite the factories' closed (and sometimes hostile) management practices, to improve service provision to young women workers. Volunteers at Mexicali-based Alaide Foppa are holding the line to ensure the ongoing presence of nongovernmental and other civic participants in "citizens' committees" and other local government advisory bodies. And maquiladora workers at Casa de la Mujer/Grupo Factor X have expanded their public policy training to include documentation of labor rights abuses, direct organizing campaigns, and community lawyering.

These organizations, both inside and outside of the United States, are working as part of a global movement to make differences in the lives of individual women and their communities. Their success in part depends on financial support from individuals and organizations in countries like the United States, where resources are relatively abundant.

How Can We Encourage and Support Global Giving for Women?

According to recent Foundation Center statistics (2002), less than 11 percent of total private philanthropy went to support international organizations in 1998. Of this, an even tinier fraction goes to support organizations led and governed by women. In the United States, the women's funding movement has led the effort to recognize how investments in women and girls can strengthen communities, build a resource base for local initiatives, and mobilize new sources of philanthropic giving. Led by the Ms. Foundation for Women, the largest women's fund in the country, women's funds now exist in almost every community in the United States, offering larger foundations and individual donors a viable vehicle for their social investments. By serving as intermediaries between the talented and creative on-the-ground women, organizations, and precious financial resources, women's funds play a valuable brokering and linking role. For those who wish to make similar investments in women and girls overseas, women's funds like the Global Fund for Women in San Francisco and Mama Cash in the Netherlands offer similar choices. Increasingly, domestic women's funds are also offering their donors the option of designating gifts overseas through Donor Advised Funds. The Women's Foundation in San Francisco has managed grants to women's groups in China and Afghanistan for this effort.

Internationally, only a handful of small foundations exclusively provide resources to women's organizations, particularly for those based in the developing world. These include the UN Women's Fund (UNIFEM), small European funds such as Kwinne na Kwinne in Sweden and WomanKind in the United Kingdom, and the two largest independent women's funds in the world—Mama Cash in the Netherlands and the Global Fund for Women in the United States. Together, these funds are only able to direct about $10 million per year to women's organizations. Most women's funds and the large private foundations are not endowed with assets that generate their grantmaking income. Instead, each, including UNIFEM, is forced to raise its annual budget from other donors. Over the years, however, women's funds have succeeded in raising awareness of the critical role and contributions of women among both individual and institutional donors. At the same time, their model of feminist nonhierarchical and inclusive philanthropy has attracted much attention and interest among women led NGOs in other parts of the world.

In 1990, the Global Fund for Women supported a fund modeled in its image in Mexico. Initiated by a local Mexican women's group, Grupo por les Derechos Humanos por las Mujeres, the first Mexican women's fund began to develop the seeds of change for a movement. Semillas (or seeds), as the fund was called, inspired others in its wake. Executive Director Emilienne de Leon notes, "Our relationship with the Global Fund for Women has meant a strategic alliance for us. In the last three years, you have increased your support, giving us the momentum to consolidate our growth process. By making a grant to Semillas, the first feminist fund in the global south, the Global Fund made a commitment to the rights of women in Mexico."

In 1992, for its fifth anniversary celebration, the Global Fund made a series of partnership awards to organizations in other parts of the world to explore the idea of "giving away money." In 1994, a team of African women first conceived of a similar fund for women in Africa, which came to fruition almost eight years later. And in 1996, a grant from the Global Fund catalyzed the efforts of a Nepali activist and women's rights leader, Rita Thapa. TEWA, the Nepali women's fund, was born that year in Katmandu, Nepal. In 1997, a second set of Global Fund Partnership grants inspired women from Mongolia and the Ukraine to move forward with women's funds in their countries. By 1999, the Global Fund and Mama Cash brought together six women's funds for a brainstorming session and by 2000, almost a dozen women's funds gathered at the first official meeting of the International Network of Women's Funds. Shirley Walters, founder and chair of the Women's Hope and Education and Training Trust, points out that "these international women's funds provide an easily identifiable way to support the work of women's groups in other countries. The Global Fund for Women is a beacon of light . . . it would be a dream to have a similar type of organization here to support grassroots initiatives to strengthen the position of women."

There are numerous ways to support funding for women internationally and not all of them require sending dollars directly overseas to the international women's funds. Important local actions can take place to support women globally. These include giving to U.S. women's funds involved in international work, donating time through participation in exchange programs, and through working to sustain global connections with sister funds and other affiliations.

One way to take local action is to support international work by forming Donor Advised Funds through a locally based foundation. Donor Advised Funds provide an alternative to direct giving or setting up a private foundation. At the Women's Foundation of California, for example, Donor Advised Funds allow donors to work actively with the foundation in selecting specific issues to address and in suggesting the particular grant recipients. In this collaborative effort, the Women's Foundation acts as facilitator, working to combine the hopes and dreams of donors with communities of women and girls that they might not have found on their own. In two instances, donors have worked with the Women's Foundation to set up funds that support work being done in other countries.

One Donor Advised Fund, the Dragon Fund, was created when a group of Chinese American women organized by the 1990 Institute and the Women's Foundation came together to devote resources to rural areas in China. The Dragon Fund team met with the Beijing-based All China

Women's Federation (ACWF), the world's largest nongovernmental organization working to represent and protect women and their rights. With valuable guidance from the ACWF, the team traveled to villages in Gansu and Shaanxi Provinces. These regions historically have been the poorest and most neglected in China, and they are the focus of the central government's western development strategy. Three programs were funded, including a Women's and Children's Training Center to offer literacy and technical training, a Women's Greenhouse to expand the local agricultural economy for the area's women, and the Spring Bud Scholarship Program, which finances the education of those one thousand girls in the Shaanxi Province.

Another Donor Advised Fund administered by the Women's Foundation is the Fund for Afghan Women and Girls. Through the fund, Afghan women and girls in Afghanistan, Pakistan, and California were granted funds to support education and humanitarian aid in the form of healthcare and shelter for women and girls as well as a sister-schools program connecting Bay Area schools with schools in Afghanistan.

Besides giving money directly to international women's funds or setting up Donor Advised Funds locally, there are other ways to support the global women's movement. Donating time through participation in exchange programs offers much-needed support to women's groups overseas and provides the volunteer with a valuable and possibly life-changing experience. The American Jewish World Service, for example, which works with many women's groups around the globe through its Women's Empowerment Fund, operates the Jewish Volunteer Corps (JVC). Members of the JVC are assigned to various nongovernmental agencies based on their skills and abilities and may provide accounting and bookkeeping assistance in Venezuela, public health counseling in South Africa, or fundraising strategies to an NGO in Thailand.

By working together and sharing information about each other's work, women's funds around the world are supporting the global women's movement. They are sustaining global connections and learning lessons from each other. Women's funds recognize that better solutions to problems often can be found by considering the global nature of issues. For example, women's funds around the world are important sources of information on the migration patterns of women and girls, whether they are refugees escaping warfare and military conflict or migrating to areas because of economic hardship. Working with Zapoteca women and girls from Oaxaca, a women's group here in the United States might provide multilingual services, since many do not speak Spanish nor English. They also might provide legal or job training assistance. At the same time, working together across borders, women's groups can look at the factors causing the migration out of Mexico, setting up economic development or micro-enterprise projects to help sustain the local women's economy. This global perspective can lead to deeper and longer-lasting social change.

This also leads us to look at other areas where similar things can happen. TEWA, the women's fund in Nepal, for example, has created a holistic way of fundraising by including the whole community. In a country dealing with a population torn apart and displaced by war, TEWA has also developed ways of training peacemakers and promoting peacebuilding. Through the global connections that women's funds have built, the lessons learned in Nepal can be shared with other countries around the globe, including the United States.

We cannot emphasize enough the need for women's global funding and the assets of women and women's funds around the world. Women's funds like those in Mexico, Nepal, the United States, and elsewhere are working together with a shared global perspective to effect significant and positive changes in the lives of women and girls. Local actions also play an important role in supporting the global women's philanthropic movement.

Women's funds offer a different way to think about philanthropy. Their emergence demonstrates that significant efforts are underway, led by innovative and inspiring women. These women take a collaborative approach rather than one that is top-down and hierarchical. For example, women's funds often support women's groups that serve as leaders in reconstructing civil society and that in times of war keep channels open for dialogue. Women's groups such as England's Global Women's Strike and Central Asia's Worldwide Sisterhood Against Terrorism and War are working toward a paradigm shift that diverts funding away from militarism and warfare toward positive social change.

The power of the United States is felt politically, economically, and culturally by other countries around the world. For people in the United States, recognition is growing slowly that we are also dependent on the rest of the world. It is becoming apparent that world affairs need to take a different path—perhaps a path led by women's vision of a world community. They may be leading grassroots organizations like those described in Nepal and Mexico, helping to create a silent revolution. These women may be in positions of power, trying to wield their influence for social justice. The global women's philanthropic movement is about funding women to work as leaders for social change in ways that affect communities, nations, and the world. Surely such a movement deserves the respect and support, financial and otherwise, of us all.

FROM CRADLE TO GRAVE
Challenges and Opportunities of Inherited Wealth

CYNTHIA RYAN

Finding a way to "own" their wealth, to accept it rather than feel ashamed of it, is a necessary first step as heirs begin to "come out" and connect with others.

Barbara Blouin, For Love and/or Money:
The Impact of Inherited Wealth on Relationships

Every woman who inherits money has a unique story to tell as well as an individual approach to spending, saving, and sharing her wealth. Nonetheless, there are common experiences and issues that many of us grapple with, and a common process that most go through before they are comfortable with their inheritance and philanthropic potential.

I was raised in a household without inherited wealth. But as my sisters and I reached early adulthood, my father's business successes increased and so did our standard of living. We enjoyed amazing vacations and the luxury of beautiful homes. Today, I often see trucks bearing the logo of the company my father grew into an international corporation. Unlike my teenage stepbrother who was born to such wealth, I came to it gradually. I believe that difference in our experience, and perhaps gender, make a difference in our respective perceptions and feelings about our situation. After talking with heirs and other women of wealth, I consider myself lucky. I have not felt unduly isolated from my peers because of money. I maintain a healthy appreciation that having more than ample financial resources is not the norm.

One of the more difficult questions that people with inherited wealth often ask themselves is why they should have so much by coincidence of birth when so many in the world have so little? A friend of mine who inherited a large amount of money attends a weeklong conference every summer where heirs discuss the impact of inherited wealth on their lives. I tease him about the irony of people getting together to complain about having too much money. But for many, inherited wealth is a problem, and ironic as it may seem, there is a legitimate need for forums where inheritors can talk freely about the real concerns that come with wealth. The reality is that wealthy inheritors often experience a sense of isolation because of our societal reluctance to discuss money. The emotional toll this takes on heirs can be devastating. In the course of conducting interviews for this chapter, I have concluded that having a healthy, satisfying life that involves inherited wealth requires a three-pronged balance among our private, professional, and philanthropic lives. If one leg of the stool is weak, the whole structure is at risk. While every life story differs, significant threads are interwoven throughout the lives of most people who have inherited wealth.

Donna Hall, president of the Women's Donor Network, works with many women of wealth and sees a real generational difference between older and younger women who have inherited wealth. It's helpful to understand that attitudes and patterns of behavior depend somewhat on age and childhood experiences. Hall describes the experience for most women over the age of forty as a "coming out" process. Unexpressed feelings of shame or uncertainty often have haunted these women while they go through the process of understanding their worth as humans as it relates to their financial wealth. Most of these women have not worked formally but have run households and raised children while possibly volunteering in their community. The women who are involved in philanthropy often do so apologetically. Women under thirty-five seem to embrace their monetary and social power much more easily. They were raised to be more independent and aware of their worth. Hall describes their attitude as, "I'm me, I'm wealthy, and I'm proud of it." They have less baggage than the women who have gone before them and see themselves as having a range of options available—from giving their money away to using it to leverage social change on a national and international scale.

Barbara Blouin, author of several books dealing with the challenges and opportunities of being an heir, defines inherited wealth as "having enough inherited money to make paid work a personal choice rather than a necessity."[1] In conducting my research, I found that having a large amount of money was not the only way that heirs identified themselves. For some respondents, a relatively small amount of money was significant; for others, the definition of "wealth" was staggering by any definition. Wealth appears to be, at least partially, a state of mind. For many, how rich or impoverished they felt emotionally during their lifetime was also a significant factor.

People of wealth have several emotional and psychic challenges to grapple with: guilt for having unearned income, fear of spending it all and having nothing left, concerns about competency regarding money management and sound investing, worries about approval or disapproval because of money, the quest to find one's rightful place in the world. While women of inherited wealth certainly share some of these issues with men in similar circumstances, certain aspects are unique to women.

Gender differences often start with how daughters are treated by their parents, particularly fathers, as compared to their brothers. This was best illustrated for me by someone who described men as biologically having a money gene that enables them, for the most part, to feel entitled to and confident about having and using money, while women often feel like they don't understand money and don't feel capable or comfortable making decisions about how their own money will be handled and spent. Women rarely take money for granted, particularly when they have financial security purely through a lucky birth. These differences change how many men and women go on to use their financial power and accompanying social standing. If women don't feel comfortable in their own skin when it comes to money, our culture only reinforces these inadequacies. Many money managers and those who support the philanthropic industry relate very differently to men and women. It is often assumed that women need to be taken care of or supervised. This dynamic is part of the larger paradigm of how men see their world. It is mostly vertical, with rank, status, age, and wealth clearly placing one in the hierarchy of power. Women interpret things from a more horizontal perspective and naturally seek to collaborate with and complement others; that is, to realize a more collective impact. Theirs is a more holistic and inclusive model.

Most women have felt disempowered at some time in their personal, professional, and philanthropic life. We look outward from these experiences and identify with others in society who are disadvantaged in some way. This may explain the differences in incentive and motivation that are apparent in regard to what women fund compared to men. Women gravitate toward personal issues and these often are reflected in the work of more progressive social change organizations. Women don't see borders, whether political or economic, as hard and fast as men generally do. With the encouragement of various formal and informal support systems, women are using their inherited wealth to educate, empower, and liberate people from the disadvantaged places in which they find themselves. Women are more often conscious of the inequalities in the grantee/grantor relationship and go to greater lengths to form a more egalitarian framework in which to practice their philanthropy.

This chapter explores these various reflections and examines the positive side of inherited wealth, as well as considering some of its challenges.

Historical Perspective

Virginia Esposito, president of the National Center for Family Philanthropy, has discussed the tradition of philanthropy as it relates to the role of women. She states that about 150 years ago, Dr. Harriot Hunt urged "daughters of inherited wealth, or accumulated labor! The wide door of philanthropy is open peculiarly to you!"[2] While this may sound progressive, in reality women at that time were not viewed as appropriate heirs or managers of family assets. Among wealthy landowners, the eldest son was considered the primary heir, and his position in the upper class was secure. Younger sons and men of no inheritance still had the opportunity to achieve power and economic security through their careers. This was not an option for women, who married to ensure social status. Their assets left the control of their fathers to become the assets of their husbands. It was not considered in the best interest of the family to have wealth leave the patrilineal line; therefore, women were excluded from inheritance. Women also were thought to be incapable of managing their own financial affairs. This perception of women as the "weaker sex" was one more justification for keeping money and property in the control of men through guardianship or marriage.

Two literary classics reveal European society's view of women and wealth. Jane Austen details the social structures in place in the late eighteenth century regarding inheritance in her novel *Pride and Prejudice.* In her story, the Bennet estate is left to a distant male relative rather than to the Bennet daughters, who must find suitable husbands to provide them with security and status. Although the status of women as property owners and heirs was beginning to be challenged in Victorian society, Charles Dickens' *Great Expectations* demonstrates the pervasive view that women were emotionally ill-equipped to handle financial responsibility. Throughout Dickens' novel we see the psychological and financial destruction of Miss Havisham, a daughter who inherits her father's estate while still a single woman. The story illustrates the mid-nineteenth-century view of women as unable to handle the control and power that comes with inherited wealth. When love enters the equation, the protagonist loses everything and becomes an example of the unmarried heiress as threat to the patrilineal system of inheritance that was being challenged in England at the time. The novel ends with Miss Havisham's adopted daughter owning the estate, but the decimated property has lost all economic value. While these novels provide a historical perspective on women as heirs, the issues and prejudices they reveal were felt all the way into the twentieth century.

In discussing the history of the women's movement, Gloria Steinheim has reminded us that "during the Suffragist Era, women used to be the property of their husbands or fathers. The movement fought for the women's right to own property and retain their own salaries."[3] What was acceptable in the nineteenth century was for women of means to be active in the philanthropic community because their participation reinforced the family's class status. Though their giving stemmed from their father's or husband's wealth, they often were committed volunteers who contributed to the more traditional causes of "noblesse oblige" such as arts and culture, health and education, and churches (although rarely have women asked that their names be on the building). Today, women who have inherited wealth give not only in these areas, they also commit resources to a wide variety of organizations and activities seeking to create social change.

For many women of inherited wealth over the last one hundred years, the idea of charity began at home early in childhood. While the approach was often patronizing and class-based, it was predicated on the idea that "to whom much is given, much is required."[4] Of course, women with inherited money often had a surname that was well known in the community as well as synonymous with power and influence. Most of these women were asked to sit on boards of local hospitals, museums, and other charitable organizations. Many of them didn't need to work and could provide valuable volunteer support and fundraising to the organizations of their choice. While this scenario is still common, many women today, particularly those in their twenties and thirties who have inherited wealth, follow a less-traditional path and run the gamut between giving away all their assets to establishing and managing their own foundations.

The Challenge of Inherited Wealth
"Affluenza" and the Cocoon Effect

Jessie O'Neill is a psychotherapist who has coined the term "Affluenza," which "simply defined, is a dysfunctional relationship with money and wealth." She describes the psychological aspects of affluenza and how they are passed on from one generation to the next. These include a false sense of entitlement, low self-esteem, low self-worth, depression, "survivors'" guilt and shame, and what she describes as a high regard for outer self and a low regard for inner self. The cause of affluenza stems from the "assumption that money can, should, and does buy happiness—what [Jessie calls] the myth of the American dream." Critical to overcoming affluenza is

CHARLOTTE'S STORY

My mother came from well-known and politically influential southern roots, with a good deal of wealth and prestige. At twenty, she married my father, a lawyer from an old Phila-delphia family, and left the South, raising my brother and me on Philadelphia's Main Line. We had a live-in cook-cum-housekeeper whom I loved. Dinner was at seven o'-clock and we met our parents every weeknight before dinner in the den where they had cocktails and my father read the evening paper. We had lots of lessons—skating, tennis, horseback riding—and lived in a particular social sphere. My brother and I both went to boarding school and I grew up thinking everyone had similar lives. I was thirty before I realized that not everyone wrote thank-you notes and followed certain rules of etiquette. My parents enjoyed the company of wealthy people like the Vanderbilts and the Fire-stones and my mother spent extravagantly to keep up with those friends. She had in-herited her own money, which she controlled. My father was generous and I always felt taken care of, although my mother instilled in me the fear that I might never be able to support myself. My parents divorced when I was fifteen and remarried each other a year later. They divorced permanently a decade later, spending money wildly in the interim. I went off to Barnard College, where for the first time in my life, I became friends with people who had different backgrounds than my own.

I've always had more privilege than money, but throughout my young adult-hood, small amounts of money were given to me whenever I needed funds. My father handled my finances and he was generous; I traveled throughout Europe for more than a year after college, which he financed. A trust established by my grandfather for my ed-ucation enabled me to earn a master's degree, and I didn't begin working until I was nearly thirty.

After my first marriage ended in divorce, I started a small publishing company, which I ran for over twenty years. It was wonderful to support myself. Now I am a fundraising and development consultant for various nonprofit organizations, and although I earn less than I have in the past, I love my work.

Remarried now, I will inherit money again when an elderly relative dies. Like my mother, I have brought wealth to my marriage. I find this liberating. Looking back, I didn't think about wealth and poverty in any broad sense until I began to explore the value system I grew up with and to explore what was important to me as an adult. I have come to realize that having inherited wealth is truly a mixed blessing.

simply acknowledging the effect it has on American culture and individ-ual families. "The most important step is the first one: to bring the condi-tion out of hiding, to name and describe it, to de-mystify it."[5]

Daughters of the rich often grow up experiencing what could be called the "cocoon effect." They frequently reside in homogenous communities that include the streets where one shops, the stretches of coastline where the family summers, and the inside of private clubs and homes in other parts of the world. Laura Rockefeller describes growing up on her family's estate as being in a "verdant cage, beautiful to the senses but in many way oppressive."[6] Although one of the most integral elements of a wealthy child's life, money is not often discussed and children quickly come to consider it a taboo subject. Many girls of wealth receive mixed messages about money while growing up. "Don't talk about it" conflicts with "Money makes you special." Guilt and low self-esteem present barriers to self-discipline and initiative.

Women especially worry about how much money is enough. The fear of being left without enough is a legitimate concern for women who have always depended on others for their income. I have spoken with many women who had very little understanding of the actual dollar amounts they were worth and when and how they could access that money. Inherited money can be difficult to access or use. More often than not, money managers are male and, perhaps through good intentions, want to protect their clients, but this attitude disempowers women. Luckily, professionals and organizations are available now that provide a range of services for women to address the questions and concerns they have about their financial literacy. For women who want to take more control of their money and the role it plays in their lives, publications, conferences, and professional support are available. Often just realizing that other women are in similar circumstances and grappling with the same questions is enough for them to start taking the steps toward truly owning their money and using the power that comes with these resources. Even if working for money isn't necessary, finding one's passion and working for the change one wants to see in the world is important to feeling like a valued member of society.

A very helpful process for individuals and families who will be undergoing the process of wealth transfer is to communicate openly and with as much neutrality as possible. Three checklists are available on the Internet that succinctly put into quiz format whether a family is prepared for the transfer of wealth (www.thewilliamsgroup.org/readiness.html). Ten questions deal with the family structure as a whole and two are for individuals to assess each heir's understanding of their "Family Wealth Mission Statement." Even if one doesn't choose such a regimented approach, the more transparency and dialogue brought to the process the better. This includes a range of relationships: parent to child, partner-to-partner, and so on. Each relationship has its own dynamic, but for the process to be a positive one, the individuals with income must be direct and honest. This only happens once they personally have come to terms with money and the role it plays in their lives.

Relationships

Like all people, women who wrestle with how best to manage the personal and professional aspects of their lives need the support of friends, family, and life partners. Yet many women feel that they have to conceal their wealth or the challenges it presents. Many inheritors so downplay or even deny their wealth that they are unable to be honest with the most significant people in their lives. As one woman put it, "The more I cared about the person I was speaking to, the more I was tempted to look away when I spoke my name because I could not bear to see myself disappear in their eyes and become the stereotype of someone spoiled, elitist, reactionary." Such concealment can lead to isolation and distrust. Women heirs often use the term "coming out" when describing their decision to

ALEX'S STORY

I am a member of Babes with Bucks. Started in 1995, it is an organization where women of wealth can gather and discuss smart investing, their role in philanthropy, and what to do with the guy who earns a lot less than you do. I grew up in a modest, middle-class neighborhood in New York. My father and uncle ran a successful business and I knew that I had wealthy relatives who ran the company in Europe. Growing up, there was very little discussion in the household about finances or inheritance, so when my father died while I was in my early twenties, I had no idea of the fortune I, as his only child, had inherited. My uncle retained control of my finances and it was several years before I knew I had a considerable amount of money and over a decade until I felt prepared to spend and manage my finances independently. It was not an easy transition for either of us. He wanted to know that I could take care of my investments, and while I respected the fact that he had invested wisely, I also felt a desire to be independent of his control. There is always an element of dependence created when one adult supervises or oversees the finances of another. I felt as though the money wasn't really mine. Every time I wanted to withdraw money from the account, he was aware of the transaction and possibly judging my decisions. In this situation, I felt I needed his approval for how I was spending the money.

My wealth has also affected some of my personal relationships, particularly with men. I found that most men were pleasantly shocked when they found out I had a personal fortune, but I also have experienced the demise of relationships due to the complexities of fiscal management. I have been engaged several times and while I would not tell friends and colleagues about their wealth. The sense of being different and the possibility of being shunned because of that difference is very strong and for many heirs yields an entirely new set of problems, particularly for women who are politically and socially progressive. Often it becomes difficult to justify working as an unpaid activist who fights against the disparity between wealth and poverty alongside women who are barely able to earn a living because of their own calling to social activism. For wealthy women in particular, the fear of being used is profound. Most women with wealth inevitably have significant relationships with people who have decidedly less money than they do. Sticky questions arise: Do you lend friends money? Do you pay disproportionately when you dine out or travel? Financial inequality has to be handled skillfully, honestly, and with a sense of humor.

In her book, *For Love and/or Money: The Impact of Inherited Wealth on Relationships*, Barbara Blouin describes the term "wealthism" coined by Joanie

---

ALEX'S STORY (CONTINUED)

say that money was the only factor in the relationships ending, it did play a role in destabilizing them. It is not easy for some men to feel secure when the woman they are involved with has a bigger bank account. I went to a lawyer to discuss a prenuptial agreement and the lawyer assumed that I was the one being asked to sign one to protect my fiancé's wealth.

I also grapple with professional and philanthropic decisions. There is the question of work. If I don't need to work for the income, how do I choose a profession? Do I want to be committed to a nine-to-five schedule? If I forgo a more traditional career path, where do I find the sense of worth and identity that is normally part of the professional experience? Will I feel a need to defend why I don't work and how do I explain it?

Once I gained control of my finances, I still hadn't found my philanthropic voice. My family had no history of philanthropic giving and within my circle of friends there were few that had disposable income to give in a substantial way. I knew I had enough that I wanted to give some away, but I did not feel comfortable openly discussing my resources. Eventually, I met someone who worked in the nonprofit world who directed me to Threshold, a foundation formed by people of wealth who want to give to progressive causes. I have been a member for seven years now and am active in their peace committee. Threshold is important to me for several reasons: It provides a safe environment where members can discuss the impact of wealth on our lives, it introduced me to a group of peers who had experience giving money to the kinds of progressive issues that interest me, it helps me organize my philanthropy, and it provides a legal and structured mechanism through which to give.

Bronfman in *The Experience of Inherited Wealth: A Social-Psychological Perspective*. Wealthism "describes a set of attitudes directed at the wealthy by the nonwealthy." Bronfman writes, "Wealthism includes those actions or attitudes that dehumanize or objectify wealthy people, simply because they are wealthy. The main attitudes of wealthism are envy, awe, and resentment. . . . Wealthism differs from the other 'isms' in that racism and sexism are perpetrated *by* those who have power, whereas wealthism is directed *at* those who have power."[7]

Guilt about unearned wealth can lead to poor decision making, and intimate relationships are tested by an imbalance in assets. (Barbara Hutton, the dime-store heiress, suffered through six marriages). Every couple has to negotiate, but the more a woman empowers herself to understand her finances, control them, and appreciate her own self-worth, the better equipped she will be to make sound decisions and healthy relationship choices.

MY STORY

In 1998, I agreed to work part-time to launch our family foundation. It was something my father had thought about for several years as the financial success of his businesses and investments increased. The majority of my family share very similar progressive political, cultural, and economic values. I have always respected my father for what he contributed to society and what he provided for us by working very hard. What started as a part-time position five years ago, is now primarily a full-time job.

Initially, we didn't create a mission statement or guidelines for our philanthropic endeavors, as we did not consider unsolicited proposals. Instead, we followed our instincts and interests and watched what developed. The primary focuses of our foundation were in the areas of human rights, and peace and security. Our grantmaking is on a local, national, and international scale. We provide grants ranging from hundreds to hundreds of thousands of dollars. The trustees of our foundation are my father, stepmother, and three sisters. A younger brother will become a trustee when he is older. Each trustee has a discretionary amount of money to award and each is encouraged to explore issues of particular meaning to them. We are encouraged to get involved locally with relevant organizations. Our philosophy is that philanthropy is more than check writing. It's partnering with organizations by sharing our time, resources, intellectual capital, advocacy, and networking capabilities. It's also about being a voice in the philanthropic community to promote the issues we care about and to advocate for public policy that supports those ideals, whether in the arts, education, the environment, or women's issues. One of the most effective ways to realize this belief is to join organizations of like-minded funders and individuals. I belong to the International Human Rights Funders Group, serve

Philanthropic Opportunities

Heather Roulston Ettinger has pointed out that "even when women inherited wealth from their husbands or fathers, there was, I suspect, a tendency to hold back from a full sense of legitimate ownership. A woman would be more likely to use this wealth to give a gymnasium in her father's name at his college than to endow a chair in the women's studies department at her college."[8]

But Marjan Sax, whose life's work has been using her inherited wealth to fund social change, wonderfully describes the dynamic of what philanthropy can be. "It's not about how we can help black, migrant, and refugee women, but how we can help ourselves by becoming more diverse."[9] Having the resources to practice philanthropy, on any scale, is a wonderful opportunity to address all the issues one cares about whether the environment, health, the arts, or human rights. As a good friend says at every board

MY STORY (CONTINUED)

on the steering committee of the Peace and Security Funders Group, and am a member of Grantmakers Without Borders, the Women's Donor Network, and Women Waging Peace. We are also members of the Council on Foundations and the Association of Small Foundations. These different organizations all have been a resource for everything from administration and accounting to site visits. My father and I together sit on nearly a dozen nonprofit boards, including Landmine Survivors Network, Physicians for Human Rights, and Women for Women International. This is the best way I know to support an organization I care about, as it involves me at every level, from fundraising to program content to finances. More importantly, it connects me to people who are working on the front lines of social change.

Besides having the wonderful experience of traveling and meeting people of passion who work for the organizations we partner with, the most satisfying aspect of our foundation work for me has been the relationships I have formed with my family by working for the foundation. I am the sole employee, and while my father and I are the most involved at this point, our family comes together to discuss and share our values and thoughts for the future. Discussions and issues about money have not always been positive in my family. There are the usual conflicts of a first and second family, including occasional resentment and misunderstanding. In some instances, communication between individual family members has had to be rebuilt. But the foundation has been a vehicle for each of us to contribute and to share what we feel are vital issues. And each of us has a sense of pride—in my father for having been able to create the foundation—and because we fund such interesting and important issues, such as land mines, advocacy, human rights, gender equality, and progressive journalism. Philanthropy has given our wealth meaning and value that extends far beyond the number of dollars we have shared.

meeting we attend together, "It is an honor, a responsibility, and a great pleasure" to be able to partner with organizations that are addressing society's problems on a local, regional, national, and international scale.

This is both a complex and essentially a simple process. First, each person must articulate her own vision of philanthropy. In this regard, women traditionally have volunteered their time, but now they have substantial financial resources at their disposable with which to create a new style of philanthropy. Women with means now have the influence to be heard; finally, they can create different paradigms of power.

Tips of the Trade

Since 1999, either alone or as part of a couple, women have donated nearly $900 million to endow the top one hundred new foundations.[10] Increasing simultaneously are the networks now available to women with wealth. Organizations such as Resourceful Women, Babes with Bucks, and More than Money enhance the process of learning how to save, spend, and share one's money wisely. Beyond giving valuable investment advice, they provide a safe place for women to speak about their concerns and to ask questions without being solicited, embarrassed, or scorned. Through conferences, workshops, and support groups, women address such issues as resources, vehicles for giving, and levels of involvement. A plethora of financial advisors, counselors, and other professionalswho respect one's values and decisions are available to provide legal, financial, emotional, and logistical support. Many women have found their voice and developed their personal framework for philanthropy in these communities.

Ellen Remmer, a professional philanthropic advisor at the Philanthropic Initiative in Boston, is also a trustee of her family foundation. She neatly summarizes the six Cs of women's giving first listed by the co-founders of the Women's Philanthropy Institute in *Reinventing Fundraising: Realizing the Potential of Women's Philanthropy*, published in 1995: Create, Change, Connect, Collaborate, Commit, and Celebrate. These actions are apparent whether women fund from a more traditional perspective or choose to fund organizations with a more radical agenda. What Remmer found most rewarding about her philanthropic activity was the way it bonded her to her siblings. "Working with my sisters and Mom on the foundation has provided incredible glue, good feeling, and pride. We have learned about each others' strengths and perspectives, been able to explore and identify strong family values and passions, challenged old roles, and learned a great deal about working together effectively." Like many people of wealth, their impetus to form a family foundation was "grounded primarily in emotional reactions to sudden new wealth . . . [they] wanted to make some 'meaning' out of [their] surplus and wanted to set an example for [their] children." As a group of women, they understood the importance of funding women and girls and "decided to focus on reducing feminization of poverty by helping girls take charge of their lives."

For those interested in starting a family foundation, the best process often begins with a conversation with a professional organization about the legal and administrative requirements. Organizations such as the Boston-based Philanthropic Initiative can provide clients with information needed to get started, including a wide range of services tailored to the level of involvement that family members want in running a family foundation. Numerous books about family foundations are also available through the Council on Foundations. Also invaluable are *A Plan of One's Own: A Woman's Guide to Philanthropy* (New Ventures in Philanthropy and the Forum of Regional Grantmakers, www.givingforum.org), and *Inspired Giving: Creating a Giving Plan* by Gary and Kohner. Family foundations require specific legalities. They have the same tax-exempt status as a 501(c) 3 charitable organization.

A family foundation is appropriate for long-term philanthropic goals because they are designed to have revenue generated from assets, ideally at a higher rate than the 5 percent per year required by law. Family foundations also pay a yearly excise tax of 1 to 2 percent of their net investment income.

Making the decision to start a family foundation should be undertaken only after serious consideration of all giving options and comparison of the various elements of each to determine if a family foundation is the right framework for personal giving.

The most important consideration is that each individual finds a means of directing personal resources that supports a personal vision for a healthy society. Some women, like Ellen Malcolm, president of EMILY's List and the new political group, Americans Coming Together (ACT), start their own organizations; others, like myself, work for their family's foundation, sit on boards of organizations, and spend time, energy, and money on behalf of issues they care about. What matters most is that each woman makes her own sound choices about giving her money away.

Owning One's Power

Women of inherited wealth still have hurdles to clear to become women with a sense of purpose. For many, childhood was a time of mixed messages about our worth and about the role of money in our lives. As young adults, we became aware of ourselves as different, and learning to function in a less privileged world was often painful. As the process of owning and con-

ANNIE'S STORY

It was my mother who came from money. She had a trust fund but struggled with her background. She seemed to want people to know that she came from old money, but that she was too "good" to be part of it. She dealt with it by being reluctant to spend money. My father came from a middle-class family. His only extravagance was gadgets. He was averse to spending money on his kids; he felt that money spoiled kids.

I knew we were comfortable most of my life. When I was around twenty, it became clear that we were a lot more than comfortable, but the implication was that it was a negative thing. When my father's company went public in the early 1990s, we had a family meeting. We were told we were going to have to learn to manage money. That seemed logical. However, what could have been a positive celebration amounted to more of a charade of mourning and guilt. My mother cried, claiming she wanted to give all the money away. How much money we had wasn't clear to me even after that meeting.

About five years later, trusts were created for each of us. I hadn't done much with it until recently, because I always felt like it wasn't really mine. There has always been so much ambiguity surrounding what was expected of us, not only with how we spent our money but how we made life choices. So not surprisingly, I feared making the wrong choices. In addition, I am a very private person, probably because I am insecure about other people's reactions to what I do, how I spend, and what others' true intentions are. I don't have a problem with people thinking of me as privileged. I do have a problem with people thinking I am spoiled. In the past, I've thought about decrying all my wealth so I could be completely independent. I wanted to free myself of a relationship with my parents on a financially dependent level, as well as from the common perception that people with money are evil and selfish. However, I enjoy the freedom and fun money can bring, as well as the good it can do. I would be crazy to give it up.

Throughout high school, college, and beyond, I have always had a job or been a full-time student, though in the last three years I have only worked independently here and there, and slowly have begun focusing more time on philanthropy. When I knew I didn't have to work because of the income I received from my trust, it was hard to justify getting underpaid and having time constraints for something I wasn't passionate about. I

trolling their wealth continues, many women find themselves struggling to enter, understand, and change the male-dominated and conservative world of investment and finance. Women are increasing their fiscal self-confidence and becoming accountable for their own inherited wealth, and they are using their inheritance in a socially responsible fashion while fostering important social change. My family's money has allowed me to work

ANNIE'S STORY (CONTINUED)

absolutely appreciate the unique position I am in because I can support causes that I believe in, spend time with family and friends, and do the things I *am* passionate about.

We started a family foundation six years ago. There are five trustees: my parents, both brothers, and myself, and we each distribute our fifth of the allocated 5 percent of the assets. We give one communal grant per year and we each take turns taking control of this process and choosing the grantee. It has been a pretty positive experience so far. In fact, the rewards of this experience have led me to focus my time on being a philanthropist. I have begun to spend more time educating myself on how to be a responsible grantmaker, which is crucial as the amount each trustee will have to give is going to increase significantly in the next year.

My oldest brother, who has been involved heavily in philanthropy for several years now, has helped me. While we have different styles and passions, it has been very positive to share in this endeavor. I am passionately interested in environmental issues. I sit on the board of a local environmental education organization and am involved in various other ways with other local organizations. I do most of my giving anonymously or through our family foundation, as I am not comfortable having my name connected to the gift. The opportunity to give has been positive in strengthening the bonds between my brothers and me.

At this point in my life, I'm pretty comfortable with the way I'm handling my wealth and how it affects my life. I have friends whom I've known for years and they know *I* know I'm in a unique situation. They have been with me throughout this financial "transformation" and seem to appreciate that I still have the same values. I feel safe with them because they understand and appreciate my philosophy about my situation. Their support, in addition to that of my husband and my brothers, is invaluable. I still struggle sometimes with what it means to me to be a young woman of inherited wealth. The greatest challenge is the envy people have of my situation and their judgment because I didn't earn my wealth. I also have to be careful about people taking advantage of me.

Having the freedom to do what I want when I want and also the time to focus on the things that interest me is a blessing. As well, through philanthropy, I meet some of the most amazing and inspiring people. It is an incredible opportunity to make a positive difference in the world.

with extraordinary people, and to feel that I'm changing the world on a practical and a spiritual level.

While many societal attitudes regarding inheritance are patrilineal and traditional, women are beginning to question the way in which money is passed on to the next generation and are exerting their influence on the process. Women are starting to question societal and family attitudes toward wealth, destroying the myth that heirs are informed about their assets and have control over them. Like Liesel Pritzker of the Chicago Hyatt fortune, who is suing her family for emptying her trust, women are legally and publicly defending their inheritance and challenging male authorities who have claimed guardianship of them.

As trillions of dollars pass intergenerationally, women will join in teaching the inheritors of tomorrow the values and skills needed to be active and productive philanthropists. Many women with inherited wealth will avoid repeating the mistakes of their parents and will be more open with their children about the realities of their financial situation. As women begin to recognize that the guilt they feel about inheriting is wasted energy, they will convey to their children that what is important is what one does with the money. A recent study by Citicorp Private Bank demonstrated that women more than men are likely to "teach kids that affluence brings responsibility" (61 to 37%) and that it is "important for others in the family to be involved in charity" (40 to 21%).[11]

PAM'S STORY

The power and wealth in my family comes from my Mom's side. She and my aunt have always sat at the head of the table and controlled the conversation. I grew up in New York City, but we had other homes, a private plane, and household staff. People recognized our name. Luckily, we traveled a lot and were exposed to the disparities of wealth in the world. We were taken out of our comfort zone and encouraged to give back to the community at large.

My Mom has always done a good job of judging how involved we should be as children. I've been attending site visits and visiting her office since I was born. I absorbed a lot and though I sometimes felt like time with us was taken away, I understood how important those responsibilities were to her. I was around ten when she started a new, progressive foundation with my aunt. I started going to foundation meetings periodically and began to understand the importance of empowering people who are disenfranchised. At fourteen, I became a junior trustee, and while I was a non-voting member, I was encouraged to give an opinion. My mom then started her own foundation whose mission is to fund NGOs that empower women to realize their potential. I don't share all the same beliefs as my Mom, but she's always open to dialogue.

I've struggled a bit in my relationships with others. When women have money, they also have power, so they have to be with men who have strong personalities and don't feel intimidated. Men want to feel like they're making a contribution. My wealth is somewhat of a taboo subject with my friends. I usually don't bring it up and they don't either. There's a lot of silence around the issue of money.

Looking Ahead

When used wisely, inherited wealth has the potential to be a powerful catalyst for positive social change. It can create and support organizations that influence how society is shaped while providing immediate hope for individuals in need. At best, women's philanthropy can create solidarity and change the global structure of inequality as it now exists.

Some time ago, I heard Karen Pittelman, an heir in her twenties, speak about an organization she founded with $3 million. The Chahara Foundation's mission "is to support grassroots radical nonprofits run by and for low-income women in the Greater Boston area." The foundation supports the efforts of the most marginalized women (women of color, immigrant women, and single mothers) to fight to shape public opinion and policy around the issue of economic oppression. I have followed Karen's course of philanthropy and found her to be inspiring. "Sometimes I thought it would be easier just to give it away, wash my hands of it in a way," she says.

PAM'S STORY (CONTINUED)

I'm still thinking about how I want to express myself philanthropically. I would like to work with my family and eventually collaborate with them more. I do like the structure of a foundation to help organize my giving. I don't like the word "philanthropist." It makes me cringe. I find guidance in the words, "to whom much is given, much is required." As a Christian, I feel redistribution of wealth is very important. It is key to my value system. Through my philanthropy, I want to address the disparity between rich and poor.

Right now, I've chosen to work on the grant-seeking side of things. For the last two years, I've worked with a nonprofit that works on agricultural issues in Latin America. I've learned how hard it is to get grants and how difficult some foundations make the application and reporting process. I think there is a lack of trust sometimes in the grantor/grantee relationship. In some ways, my professional life of grantwriting and working with nonprofits has started to merge with my personal involvement with my family's philanthropy. I'm now in my late twenties and in the stage of owning one's power.

I believe that progressive organizations can't do their work without also getting involved with advocacy. As women of influence, it's important that we not stand still during attacks on what we believe. We need to have our own positive agenda. We need to be pro-active. Coalition building takes time and effort, but as progressive individuals, we need to work together toward effective strategies. We have to leverage our wealth to help get the issues and organizations we support well-funded. It will take substantial resources and long-term commitment to build the capacity of the social justice movement. I'm willing to devote my time and money to that.

"Now I'm creating a resource instead of an erasure. A lot of people like to give their money [away] but they aren't interested in surrendering the power that goes with it. But redistribution of wealth means changing the dynamics of power, too. If the same small group of people hold on to most of the wealth generation after generation, it is very difficult to make social change. And so they train their children to be silent about money, to accept and perpetuate their values, and most of all, to believe that they are entitled. That's why I think people with inherited wealth can have an enormous role to play in bringing about change. If we buck against what we've been trained to, if we say we are not going to just go along with a system that may have worked for our families but which is drawing blood from most people, it breaks a cycle. It changes the flow of power."[12]

My hope is that my family's legacy is one of shared values and the spirit to participate fully in the world to make it a better place. I think future generations of trustees in our family foundation will appreciate not only the freedoms and opportunities that money has provided them, but also the special responsibilities it has created and the engagement it has allowed.

As Arthur C. Frantzreb has noted, "The act of philanthropy is a spiritual act, an expression of caring for one's fellow human beings. It is a belief in the future that the future can be good. It is investing in that future. It is helping to make the dream come true."[13]

NOTES

1. *The Legacy of Inherited Wealth*, edited by Barbara Blouin and Katherine Gibson (Blacksburg, Va.: Trio Press, 1995), 3.

2. Quoted in *Family Giving News*, NCFP, August 2002.

3. Businessweek Investor interview by Toddi Gutner, "A Feminist Icon Reflects on Money," Businessweek Online, September 17, 2001. URL is http://businessweek.com/magazine/content/01_38/b3749111.htm.

4. St. Luke 12:48.

5. Website: www.afluenza.com.

6. Vance Packard, *Ultra Rich: How Much is Too Much* (New York: Little Brown, 1989), 80.

7. Barbara Blouin, *For Love and/or Money: The Impact of Inherited Wealth on Relationships* (Ann Arbor, Mich.: University microfilms, 1987). Emphasis added.

8. Website: www.votd.com/etting.htm.

9. Website: www.learningtogive.org.

10. Jankowski Associates, Inc. 2001. Reference to the figures given came from a report that can be found on their website. URL is http://www.grantsdirect.com.

11. Citicorp Private Bank Web site at www.citigroup.com/citigroup/press/020805.htm.

12. *Sojourner Magazine*, 25, no. 9 (May 2000).

13. Website: www.philanthropicgift.com.

PUTTING OUR MONEY WHERE OUR MOUTHS ARE

Sharing Earned Income

꧁꧂

MARGARET TALBURTT, JUDY BLOOM, AND
DIANE HOREY LEONARD

W omen's philanthropy has a history of being categorized and stereotyped to legitimize discussions surrounding women's motivations and actions. "Reach a woman's heart and you'll have her checkbook" or "Women give time not money" or "Put the starving child or sad puppy on the picture and she's yours" are repeated and accepted truisms. As more research is conducted on women and philanthropy by organizations such as the Women's Funding Network and the Center for Women's Business Research (CWBR), as well as the Women's Philanthropy Institute and private investment and marketing firms, data are available that refute many of the stereotypes about women's giving, particularly about giving by women from their own earned assets. A more comprehensive picture of women's philanthropy now exists. This chapter will explore the realities of women's philanthropy as detailed in research and the examples set by five women philanthropists.

Data from several Center for Women's Business Research studies assert that, as the number of women business owners grows, the number of women considered to be of high net worth due to their own earned assets also continues to increase dramatically. According to a 2002 CWBR report, there were an estimated 6.2 million majority-owned, privately held women-owned firms in the United States at the time of the study, employing 9.2 million people and generating $1.15 trillion in sales a year. It is estimated that this 14 percent rate of growth in the number of women-owned firms is double that of the national estimate for new businesses in the United States.[1] In addition, there has been a surge of high-net-worth women. Between 1992 and 1995, the number of women with assets greater than $600,000 grew by 19 percent and the total value of these assets increased by 27 percent to $2.3 trillion. In the past, the wealth was assumed to be from inheritance. This is simply not the case today.[2]

This continual growth in female assets means an increase in the number of women who have the influence and ability to decide where their philanthropic dollars—that is, their earned assets—are best used. Contrary to popular belief, women give proportionally as much money as men do in their philanthropic efforts. While women and men business owners participate more as a group in philanthropic giving than U.S. households in general, CWBR reports that female business owners give more to charity than their male counterparts. According to Nina McLemore, chair of the National Foundation for Women Business Owners, "Nine out of ten business owners (92 percent of women and 88 percent of men) contribute money to charities, compared to 70 percent of all U.S. households surveyed by Independent Sector in 1999."[3] Another CWBR study of high-net-worth individuals (those worth $5 million or more) found that 58 percent of women wanted enough wealth to be able to give money away compared to only 39 percent of the men.[4] Clearly, women exceed men's giving by both intention and behavior.

Beyond comparing male and female business owners, there are also differences in women's philanthropy patterns between female business owner and women who are not business owners. According to "Philanthropy Among Business Women of Achievement," a report by Independent Sector, women business owners are almost twice as likely to make charitable contributions as are women as a whole. Specifically, 92 percent of female business owners' give to charity while only 52 percent of women in general do.[5]

While examining participation in philanthropic efforts is informative, it is also important to explore the potential impact the philanthropic participation of these women has. According to 2002 CWBR data, over 50 percent of those categorized as high-net-worth contribute in excess of $25,000 annually to charity. This figure includes the 19 percent of high-net-worth female business owners and female executives who contribute $100,000 or more to charity per year.[6] One study found religious organizations, local community services, and youth organizations to be the top three recipients of the gifts for both men and women.[7] However, another study of women only found that more than 50 percent of the businesswomen surveyed supported education-related groups, 42 percent gave to women-related causes, and 41 percent supported the arts.[8] This would seem to indicate that women with assets may have a particular commitment to women and girls.

Defining philanthropy can mean more than just the giving of one's money to a cause, but also the giving of one's time. When looking at business owners' personal philanthropy, women are just as likely as men business owners to be involved and engaged at some level within the organization to which they make their gifts. However, women business owners began their volunteerism at a younger age, and in greater numbers, than did male business owners. According to CWBR data, 48 percent of women business owners began volunteering as young women, while only 40 percent of male business owners began volunteering as young men.[9] Another difference between the involvement of women and men business owners in their personal volunteerism is evident in the roles that they tend to play within the organizations. Female business owners have a higher tendency than male business owners do to take on board leadership roles within the nonprofits in which they volunteer their time; 94 percent of women serve on boards compared to 83 percent of men.[10] In today's nonprofit experience, board leadership can be correlated strongly to significant donations.

There are many different theories about women's philanthropic motivations. Only a small minority of women business owners is motivated in their giving by the desire to be recognized for their efforts. Of the business owners surveyed by CWBR, only 8 percent of women business owners, compared to 12 percent of male business owners, ascribed their philanthropy to the economic returns that could be gained for their business. Rather, more than 50 percent of women business owners reported that their business philanthropy and voluntarism were motivated primarily by social responsibility. The remainder of the respondents noted that both factors led to their business philanthropy.[11]

The motives for philanthropic efforts by high-net-worth men and women who have earned their own assets vary, but according to a 2002 study conducted by Harris Online, the most significant motivator for women in their philanthropic efforts is the desire to give to social causes in which they believe strongly, 86 percent compared to 66 percent of the men. The next most important reason given was personal experience with the organization, which was rated nearly the same for both men and women (+/− 55%). Use of the money for tangible results and charitable giving as part of a family tradition were factors of approximate equal importance to both men and women in shaping their attitudes toward giving.[12] Even more interesting is the difference between men and women related to feelings about the tax benefits of gifts. As reported in the same study, 40 percent of wealthy men are motivated to make a gift by tax and estate laws compared to only 25 percent of women. It would seem that mission and the tangible work of the organization are extremely important to women donors of wealth.

Christine Grumm, executive director of the Women's Funding Network, offers an additional reason to explain women's giving. Women, she says, tend to be more motivated by specific causes than men are because on the whole, women are more likely to have needed the services of a non-profit group themselves, or to have been close to other women who did.[13] While this is not listed as one of the top three reasons for philanthropic giving in the Harris Online study, it is believed by researchers to be a factor in many women's motivations. Finally, it is also clear that women are motivated to give when they are asked for a gift, which was much less likely to happen in the past when it was assumed that women did not have the assets to donate.[14]

In summary, the trends discussed here characterize women's philanthropy as being multiple and varied in motivation, but driven by social change as the perceived goal of giving. Women with assets, many of whom earned those assets as business owners or highly ranked executives, are more likely than men to put money and time into organizations that affect social change. The following case studies of successful women using their own earned assets to make a difference showcase the power behind women's philanthropy and add insight to the statistics and studies.

Kathy Levinson

Kathy Levinson is a former vice president of Charles Schwab and has been president of E*Trade Securities and president/CEO of E*Trade Group. Living in California, she currently spends most of her time engaged in philanthropy, community service, and activism. Her philanthropy has changed substantially over the last decade as her own personal involvement has grown.

Unlike many of the respondents in the previously cited studies, Kathy does not remember giving as a child. Until three years ago, she described her philanthropy as "transactional," that is, she gave because a friend was involved or because the literature caught her eye. But as her personal assets grew, her philanthropy did as well. She now has very clear goals and objectives and spends time thinking about the best ways to achieve those goals. Her development vehicle has a mission and she looks at requests in relation to that mission. Her business card presents her work as "strategic philanthropy and investment."

For years, Kathy resented the monied powerful. "I was an activist, 'scratching up' from underneath." Having acquired her resources through her successful business ventures, she knew that money could be used for social change. There is no guilt attached to her philanthropy. "I want to change the hearts and minds of my target audience." Her giving today has three focal points, all related to civil rights. Her priorities are girls in leadership, Jewish causes, and gay and lesbian causes. She particularly likes to fund programs that address two or more of these issues. While she still uses a small amount of her resources to support friends' projects, the majority of Levinson's philanthropy is aimed at organizations that work to change laws and behavior, especially the educational elements that change people's attitudes.

"Philanthropy is like anything else; it is a learned skill," says Levinson. Just as a sport is not mastered in one session, neither is strategic giving. She feels it is normal to ask questions and to not know everything at once. In addition, she believes there are lots of opportunities to learn. For her, money took a significant amount of time to acquire; therefore it is just as appropriate to consider carefully to whom, when, and how it is dispersed. She advises "Be thoughtful, not afraid to learn; be intentional and avoid the tendency women have to be shy or anonymous." Kathy does not feel the obligation for her name to be visible, but it is important for her to have an impact. If the use of her name can lead to a better outcome, she is happy to have the visibility. For example, one of her political causes has a Leadership Council that is 90 percent male. She is the first woman in this "club of givers" and feels it is significant that her name is there.

The value of restricted gifts also has become clearer to her, because such gifts create an opportunity and willingness to engage in dialogue. Conversations about the gift are often more stimulating than the gift itself. "When you force people to dialogue and challenge their ideas and they can talk without begging, you increase survival and caring." She is passionate about this type of conversation: Her point is to touch the world, not to write a check to end discussion. She says *how* you give and *that* you give are more important than *what* you give.

Today, Levinson's philanthropy is much more sophisticated than it once was. Her gifts range from $100 to seven-figure donations; there is no typical gift. She is open to new ideas about how to construct a gift to achieve her goals, such as working together through multiple organizations rather than giving money to one specific organization. She has been exploring new ways of giving to leverage the same amount of money and make it go further. Matches, charitable remainder trusts, and donor advised funds are all vehicles she considers to maximize the impact of each dollar.

Over time, Levinson has expanded the relationships among her financial support, time, and personal involvement to maximize the impact of her giving. She would like to think of a world with equal rights and access for all, a world more conscious of differences, more welcoming rather than exclusionary. It is important to her that her two young daughters observe and learn about philanthropy through her model; she wants it "imbedded in their DNA." To that end, she and her partner involve the girls in decision making about gifts to particular causes as well as asking them to contribute their own money. It seems the lesson has been mastered: When one of her daughter's said she'd like to win the lottery, her mother asked what she would do with a million dollars. Her daughter replied matter-of-factly, "I would give it away, like you do."

Lekha Singh

In 1988, Lekha Singh helped to start a very successful software company that provided her with assets for her philanthropy. She went on to become the founder and CEO of the i2Foundation, which promotes advancements in education, technology, environmental practices, medicine, and economic opportunity.

Born in India, Lekha has a very distinct memory of the first time she made a gift from her own resources. At perhaps the age of three or four, she saw a beggar in the streets and was so moved she tore the rupee (dollar) she had in her hand in half and made her first gift. Another distinct memory that was to have later consequences was seeing a woman beaten publicly when Lekha was eight years old. The image never left her and it spawned a lifelong commitment to addressing domestic violence issues.

For Lekha, philanthropy is really a love of community. Early on, her philanthropy was emotionally driven. "I had a lot of spontaneous enthusiasm and I wanted to end the suffering I saw." But she now feels that her activity is more focused; a balance between the heart and the mind. "I believe that what you do on the outside is based on what you feel on the inside, yet due diligence is critical to a successful outcome." For all her passion, Singh's entrepreneurial experience has taught her that good business principles are extremely important to successful program outcomes. "Giving is a balancing act. It's a balance between mind and heart, between organizational capacity and organizational vision, between urgency of need and long-term solutions. To give in the right way is an art," says Singh.

While women's issues have always been at the root of her philanthropic concerns, she currently is focused on addressing the issues of hunger and poverty, which, she notes, are definitely women's issues. Combining her technological background with this substantive cause, Singh hopes to enhance the efficiency and effectiveness of program delivery while improving the standard of living for millions of people around the world. Since 1996, for example, her grants through the i2Foundation have resulted in forty million meals served to those in need.

Lekha feels that her gender definitely has played a role in her philanthropy. She describes a nurturing response that makes her want to help. But as she has grown as a philanthropist and as a businesswoman, she finds that her confidence and risk-taking have also increased. "I am bolder now because I know that old solutions don't work. . . . You have to take risks to see greater results."

Like Kathy Levinson, Lekha counsels new philanthropists to have the confidence to say no to requests that are not a part of an established mission. Before making gifts at this point in her life, Singh is more thoughtful about the vision, operations, and strategies a potential grantee proposes. The size of her gifts varies with the request and whether she believes that money is actually the best solution to the problem described.

Her advice to a new philanthropist is to start with compassion. Singh believes that giving is personal. Early on, she says, stick to one priority and don't give up when the going gets tough. Her experience has also taught her that you can't treat symptoms; for real social change, you have to go to the root of a problem.

Lekha Singh is a global philanthropist. Holding on to the sensitivities that marked her early life in India, she has added entrepreneurial skills honed in America. Her goals for social change affect nations throughout the world. The i2Foundation is a testament to the belief that the dreams of girls become the visions of women.

Laura Scher

Laura Scher is co-founder, CEO, and chair of Working Assets, a long-distance telephone company that offers its members the opportunity to "use their phone as a tool for building a better world." Begun seventeen years ago, Working Assets asks members to nominate nonprofit, progressive social change organizations to receive donations taken from a percentage of every telephone transaction. In 2002, that strategy resulted in nearly $6 million divided among fifty organizations. Laura Scher has combined her personal sense of giving with her business to create a unique and significant philanthropic organization.

The main goal of Working Assets contributions is to educate its public to bring about social change. Staff does due diligence on all nominated organizations. Over the last seventeen years, Working Assets has shifted away from environmental concerns to human rights and social justice.

Scher's belief is that one should "consider the political ramifications of all actions."

Scher's vision for the future of philanthropy is to effect "major social change, societal change." Although philanthropy is a word she thinks of as "being what wealthy people are engaged in," values drive her corporate and personal giving. She supports smaller organizations and looks to the organization itself rather than to its specific projects.

Over the years at Working Assets, Scher has learned about "amazing people doing amazing things. . . . There are wonderful groups working [for change] and although one might not agree with every tactic or strategy, I am not so egotistical as to have to start a new organization to accomplish my goals."

Scher learned a great deal about philanthropy from her parents and hopes to set a similar example for her children. Her mother and father both served on boards and donated regularly to nonprofit organizations, helping to establish the values that now drive her philanthropy. Today, she teaches her own children by action and service. It is this strategic and values-driven giving that characterizes Laura Scher's commitment to social change.

Murem Sharpe

During the 1990s, Murem Sharpe was a founding vice-chair and active member of the President's Council of Cornell Women, an organization at Cornell University, her alma mater. While not her first donor experience, it was one of critical importance to her. The Council was one of the first in the nation to spark significant giving to a university by proving that women had the resources and the will to be major donors. Specifically, this group established the Affinito-Stewart Grants program, which awards grants of $1,000 to $8,000 to Cornell assistant and associate female faculty for research in their fields of study. Since its inception in 1992, the program has funded more than $262,000 to 121 women faculty at Cornell.

Sharpe credits her parents with instilling a sense of giving. Both contributed their time and talents to causes they believed in, and she and her husband have continued this tradition along with their two teenaged children. Sharpe is currently CEO of a consulting firm she founded, B2B Quarterback, which provides outsourced marketing and business development services to high-growth companies. Previously, she held executive and general management positions at several Fortune 500 companies.

Unlike many donors, Murem has a strong preference for endowment giving. This type of gift offers her a lasting sense of investment in the sustainability and long-term success of the organization she supports. Although the short-term monetary benefit may be minimized, over time these gifts contribute more to the stability of an organization.

Her first gift to an endowment, which was also her first sizable personal gift, was to the Stamford, Connecticut, YWCA. (At the time, she served as president of their board of directors.) As she considered her gift to that campaign, she reflected on both the amount and the different options for making a gift. She educated herself on the advantages of cash versus stock, multi-year versus one-time gifts, and other donor prerogatives. This analysis typified Sharpe's subsequent gifts.

Sharpe advises other women donors to practice "serial monogamy" in their philanthropy: She suggests choosing "one or at maximum two organizations at a time instead of spreading yourself too thinly . . . In this way, you can build relationships that last longer and have greater meaning . . . as well as having more impact on the organization." This combination of hands-on involvement at significant gift levels parallels the confidence and strategic commitment that have made her a successful businesswoman as well as philanthropist.

When choosing a cause for her philanthropic efforts, Murem looks for a compelling case, leadership respectful of diversity, management and board strengths, and the potential for new levels of organizational growth. In turn, she gives of her time, talents, and resources. These characteristics define a philanthropist to her but she still feels the term "typically describes someone older," like her role models, who are "philanthropic in their activities and attitudes."

Like other donors, Murem Sharpe is committed to social change. Her understanding of the importance of long-range giving distinguishes her approach to philanthropy and her commitment to social change through capital investment, a strategy familiar to her as a business executive.

Lily Kanter

Once on the cover of *Time Magazine* as a "new philanthropist," Lily Kanter made her presence known at a youthful age. Her resume includes serving as a retail industry expert for Deloitte & Touche, IBM, and Cooper & Lybrand before landing at Microsoft, where she rose to become the western manager of E-commerce. Now retired from corporate America, Lily is married, a mother, and owner of her own business, Mill Valley Baby & Kids Company.

Reared by parents who were tireless community suporters in Kansas City, Lily began serious volunteering at the age of ten. Later, she became involved in Democratic politics and activist groups in college. Her commitment to volunteerism has continued and has been a bridge to her philanthropy, although she finds the word a bit elitist. She would rather describe herself as "a social entrepreneur focused on making the world a better place."

Making serious use of her own resources began at Microsoft when she gave 50 percent of her adjusted gross income away, in part because she would rather "give to charity than the government." After that, Kanter established her own foundation and gives away 5 percent of its value each year. Her gifts range from $100 to $10,000.

Initially motivated by whatever touched her heart, Kanter is beginning to establish criteria and focus for her giving. She prefers organizations with low overhead and little bureaucracy; she is not patient with wastefulness. She funds what she believes is important in life. For her, this includes Jewish causes, gender issues, and the World Institute on Disabilities. She is interested in women's issues because she sees women as "the people to lead change in the world."

Kanter is credited with starting Social Venture Partners (SVP) in the San Francisco Bay Area. SVP takes a collaborative approach that educates "investors" about causes and pools their resources for giving to charitable organizations. There is peer pressure to get involved. Kanter still serves on the SVP Board, which grants $250,000 a year.

Her advice to other women givers is to "get involved in a hands-on way. Pick a few nonprofits that inspire you and get on the board or chair a committee; stay connected. If you just write a check, it is too easy to forget the cause."

Lily Kanter knows that her individual philanthropy may not be enough to change the world entirely. However, as a donor, she "gives money to ignite activism and inspire others to join her in contributing to a worthwhile cause." She hopes to see a change in people's priorities to make the world a better place.

Conclusion

Clearly, all the women profiled here have visions for the world that require social change. Earned assets have given them the means to nurture and create change, and their business experience has given them the skills and confidence to foster that social change. Their philanthropy is shaped by their gender as much as it is by their energy, clout, commitment, and assets. There is every reason to think that as more women accumulate assets in the future, the cumulative impact of their philanthropy will be significant.

NOTES

1. "One in 18 U.S. Women Is a Woman Business Owner," *Center for Women's Business Research/Research,* July 16, 2002, p. 1.

2. "Giving Large," *Working Woman,* December/January, 2000, p. 16.

3. "Survey Finds Business Owners Are Philanthropic Leaders," *Center for Women's Business Research/Research,* November 14, 2000, p. 1.

4. "Men and Women and Their Money," *New York Times,* December 22, 2002, Business/Your Money, p. 22.

5. "Women Executives Said to Give More," *The Chronicle of Philanthropy,* November 18, 1999.

6. "Key Facts 2002," Center for Women's Business Research, 1411 K Street, Suite 1350, Washington, D.C., 20003-3407. 2002, p. 2.

7. "Survey Finds Business Owners Are Philanthropic Leaders," p. 3.

8. "Business Women of Achievement Are Independent Philanthropists," *Center for Women's Business Research/Research,* November 12, 1999, p. 2.

9. "Survey Finds Business Owners Are Philanthropic Leaders," p. 3.

10. Ibid., p. 2.

11. Ibid.

12. "Tax Incentives Move Women Less Than Men," *Philanthropy Journal,* April 16, 2001.

13. The online Harris data came from an article: Elizabeth Greene, "Study Finds Differences in Giving Patterns Between Wealthy Men and Women," *The Chronicle of Philanthropy,* May 3, 2001.

14. "Business Women of Achievement Are Independent Philanthropists," p. 2.

THINK BIG, SPEND SMALL

The Impact of Woman-to-Woman Small-Scale Support

꿍

ZAINEB SALBI

Never believe that a few caring people can't change the world. For, indeed, that's all who ever have.

Margaret Mead

One of the simplest definitions of the term "philanthropy" is "goodwill to fellowmen."[1] However, philanthropy is not just a term, but is also a concept that carries with it certain inferences, and without a more inclusive reading of what exactly constitutes a philanthropic act, it becomes only too easy to associate philanthropy with the stereotypical image of the very wealthy, often male individual who makes sporadic, but large gifts of money. In spite of this stereotype, it does not always require millions of dollars to make an impact in this world. Sometimes a small contribution, which may require even more sacrifice on the part of the giver than a large donation, is more than enough to lead to significant change.

I am a witness to and a participant in this phenomenon. In 1993, I was twenty-three years old, recently married, and a student. My husband was a student as well, and both of us were also working. We did not have much money at all, but we were so passionate about the need to help women survivors of rape camps in Bosnia-Herzegovina and Croatia that we could not justify our inaction, and together we founded an organization called Women for Women International (Women for Women in Bosnia at the time). I quit my job so I could completely dedicate myself to building Women for Women International (WWI), which meant living without any compensation for the first three years. My husband made his own sacrifice by prematurely ending his doctoral program at the University of Virginia in order to work full time to support the group's efforts. We did not have a wealthy family to support us and, like us, most of our friends were at the beginning of their careers and did not have much wealth to spare. Our funds may have been extremely limited, but our passion was boundless.

The first program that we designed was geared toward allowing other people from a similar economic class to contribute to social change; a program that would offer direct support and be emotionally satisfying without requiring that donors interrupt their lives. Calling this facet of our organization the Sponsorship Program, we initially linked women in North America with women survivors of the war in the Balkans but eventually expanded this program worldwide. Each sponsor commits to sending $25 a month to the woman she is sponsoring along with a letter to establish a personal communication link between the two women. The program appeals to thousands of women in North America who view the Sponsorship Program as a very concrete way to make a difference in one person's life for the price of a dinner and a movie.

Thousands upon thousands of women committed to the goals of Women for Women International over the years, eventually transforming the group from a basement operation running on personal credit cards to a multi-million dollar program with more than forty thousand women as part of its global network. Since 1993, WWI has sent more than $9 million dollars in aid and loans to more than twenty thousand women in Bosnia, Kosovo, Rwanda, Nigeria, Pakistan, Afghanistan, and Colombia, affecting each women's life in a positive and sometimes life-changing way. As a result of my experience, I've learned and, I hope, taught others that it does not always take a lot of money from a single individual to change the world. Rather, a passionate belief in what you are doing can fuel even the biggest dreams and lead to success.

Despite the success, I am not the first woman to experience the power of grassroots philanthropy and I am only one of thousands who have learned that making a difference in the world does not necessarily require a fortune. Women historically have used philanthropy as a means to gain authority, social and economic, in a male-dominated society.[2] As a consequence of not being able to depend upon financial donations as a mode of philanthropy, women also often have pursued different forms of philanthropic activities from those utilized by wealthy men. Recent scholars of philanthropy have identified six characteristics of women's philanthropy that have been widely accepted by the nonprofit community as the defining components of women's philanthropy.[3] Known as the six Cs, these characteristics are generalizations in a sense, but also provide a very useful framework with which we can explore women's grassroots philanthropy. The six Cs are Change, Create, Connect, Commit, Collaborate, and Celebrate.

This chapter examines the presence of all of these characteristics in grassroots philanthropy, but will focus largely on the second C, Create, by exploring the creative ways in which professional women as well as those with limited income, including students, single mothers who are struggling to make ends meet, and others who contribute to the philanthropic world, make their own niche in promoting social change in their communities as well as worldwide. These are the women who refused to limit themselves to the limitations of their income. A $1 contribution is indeed different than a $100,000 contribution, but the spirit that leads to that $1 contribution can be as powerful as the one that that initiates the $100,000. Sometimes it is even more powerful.

Getting In Deep

We can all be philanthropists, whether we have $25 or $25 million to give. The size of the gift isn't what makes you a philanthropist, it's your attitude and values.

Marie Wilson, "The White House Project," Taking Charge:
How Women's Funds Are Changing the Face of Philanthropy

Alice Wells lives in Phoenix, Arizona, and has been a member of Soroptomist International since 1980. Soroptomist International (SI) defines itself as a global voice for women working through Awareness, Advocacy, and Action with more than ninety-seven thousand members in 120 countries. Its mission is to advance the status of women and girls and cooperate with intergovernmental and other organizations for the advancement of international understanding, goodwill, and peace.

Alice originally joined the group to meet other women involved in education, as she was a curriculum administrator at the time. She didn't know much about Soroptomist International but was drawn to the community service aspect of the organization. Ultimately, the group provided her so many opportunities to make a difference in her community that she feels that she learned much more from her membership with Soroptomist International than any graduate school could have taught her.

Alice tells of one particular story that she feels exemplifies the impact that professional women can have through their work with Soroptomist International and that also fulfills all of the six Cs. At the time she began

WOMEN FOR WOMEN INTERNATIONAL

Women for Women International provides women survivors of war, civil strife, and other conflicts with tools and resources to move from crisis and poverty into becoming self-sufficient and active citizens who promote and protect peace and stability.

Women for Women International works on two different levels: one-on-one linkages and individual-to-community connections. Through the Sponsorship Program, Women for Women International links women in the United States with women in Bosnia, Rwanda, Kosovo, and Nigeria, and Afghan refugees in Pakistan who have survived and are surviving violence, and the resulting political, social, and economic upheaval associated with it. Each sponsor sends her matched "sister" $25 a month along with a letter to establish a communication link between the two women. Aside from the emotional support, the Sponsorship Program provides very direct financial support to help sponsored women meet basic needs for themselves and their families. Women for Women International asks for a minimum one-year commitment for sponsors in this program.

Our Global Voices Program creates an individual-community connection. This program links individuals from different parts of the world with a particular community in the countries in which we work. In particular, this program allows Women for Women International to provide a variety of services to the sponsored women, their families, and their communities. Provided services include, but are not limited to: training in technical and employable skills, sessions on defining women's role and value in society, business training, leadership training, and assistance in starting income-generating projects through the provision of micro-credit loans. Individuals' $25 monthly contributions allows us to continue our operations in the countries in which we work, while also enabling us to respond to crisis situations in a timely manner.

For more information on Women for Women International, visit www.womenfor women.org

her membership, Phoenix only had one child-crisis center. In the midst of a discussion with one of her friends about children in crisis, she realized that many more children needed a safe place to go in times of crisis that what was available (Change and Create). Alice decided that this would be a perfect issue for Soroptomist International to address and brought the idea to her local club (Collaborate). Her peers agreed with her and began working to start a child-crisis center (Connect). This abstract conception of an unfulfilled need grew into a physical center in one house, and then two houses, and has recently moved into a multi-million dollar facility. After getting the project started, Alice was able to step back and let experts in the field take over, but she is particularly proud of the fact that a simple idea was able to grow into an actual child-crisis care facility (Commit).

Aside from allowing her to make a contribution to her community irrespective of her income level, what Alice likes most about Soroptomist International is the fact that it allowed her to turn a good idea into reality. Alice has a full-time job and is always very busy. Being able to participate in a project that helped so many women and children made a huge difference for her. Soroptomist International also gave Alice an emotional connection and sense of belonging to her community rather than simply writing an impersonal check. Building relationships and investing in the social formation of the community is often at the front agenda for women (Celebrate). As others have noted, women often have "very personal motives and an ethic of personal commitment in their giving."

As mentioned earlier, women donors generally seek a higher level of involvement in the groups that they support than do men. According to the Independent Sector, 62 percent of women volunteer compared to 49 percent of men. Volunteerism is only one of the ways where women contribute in ways other than financial contributions to the causes they are supporting, but volunteerism has a significant impact on the functioning of nonprofit organizations. In 1996, there was an economy-wide estimate of 20.3 billion volunteer hours, which is equivalent to 10 million full-time workers. Even if each of these workers had only been making minimum wage, organizations saved over a $100 billion in wages.[4] The Independent Sector also reports that women feel duty bound to contribute to their communities. In particular, 47 percent women believe that contributing to different causes is a moral requirement as opposed to 39 percent of men.[5] In general, women report a greater need for tangible involvement in their chosen causes and there are many manifestations of this need.

Sharon Dawson comments on her experience with sponsoring a woman through Women for Women International's Sponsorship Program by saying: "The part that touched me was that I wasn't just going to send money into some pot . . . I was going to be sending $25 a month, but I'd also be corresponding with [the beneficiary] through letters. There was a face, a story, and an outcome that I could be a part of." Like Sharon, many women want to see concrete results for their contributions. They want to make a difference by being involved in the organization they are supporting rather than by simply writing a check.

Deborah McKinnon, a fifty-one-year old attorney with a trade association, demonstrates this point when she talks about her involvement with Soroptomist International. She says: "I became a donor out of a sense that it is the right thing to do . . . the opportunity to support the mission not only through a cash donation but also through action and hands-on service to support the ongoing mission and work of the club and the entire international organization. To paraphrase, give locally, help globally."

What Deborah likes about Soroptomist is their shared commitment to enhancing the quality of life and encouraging the livelihood of women worldwide through economic and social development, health, education, and environmental initiatives, while respecting local and indigenous cultures and values. However, Deborah also feels that she has benefited greatly from the lasting friendships that her membership creates by introducing her to women and communities across the globe.

Deborah eventually became involved in the organization's leadership as well as its hands-on service projects at the club and regional level. She defines philanthropy as the "ability to give willingly and freely in huge increments to support identified concerns important to the donor." Deborah has found that her involvement as a member of SI, and her eventual position as president, have had as large an impact on the functioning of the organization as a cash donation. As a matter of fact, she argues that the word "philanthropy" cannot be limited to financial donations only. Philanthropy, according to Deborah, involves a higher level of involvement in the social cause one is supporting. A misdirected focus on large gifts of money negates the many positive and important works that have been undertaken by women of all social classes and ignores the creativity employed by these women in order to enact social change.

Size Doesn't Matter

Women do not always give only because they have "extra" money. According to the Center for Women's Business Research, 40 percent of women donors donate to "give back." Pamela, explaining her attitude about giving back in a letter to the woman she is sponsoring in Nigeria through Women for Women International's Sponsorship Program wrote:

> I want to tell you the reason I chose to be a sponsor. Not so long ago, I was a woman in great need, like yourself, and a complete stranger heard that I was living in an apartment without any heat, which in my country in the winter means it can get very cold. She wrote to me and asked if I would accept a small amount of money every month to help pay my heating bills. She continued to send me this money for many months, until I was back on my feet again. I never met her in person, never even spoke to her or saw her picture, but I always said that if I had the chance, I'd do the same for someone else someday, sharing that same kindness with others, as a way of extending hers. I hope you understand why this

SOROPTOMIST INTERNATIONAL

Soroptomist International (SI) is a global voice for women working through Awareness, Advocacy, and Action with over ninety-seven thousand members in 120 countries. Its mission is to advance the status of women and girls and cooperate with intergovernmental and other organizations for the advancement of international understanding, goodwill, and peace. Soroptomist, coined from the Latin "soror" and "optima" (the best for women), was founded in 1921 in Oakland, California.

The world's largest classified service organization for executive and professional women, Soroptomist International comprises four federations: Soroptomist International of the Americas (SIA), Soroptomist International of Europe (SIE), Soroptomist International of Great Britain and Ireland (SIGBI), and Soroptomist International of the South West Pacific (SISWP).

Professional and executive businesswomen of all ages and ethnic groups and from all walks of life and cultures belong to Soroptomist. Included in the more than thirty-five hundred occupations and professions represented in Soroptomist are university presidents, farmers, office managers, business owners, physicians and other health care professionals, educators, accountants, and attorneys. The Soroptomist branches are known as leaders in their fields.

Soroptomist accomplishes its community service goals through its six programs of service: Economic and Social Development, Education, Environment, Health, Human Rights/Status of Women, and International Goodwill and Understanding.

For more information on Soroptomist International, please visit their Web site at www.soroptimist.org

is important to me, and see that I also know what it's like to need assistance from others sometimes, even from strangers you'll never meet.

Joyce is another woman who is helping another woman in another part of the world as a way to give back to those who have helped her when she was in need. Her personal connection and the emotional investment that she has in this process are loud and clear in her letter:

> When I was nineteen, due to some hard times in my family, I was on my own. I decided that college was my best chance to make a secure future for myself, and with the help of loans, scholarships, work-study programs, and other aid I was able to support myself and earn my degree in four years. So with the help of others, I made it through. That's why I'm participating in Women for Women International—to give to others, as others gave to me so long ago.

I don't know about Pamela or Joyce's current financial situations. But I do know of many women who did not let their financial limitations hold them back from helping others in need. They are part of the 9 percent women donors who donate to answer a need and the 8 percent who donate to help others. The income level of these women has never stopped them from contributing nor has it stopped them from making a huge financial and social difference as a collective of individuals. In fact, 7.3 percent of Women for Women International's donors make under $25,000 in annual household income; 22 percent make less than $50,000, and another 22.2 percent make between $50,000 and $75,000. Most can be categorized as limited-income or middle class. Yet, all have made significant contributions toward creating social change not only in their local communities but also around the world.

I mentioned earlier that Sharon Dawson in San Francisco felt very strongly about sponsoring an individual woman. Sharon followed through on this commitment despite the obstacles life threw in her way. Sharon continued to sponsor her sponsored sister in Nigeria even after she lost her job as a computer software engineer and despite the break-up of her engagement. Financial restraints were issues that she had to think about, but she did not let these restraints stop her from continuing her support to the woman she is sponsoring. In commenting on that, she says, "I redid my budget and thought to myself 'I'll find some way to do this.' I was scrimping and saving, and I still am, but I'm not going to stop. My worst day is nothing compared to what they go through on a normal day."

Getting Together is More Fun

I shared what I saw and heard with my family and we all agreed that in lieu of buying holiday gifts for each other this year, we would send a donation to Women for Women International.

Jane, a sponsor with Women for Women International

According to Raquel Newman, "women seek a more personal connection with their cause and require a longer nurturing process and more education in order to make a charitable gift to an organization or devote themselves to a cause."[6] This need has coalesced with a desire to give in a collaborative fashion, leading to a form of collective giving that is known as a Giving Circle. Women largely have dominated this phenomenon in philanthropy, but historically communities of color often have depended upon collective giving. Recently, in East St. Louis, one of the most impoverished and segregated communities in America, members of the community managed to raise over $300,000 for a girls' and boys' club.[7] This is an excellent example of the potential power of collective giving, but Giving Circles also provide an example of this power.

Members of Giving Circles invest time in learning about the issues that they are interested in supporting, and they use their combined resources to support these causes financially. However, they often donate their time and skills to these organizations as well. Alison Goldberg, the founder of a Giving Circle in Boston known as the Kitchen Table, describes the process the group goes through before deciding on an issue or on the group they want to support:

> [We] get together once every month and a half. At the beginning of the Circle, we invested a lot of time talking about our political beliefs, the meaning of giving, and how we want to shape our giving trends. Investing in this time was very helpful. It was great to get a chance to talk to people about their giving ideas and learn from them. It was also very nice to do site visits with other people to the groups we were considering to fund. Having the freedom to give with friends was very nice.

The Kitchen Table includes ten members with different professional backgrounds. They include a lawyer, an artist, and a woman who works with a nonprofit. All members are younger than forty-five years old. They all have equal votes regardless of the amount they give. There is no minimum amount. The donations range from $100 to $5,000.

The social aspect of giving is yet another incentive for women to pull their resources together as they seek to make social changes. Marie is part of a group known as the Bus Stop Moms. Marie talks about the emotional connection she felt with all the other moms and their daughters as they

THE KITCHEN TABLE, BOSTON

Their name represents the symbolic "four legs" that hold up the Kitchen Table (and what they strive to achieve): to build a community of women with diverse experiences, to expand their network of people involved with social change, to learn through this experience of giving, and to give dynamically with community representation. The group currently consists of fifteen members, ages twenty-six to forty, with varying levels of income; some have significant wealth now or will in the future. The amounts members give vary from around $100 to $5,000. Two co-chairs and volunteers run it. The current focus areas are poverty and education. They planned to make their first grant of around $10,000 in the spring of 2002. The Kitchen Table began an application process for their first funding round with a deadline of July 15, 2002.

tried to raise money to sponsor a woman and her family in Kosovo through Women for Women International. In describing her experience, she wrote to Arife, the woman she is sponsoring in Kosovo, saying:

> When we heard of your terrible suffering in all the news stories in the papers and on TV, I felt full of sorrow for all of you who were forced out of your homes and suffered the loss of loved ones and everything else you have endured. I wanted to help to send money, but I couldn't do it alone. So many mothers in our neighborhood got together and held a benefit garage sale to raise money to sponsor a family. Many women and girls helped—mothers, grandmothers, daughters, and sisters. We were thrilled to make enough to sponsor you and your family for a year. I know it's not much money, but I hope it will help you in rebuilding your lives. I cannot imagine what you have been through. I think of you often in my prayers.

Sarah Feinberg is another person who managed to combine the satisfaction of getting together with other people and establishing new friendships with the joy of giving despite a limited income. Sarah established a giving circle known as Tzedakah Collective when she was twenty-five year old back in 1999.[8] At the time, Sarah had recently moved to Boston from New York City to attend Boston University's MBA program. Sarah explains:

> [About the time I moved to Boston] I read about a Giving Circle in New York that a friend was involved in. I showed the article to a business school friend who was immediately excited about starting such a group in Boston. As students we had little time or financial means to give to the community. Starting a giving circle seemed like a good way for us to use our limited resources in a way that could benefit the local Boston community we were taking so much from while in school.

Although the project began only with women in Sarah's class, it eventually expanded to other professional young women.

The average age of the members of the Tzedakah Collective is between twenty-five and thirty-five years old. The Collective, which continues to operate and grow, has an average of ten members in any given year, all of whom are women. Members of the group are diverse in their religious, ethnic, and sexual orientation backgrounds. While members started by donating about $10 per month per member, they have been able to increase their monthly contributions while maintaining equal votes for all members regardless of the amount of contribution. In the first year of operation, the Tzedakah Collective collected $500, which they donated to the Elizabeth Stone House in Jamaica Plains, Massachusetts. This amount increased to $1,200 in 2001, which they donated to Suited for Success in Jamaica Plains.

Like the Kitchen Table, the Tzedakah Collective invested the necessary time to learn about philanthropy and the particular issues and causes they were interested in supporting, be it domestic violence projects, vocational skills training, or issues of co-existence within the Boston community. In the process of creating lasting change in the community, these women also formed lasting and fulfilling friendships. When commenting on her experience as a founder and member of the Tzedakah Collective, Sarah says: "It allowed me to know my classmates who became my best friends. It enabled us to develop communication with each other that we wouldn't have otherwise. Furthermore, this experience helped keep me in touch with my classmates even though we graduated awhile ago."

Conclusion

When I was fifteen years old, my friends laughed at me when I told them that I wanted to help women from around the world. When I was twenty-three and had just started a group to help women from around the world, a different set of friends laughed at me for starting a career of service from a negative financial state. Later, when President Bill Clinton and Mrs. Hillary Rodham-Clinton honored my work with Women for Women International at a White House ceremony, people around me began to take notice that perhaps it was possible to help others even without great financial resources. Since then, thousands of women have been helped

WHAT ARE GIVING CIRCLES?

Giving Circles—a kind of social investment club—are an enormously powerful way to effect social change and pave the way for a new frontier in philanthropy. Giving Circles enable a wide range of people to give voice to their values. In the same way that venture capital supports innovation in the business world, Giving Circles use a model of "venture philanthropy," infusing nonprofits with financial and intellectual capital, resources, and contacts. Joining or forming a Giving Circle provides its members with a hands-on opportunity to explore and collaborate with others who share the desire to make focused, social investments with impact. Across the country, all kinds of people are forming Giving Circles, and working together to make a difference.

For more information on Giving Circles, please visit the following Web site: http://www.givingnewengland.org/

through our programs and the laughs have changed into support as people begin to recognize the power and contagion of passion and commitment.

Money is important and by no means am I denying its impact, but it can't be the only drive to philanthropy. Like Deborah McKinnon, I believe that the concept of philanthropy cannot be limited to large donations or even to financial support alone.

What I have learned in my experience with Women for Women International is that philanthropy involves so much more. It involves an investment of emotion and time, in addition to the financial investment. The women quoted in this chapter did not have unlimited sources of income. They all have to work for a living. Some are struggling to make ends meet, while others are more comfortable. Nevertheless, all have found creative ways to make an impact on the issues they care about, whether by responding to crisis in their community or in some other country. Ultimately, it is their individual sense of moral responsibility rather than their financial largess that has led them to action, and that is what philanthropy is all about.

ACKNOWLEDGMENT

The author wishes to acknowledge the contribution of Jess Sucherman, Researcher.

NOTES

1. Diane Newman, *Opening Doors: Pathways to Diverse Donors* (San Francisco: Jossey-Bass Publishers, 2002), 11.

2. Kathleen D. McCarthy, "Parallel Power Structures: Women and the Voluntary Sphere," in *Lady Bountiful Revisited: Women, Philanthropy, and Power*, ed. Kathleen McCarthy (New Brunswick: Rutgers University Press, 1998), 1.

3. Sondra C. Shaw and Martha A. Taylor, *Reinventing Fundraising: Realizing the Potential of Women's Philanthropy* (San Franscisco: Jossey-Bass Publishers, 1995), 8.

4. Patti Poblete, "Sisters and Samaritans," *San Francisco Chronicle*, January 27, 2002.

5. Kay Sprinkel Grace, "Ten Things You Should Know about the Impact of Women on Philanthropy," *Contributions Magazine* (November/December 2002).

6. Poblete, "Sisters and Samaritans."

7. Mike Harris, "United Way Hopes to Raise $1.1 Million from Blacks Here," *St. Louis Post-Dispatch*, September 17, 2002, 3.

8. The word *tzedakah* is found in both Hebrew and Muslim traditions. The closest translation is "righteous giving." According to Sarah, the connotation with the word *tzedakah* is more than just charity. It includes working to make the world a better and more just place—one of the goals of the Tzedakah Collective.

WE ARE OUR
SISTER'S KEEPER
Role Models, Success Stories, Inspiration

HELEN LAKELLY HUNT AND KANYERE EATON

In living up to our name, "The Sister Fund," we hope to model the
ethic of mutuality and sisterhood that characterizes the broad work of
women's funds. In doing so, we join hands with a network of collaborators in the struggle for fullness of life for women and girls. In this chapter, we will share some of our continuing journey toward realizing the ideal
of being our sister's keepers. Most of the chapter is written in our combined voice. The few segments that reflect our individual voices are introduced with our names.

The Sister Fund supports social justice work that addresses the needs
and concerns of women and girls locally, nationally, and internationally.
There is an undercurrent of spirituality in our work—one that we have
sought to articulate in our publications and grantmaking practices. We believe the struggle for social justice, economic equality, and the eradication
of violence is sacred work. We support women of faith who are struggling
to promote women's rights within their religious contexts, recognizing that
much of the work that takes place on the earth to promote the rights of
women is rooted in the deepest and most compassionate aspects of world
religions. The Sister Fund makes explicit the power of faith in feminist
activism.

At the Sister Fund, we embrace a cosmology that life is delicately interconnected, the maintenance of which requires active care for the connections. It is our belief that the Spirit of God exists in relationships that
are mutual, honoring, and have dignity. We feel that the suppression of
women's voices and the exclusion of women from policy-making decisions
are violations of the sacred order of life. We believe our work is to rein-

state the justice and beauty inherent in life. Caring for one another is a mirror of what we want to achieve in our world—our sisterhood and faith fuel our social activism.

Several examples in this piece are derived from the biblical scripture, primarily because we are Christian—an ordained minister and a feminist theologian. It is important to mention, however, that the circle of women who enrich our work and our journey with stories, prayers, and rituals come from myriad religious, cultural, and philosophical traditions.

Our Sister's Keeper

The biblical narrative of the first family as recorded in Genesis suggests that fraternal conflict is not a new phenomenon. In that story, Cain's jealousy and resentment toward his brother escalates to fratricide. An ancient precursor to the "every man for himself" mentality, his defensive retort, "Am I my brother's keeper?" suggests that he should not be responsible for the well-being of his brother. Cain's denial of responsibility for his brother's demise is characteristic of oppressive social structures that historically have undermined paradigms of wholeness, connection, and cooperation. By placing premium value on the personal, these structures preclude the possibility of creative expression that emerges from the convergence of differing voices and multiple realities.

Cain's question, a sentiment of singularity, reflects the familiar and prevalent paradigm of the celebrated self. It is the antithesis of the energy and passion that ignited the first wave of feminists. While the notion of being "my brother's keeper" was distasteful to Cain, the ethic of being "keeper," supporter, sister, and collaborator with other women, was the hallmark of early feminist activism. In 1837, black and white women organized and conducted the first political convention of women in the history of the United States. Sarah Forten crafted an emblem that came to signify their commitment to sisterhood.[1] Portraying an enslaved African American woman, it was scripted with the words, "Am I not a woman and a sister?"[2]

What did they mean by sisterhood? These early abolitionist feminists understood the inextricable, liberating link between equal rights for white women and social justice for enslaved, black women. Both white and black women were assumed to be and treated as the property of white men. Undaunted by a racist, sexist culture that was hostile to empowered women and racial integration of any sort, these women converged to forge a sociopolitical agenda that regarded black and white women as sisters and co-journeyers in the struggle. Their consciousness of community stretched beyond what was normative, to embrace the reality of a shared destiny.

Black and white women saw themselves as one blood related to each other socially, spiritually, and psychologically. Each woman's experience was shared mutually. Each woman's plight had implications for the other. They were *sisters* and rightfully each other's keepers.

While Cain uses the term "keeper" with facetious contempt, the ideal of being a keeper, supporter, and advocate of other organizations with women and girl-focused agendas is immensely appealing to progressive women's funds like the Sister Fund. The *American Heritage Dictionary* defines the word "sister" as "a girl or woman who shares a common ancestry, allegiance, character or purpose with another."[3] For centuries, women have defined the concept of sisterhood in a way that transcends mere biological ties, to embrace a sense of unity in diversity. Progressive women have long considered the significance of political, socioeconomic, and spiritual alliances in shaping feminine realities and relationships.

The experience of sisterhood facilitates a deeper and more personal understanding of the importance of right relationship. Healthy, organic connections with sisters flourish in our lives as we open ourselves to be witness to one another's experience, allowing our own perceptions of life to be broadened through the lens of relationship. In this sense, justice is an issue of right relationship on both micro and macro levels. We begin our work on justice issues as we develop relationships with one another.

For us, sisterhood is embodied in the way we seek to listen, give, and share with our sisters. Acting as "sisters and keepers" requires that we both offer what we have, and receive what our sisters bring. So rather than working with grantees in detached and hierarchical ways, we seek to lift up an ethic of mutuality, embracing opportunities to collaborate or be "co-laborers" with those on the "front lines" of justice work. Our grantees teach us what is happening within their sphere of the movement to gain equal rights and opportunities for women and girls. Their involvement with various activist communities and social justice initiatives enables us to keep a vicarious "ear to the ground." We stay apprised of the challenges and opportunities facing grassroots women and girls, by listening to them and while we operate using clearly established guidelines, we are open to the change and evolution that accompany the dynamic nature of being in relationship with activist women.

History of the Sister Fund

The crystal we value at the Sister Fund evolves from the "life for me ain't been no crystal stair" philosophy that Langston Hughes voices in his legendary poem about a black mother and child. We know that a legacy of oppression has left most women and minorities without the resources

they need to live powerful and empowering lives. Thus, we are commit-
ted to helping our grantees climb as high as their dreams and visions take
them. It is a rightful and righteous part of our history.
Dr. Evelyn White, Professor, Mills College, Sister Says! *Spring 1994*

Helen: In 1981, my sister Swanee and I responded to an insistent and shared philanthropic impulse. Raised in a family of wealth that did not encourage the financial autonomy of its female members, we committed to learn how to find better relationships with family re-sources. We shared the work of grantmaking for ten years in close dialogue with grantee activists through the Hunt Alternatives Fund. After the first decade, Swanee retained the name Hunt Alternatives Fund and expanded her programmatic emphasis to include more international grantmaking. Deeply moved by the work of the emerging women's funding network, I wanted to help grow the expanding network—the sisterhood of private women's funds—and established the Sister Fund in January of 1993.

Named in honor of the sororal bond shared with Swanee and other sisters in the struggle, we modeled the Sister Fund's governance after the public women's funds. Kimberly Otis provided the organization with attentive, dedicated leadership as its executive director from 1993 to 2000. During its first ten years, the Sister Fund sought to live out its commit-ment to honoring the diverse gifts, talents, voices, and contributions of sisters in the women's movement through the conscious solicitation of activist women, as members of the staff and board of directors program. The Sister Fund's grantmaking practices have been shaped and influenced by women who were mothers, poets, theologians, advocates, activists, philanthropists, lesbian and straight, artists, film makers, journalists, educators, ministers, sisters, and friends from a diversity of racial and theological perspectives.

The Sister Fund is committed to social justice and spirituality within the women's movement locally, nationally, and globally. We fund in the area of AIDS, cultural empowerment, health and safety, economic justice, media, social justice, women's funds, and philanthropy. We made the issue of spirituality both a programmatic priority and a funding strategy area. Of the synergy between spirituality and justice, former Sister Fund board member Leah Wise of the South East Regional Economic Justice Network says, "Spirituality and justice don't exist without each other. To achieve justice, to create compassionate community, one must organize with kind-ness; to establish peace, one must be peace. We need to be life-affirming, so that we can guide each other toward healthy relationships and healthy communities."[4]

Many feminists are ambivalent about organized religion and spiritual-ity because traditional religious institutions have been ardent opponents of women's rights. However, women's personal faith has, at times, cat-alyzed and sustained feminist activism. A growing number of women in the women's movement want to acknowledge the faith that fuels their work for equality, and the Sister Fund aligns itself with this impulse. We fund the work of women combating patriarchy in religious institutions and we encourage efforts that strengthen both the leadership and voices of women in places of worship. Our recent efforts have been in support of the movement for gender equality in the Catholic Church and in augmenting the prophetic messages of women theologians from varying religious traditions.[5]

Kanyere: For the past three years, Helen and I have been partners and collaborators in the creative and intuitive work of shaping the soul and process of the Sister Fund's grantmaking. Coming from a background in ministry and social work, I was attracted to the Sister Fund's strong history of support for disenfranchised women and girls, its emphasis on the inextricable link between spirituality and social justice and its commitment to the development of honoring relationships with grantees. As director of a multifaceted social-service ministry at the Riverside Church in New York City, I was familiar with the challenges of grantseeking and knew well the difficulties inherent in forging relationships with elusive grantmakers. The Sister Fund's mission celebrated a different and dynamic way of being in a funding relationship—one I embraced.

In the early months of my employ, Helen and I talked at length about our shared vision for partnering with grassroots activist women in ways that would further empower their impact in the world. Imagining how we might strengthen their programmatic capability and offer refreshment in the face of burn-out, we dreamed aloud of organizing retreats for grantees in Abiquiu, New Mexico. We shared the yearning to see secular and faith-based feminists collude and co-create a woman-centered social agenda—one that would take into account the economic, political, and spiritual realities of our day. We see our work as a small, but uniquely important part of a web of support being woven by hundreds of women's funds and thousands of grassroots organizations across the world.

The "Sistering Fund": Being a Sister to Our Grantees

Spirituality is rooted in a deep sense of trust in and between women, the spirit of oneness that infuses our work, uniting those who seek and those who give.

Kavita Ramdas, President, Global Fund for Women,
New York State Bill A10807

We see ourselves being sisters to others in three ways. First, we are sisters to our grantees. Second, we are sisters to other donors, and finally, we are sisters to other women with whom we collaborate regularly. We will elaborate on these ways of sistering in the next three sections.

Since we are a small foundation with a modest budget, we augment our grantmaking with other kinds of support, including strategic funding, programmatic initiatives, sharing of space, and incubation support. In addition, our tri-annual newsletter, *Sister Says!* exists to amplify the voices of our grantees, highlighting the social change work they do in local, national, and international communities. We work closely with our talented staff toward the goal of supporting justice and fullness of life for women in our society, but we all agree it is the Spirit in our midst that moves us forward.

Strategic Funding

The mosaic of Sister Fund grantees is rich with diversity. Our primary interest has been funding women with the least access to economic resources. Women of color and faith, such as Reverend Rosa Caraballo, founder and director of Bruised Reed Ministry in the South Bronx, and Reverend Henna Hahn, founder of the Rainbow Center in Flushing, Queens, are courageous advocates of the disenfranchised women across the city of New York. Unwilling to limit their ministries to the pulpit, these women bring to the fore the plight of the growing number of women who are incarcerated, living with HIV and AIDS, homeless, battered, or abandoned. As a foundation interested in "hearing the other into speech," we have learned many valuable lessons from their experiences and we have gained transformative inspiration from their stories.[6]

Reverend Annie Bovian, executive director of Women's Advocate Ministry in Jails and Prisons (WAM), provides ongoing support and advocacy for women who have been detained by the penal system. WAM assists incarcerated mothers in maintaining and retaining contact with the children and other family members they leave behind while serving their sentences. Having visited incarcerated women in the Bedford Hills Correctional Facility with Annie, we increasingly became aware of the challenging chasm between need and services her small organization seeks to breach. Annie exposed the practice of shackling pregnant, incarcerated women while they were in the process of delivering their babies. Several articles that she wrote on the subject came to the attention of Amnesty International, resulting in the institution of a bill forbidding this practice.[7] For Annie, service to incarcerated women is service to God.

Programmatic Initiatives

At times, the Sister Fund initiates a special programmatic thrust. In 1995, Sister Fund board members began to consider the potential impact of the Fourth World Conference on Women, where women from all over the world would converge and share strategies to affect national and international policy on every major public issue. Understanding the unique opportunity for collaboration, the board committed $250,000, half of the annual grantmaking budget, to support broader participation of grassroots women. Staff and board members convened dialogues, organized panels, and participated in discussions, both before and after this historic event.

At this conference of thirty-five thousand women from 189 countries, our grantees were able to network with women worldwide who were experiencing similar issues. Given the fact that most of our funding is domestic, we felt that this was a chance to have international impact. Of the relationship between the local and global, Charlotte Bunch, executive director of the Center for Women's Global Leadership said:

> Because the local and the global are mostly seen as separate spheres, we often have trouble determining what local actions will have the greatest impact globally. Women's activism in the United States must be both local and global to succeed. Only through such a process can feminists address not only the needs of each situation but also the larger global structures creating many of these conflicts.[8]

The Beijing conference was the first of its kind in which the topic of spirituality was addressed formally on the agenda. Panel discussions led by Betty Friedan, Hyun Kyung Chung, Riffat Hassan, and Helen LaKelly Hunt brought the correlation between certain fundamentalist sects and women's oppression into focus. It also highlighted the justice and gender equality work being done by liberation theologians throughout the world. Participating in this international conference was a unique and valuable opportunity for Sister Fund grantees, staff, and board members.

Sharing Space

The Sister Fund office is situated on the lower east side of Manhattan, near Union Square, a location our New York–based grantees find easily accessible via public transportation. We share a floor and conference room with the Astraea Lesbian Foundation for Justice, and our joint space has been utilized by a number of women-focused organizations, including the Latina Roundtable, the Beijing Plus Five Committee, and the Family Health Project team, headed by Sister Fund founding board member, Suki Terada Ports. We enjoy creating a venue on our floor in which sisters can show their artwork. Our office space has been used as a gallery for the paintings of sisters we know, including former Sister Fund board member Harilyn Russo and artist Aisha Cousins. A life-size portrait of Harriet Tubman retains a place of prominence in our shared conference room, a creation of Rikki Asher, a student at the Union Theological Seminary.

Incubation

In 1995, Reverend Linda Tarry-Chard, Sister Fund founding board member, was asked by a local social activist to collect fifteen thousand black dolls to give to children living in South African townships. Living under apartheid rule, they had never seen or played with dolls in their own image. Linda single-handedly began to collect black dolls, and over the years her efforts grew into the Project People Foundation (PPF), an economic development organization that facilitates the move from "charity to commerce" for the African women it trains to make black dolls and other products. We incubated this effort between 1995 and 1996, offering space, access to office equipment, and technical assistance.

Women for Afghan Women (WAW) is a recent grantee of the Sister Fund—one that had its genesis in our office. A small, New York–based nonprofit, it exists to promote the agency of local Afghan women through the creation of safe forums where they can network, develop programs to meet their specific needs, and participate in human rights advocacy in the international sphere. In WAW, Jewish, Christian, Muslim, and Hindu women join forces to educate and advocate for the rights of Afghan women, the vast majority of whom are devout Muslims. Dedicated to the empowerment of Afghan women in New York and Afghanistan, this organization is an example of the transcendent ethic of sisterhood.

The Sister Fund has given space, technical support, office supplies, staff mentoring, and funding toward the start-up of this organization. After the tragedy of September 11, 2001, Sunita Mehta, director of grants and programs at the Sister Fund, helped WAW host their first conference in New York City and edited the book *Women for Afghan Women: Shattering Myths and Claiming the Future* (St. Martin's Press), which resulted from the conference. We lent staff support to WAW's third conference, "Women and the Constitution: Kandahar 2003," held despite security threats in the Taliban stronghold of Kandahar.

Few things are more encouraging for progressive women than to see their daughters take up the banner for social equality. We've been delighted to offer support to the early efforts of the Third Wave Foundation—the only national activist foundation that supports young women between the ages of fifteen and thirty through grantmaking, public education campaigns, and networking. Co-founded by founding Sister Fund board member Catherine Gund, Third Wave found a two-office home in our space, which they occupied for three years. Their work and vision for young women's empowerment has had national impact.

Wanting to make our space available for meetings, grant-related research, and programmatic planning sessions, we have established a small resource room where grantees come to review periodicals and seek information from other philanthropic entities. We offer technical assistance workshops and educational sessions with topics determined by the expressed needs of our grantees. In addition, each year, our grantees are invited to attend Summer at Sister Fund workshops, which feature interactive learning sessions on fundraising, board development, program evaluation, and developing effective media messages. This year, we concluded our Summer at Sister Fund series with a well-attended, grantor-grantee dialogue.

Amplifying Voices

The Sister Fund publishes a tri-annual newsletter entitled *Sister Says!* Many foundations produce an annual report to publicize their grants; however, we were clear that our purpose was not to speak for the grantees, but to let them speak for themselves. The first issue of *Sister Says!* was devoted to our commitment to diversity. Other newsletter issues over the years have addressed themes such as women's media activism, the rising incarceration rate of women and girls, issues around women and disability, the World Conference Against Racism, and grantee responses to the catastrophe of September 11. Our Fall 2002 newsletter featured the voices of donor activists such as Abigail Disney, founder of the Daphne Foundation, Tracy Gary, founder of Changemakers, and Cyndie McLachlan, founder of Girl's Best Friend Foundation, sharing their experiences with women's philanthropy.

The women who have staffed the Sister Fund over the years have been ardent feminists and activists in their own right and the temptation always exists to publish our own editorials in the newsletter. However, in publishing *Sister Says!* each year, and thus delivering the voices and priorities of our grantees to other funders and nonprofit organizations, we hope to be a true sister rather than a big sister. Not only do we consider our approach less hierarchical, but it is also our celebration of the fact that the grantees are experts in their own fields. We simply serve as their megaphones.

Two excerpts from *Sister Says!* serve to illustrate grassroots women's wisdom—powerful words from powerful women. The first was written by Frances Kissling, president of Catholics for a Free Choice in the Spring 1996 issue:

> It is our job as feminists to take injustice out of darkness and expose it to the light of day. For centuries, women and men in the church who have spoken and gone against the church have been punished and suf-

fered in silence. Our religious leaders are trained to submit—supposedly to the will of God, but most often to the will of men.

And from the Spring 1999 issue, written by the late Ingrid Washinawa-tok, former executive director of the Fund for Four Directions:

> The right of all peoples to self-determination, as set forth in international law, cannot be realized while women continue to be marginalized and prevented from becoming full participants in their societies. And if the women's movement is to continue to grow and expand globally, it must address the fundamental issues that are being addressed by indigenous women and women of color—women who comprise the majority of the world.

Being a Sister to Other Donors

Woman is a glorious possibility . . . the future of the world is hers.
Matilda Joslyn Gage, Quoted in Sister Says!, Spring 2003

In the late nineteenth century, Matilda Joslyn Gage, an advocate for women's equality, highlighted the fact that women's rights and suffrage associations were largely neglected by women donors, saying, "Almost every daily paper heralds the fact of some large bequest . . . by rich women; but it is proverbial that they never remember the women's suffrage movement that underlies in importance all others. Is it not strange that women of wealth are constantly giving large sums of money to endow professorships in [men's] colleges yet give no thought to their own sex—crushed in ignorance, poverty and prostitution—the hopeless victims of custom, law and Gospel, with few to offer the helping hand, while the whole world comes to the aid of the boy and glorify the man?"[9] Matilda's despair over the lack of models of women's funding began to be addressed systematically, close to a century after she penned these words.

For years, women mobilized their energy, creativity, and time on behalf of women-specific causes, but few gave money. In the late 1980s, a vision of women funding women emerged. Women began to leverage their financial resources in support of social, economic, and political agendas by, for, and about women. As an historic impulse, women's funds, both public and private, began to proliferate. By bringing financial power to the sense of sisterhood that had long existed and flourished in women's cultures, these donors added fuel to the engine of the women's movement. Today, there are approximately one hundred women's funds in several countries. They give away approximately $30 million annually to women and girls.[10]

Helen: Here at the Sister Fund, we have committed to strengthening the voices of women by nurturing this growing network of women funding women. Toward this end, we funded the first meeting of the National Network of Women's Funds (renamed the Women's Funding Network) in 1986. I had been on the founding boards of the New York Women's Foundation in 1985 and the Dallas Women's Foundation in 1987. A few years later, I served on the board of the Women's Funding Network and the Ms. Foundation for Women. I have been able to witness first hand the need to help donors move into strategic alliance with one another, as well as the dynamic synergy created when donors come together to amplify one another's resources. Donor cultivation and education is a critically important task for the women's movement, and we look for ways to support this when we can.

Women donors nurture others, but who nurtures women donors? The Sister Fund has maintained the goal of supporting women donors in as many ways possible. We have partnered with the Women's Funding Network in a collaborative venture to encourage potential donors to systematize their giving through private funds. Instructional resources, including a track for private foundations at WFN's annual conference and a section on private foundations in their revised women's fund manual, will be made available to emerging feminist philanthropists. My home in New Mexico is used occasionally as a retreat site for small groups of women exploring the options of creating giving circles and donor advised funds.

Women's funds potentially can be more effective than individual donors because they help women leverage each other's money and amplify each other's resources, time, and social-change investments. We are well-served by considering the transformative strength and societal influence made possible through our cooperation and collaboration. Ecclesiastes lauds the value of friendship and collaboration with these words: "Two are better than one, because they have a good reward for their toil. A threefold cord is not easily broken" (4: 9–12). When we support the work of women's funds, we support ourselves, our daughters, our nieces, our aunts, our friends, and our sisters. We are our sister's keepers.

Being a Sister to One Another

We are, therefore, I am. (www.elca.org)

Kanyere: Many organizations espouse the mission of empowering women, but because a number of women unwittingly have internalized the pervasive and oppressive elements of patriarchy, we sometimes project that oppression onto the people nearest us. As a result, women sometimes undercut and disempower one another in the very organizations that try to promote fullness of life for women and girls. At the Sister Fund, we want to be more conscious of such tendencies as we work to actualize the mission of sisterhood. I have the privilege of working closely with three women whose commitment and skill inspire me daily. They are Sunita B. Mehta, director of grants and programs; Ann Maldonado, grants administrator; and Kaliah Henton, executive assistant. Together, we formulated an informal set of office ethics by which our professional relationships are governed. These ethics include:

- The co-creation of the programmatic flow of our work. We engage in planning retreats twice a year to process new ideas, assess grantee feedback of our activities, and give one another feedback on ways to enhance our performance.

- Efforts to function more horizontally than hierarchically. We work together on projects and often assist each other in tasks that are not listed formally on our job descriptions. For example, Kaliah may write a newsletter article on a topic that piques her interest while I take telephone messages. When we engage in each other's responsibilities, we gain empathy for one another.

- The practice of being sensitive to each other's most pressing need. On occasions when one of us is having a crisis, we blend the personal into the professional and reach out not only to offer a listening ear, a hug, a card affirming our friendship and support, and a prayer, but to be physically and emotionally present in each other's support network. We have organized each other's weddings and birthday parties, helped organize family funerals, and traveled considerable distances to be present with each other in times of joy and sorrow. In short, we encircle each other with sisterhood.

- The incorporation of humor into our workdays. Funny stories about the antics of staff members' children abound! Our consultant of ten years, Stephanie Clohesy, is gifted in so many ways, including her ability to shift our perspectives during those occasionally intense interactions with a humorous word. What kind of a revolution would we have without dance or laughter?

Taking time to talk, listen, share meals, laugh, retreat, and dream in the company of sister-colleagues are small, yet significant practices that we employ to nurture healthy, cathartic connections. In doing so, we have come to understand ourselves better as sisters who support each other's actualization. It makes no sense to work to empower women on the outside, if we aren't doing this every day in our own office. We want our mission to be congruent without and within. This view of the world as a circle of sisterhood is a stark contrast to our Western, Cartesian, notion of "I think therefore I am." Our view, reinforced by a traditional African perspective is: "We are, therefore, I am."[11]

"Speech Is Silver, But Silence is Gold"

Our struggle is about creating violence-free families. And then violence-free streets. Then, violence-free borders. In that order. Because the root cause of the problem is persistent inequalities and growing inequalities.

For us to realize our dreams, we must keep our heads in the clouds and our feet on the ground.
The late Bella Abzug, Women's Environmental Development
Organization, quoted in Sister Says!, Summer 1998

Helen: My partner in love and life is Harville Hendrix, author of the best selling book, *Getting the Love You Want* (Henry Holt & Co., 1988). His work on this book served as a catalyst for the emergence of his theory of Imago Therapy, which teaches dialogue to people with marriages in conflict.[12] Harville and I have talked about the applicability of the Imago model for the women's movement. Women promote the ethic of dialogue but often lack the skills to live out this ethic. He and I enjoyed working together to teach dialogue at the Sister Fund, to the staff and several groups of grantees. I witnessed the Sister Fund slowing down and learning to listen to each other. It is in that spirit that we want to listen more deeply to our grantees. Together, we are expanding the Imago method of dialogue into "Communalogue," which we believe will be a way for nonprofit boards and staff, and perhaps warring nations, to resolve conflict and heal rupture.

Traditionally, importance had been placed on speaking, while the value of listening is often minimized. Speaking is perceived as active; listening, as passive. Speaking is rewarded while listening is overlooked. We'd like to challenge these concepts. As Patriocinio Schweickart writes, "speech is silver, but silence is gold."[13] Listening is meaning-making. Being heard is essential because it gives the grantee the reinforcement needed to strengthen her voice. It empowers her. It makes her visible. In right relationship, listening enriches both sides. When we can hear one another, we move in the direction of right relationship. As a foundation, we feel one of our most important tasks is listening. By listening to the women who work to empower others women, and learning more about their needs, we seek to develop a relevant programmatic curriculum that will enhance their day-to-day endeavors. At the Sister Fund, we are learning to place increased value on the significance of listening.

With the intention of making space for listening, sharing, and relating, the Sister Fund invites new grantees to an informal reception in our office to talk about the challenges and triumphs of their work, and to describe their motivation for continuing the struggle to achieve fullness of life for women and girls. At these gatherings, grantees meet one another as well as our staff, founder, and trustees. The routine of sending a check in the mail with our best wishes did not satisfy our desire to connect with grantee sisters.

Once we have introduced ourselves, our programs, and our space, we invite grantees to share their thoughts about how a funder might be a sister to her organization. Some have expressed that they would like us to advocate for them with other funders. Others request more strategy sessions with similar, women-focused nonprofits. Some grantees noted that they felt isolated in their efforts and worn out from the demands of sustaining arduous social justice struggles. These women asked us for soul care programs and initiatives focused on building and refreshing the spirit. We are most fulfilled as grantmakers when we are able to make meaningful connections with our grantee sisters.

Helen and Kanyere, Sisters in Collaboration

A most rewarding aspect of our work with the Sister Fund is the relationship we enjoy as co-creators of the unfolding; dynamic vision of the foundation. We share deep spiritual roots that are nourished and sustained by our faith. Ours is a mutual sense of pride in seeing women and girls flourish and actualize when provided with the appropriate resources and opportunities. We both acknowledge a sense of call to be agents of change in the society and culture so that the circumstances that negatively affect women's lives will become more just. We agree that spirituality underlies transformation and that right relationship can bring about life-changing connection. We share the discipline of prayer and cherish the notion of infinite possibility when human agency colludes with the plans and courses of divinity.

Being each other's keeper requires that we empty ourselves to hear and try to empathize with each other. Being each other's keeper has meant that we tell each other the truth and are candid about our differences. Being keepers to one another means affirming one another's successes. It is relationship that makes our experience of the Sister Fund rich, rewarding, and fulfilling, and we are grateful for the divine orchestration that caused our lives to intersect.

Conclusion

Entreat me not to leave you, or to turn back from following you! Where you go, I will go; where you lodge, I will lodge; your people shall be my people, and your God my God.

Ruth 1:16

The competition and resentment characteristic of the fraternal relationship between Cain and Abel will not promote the healing work of women's funds or support the precious lives that these organizations help to sustain. A new paradigm is needed—one that exalts the kinds of relationships that forge and nurture meaningful connection. A tenacious spirit of sisterhood stands in resistance to traditional patriarchal values, asserting instead an ethic of mutuality, an impulse toward reciprocity, and a desire to be in right relationship. The biblical story of the bond between Ruth and Naomi is a valuable model of sister support.

When Naomi's husband and married sons die, she leaves the foreign country of Moab where they were residing, with plans to head home to Bethlehem. Feeling that she has nothing left to offer her daughters-in-law, she urges them to return to their own families in Moab. One agrees to return to her own people, but Ruth feels that she is already with her kin, in the company of Naomi. Without biological relation or moral obligation, Ruth vows her unwavering commitment to accompany and support this older, vulnerable woman. Youthful vigor renders Ruth the more able of the two to support their household. Wisdom, intuition, and experience provide Naomi with the insight to advise Ruth until she finds stability and comfort in a marital relationship. Together, they forge a meaningful and productive reality for themselves and a secure future for the generations that will follow.

Often we are reluctant to use words like "covenant" and "commitment" when we talk about relationships with other professionals. Recently, a colleague shared her struggle in introducing the language of "loving kindness" to the board and staff of the century-old organization she led. Reflecting on its original mission and vision, she discovered that its founders used such language when establishing the work and the ethic that directed it. Many thought it was inappropriate to use the term "love," preferring "concern" or "consideration." The trouble is, concern flounders and grows thin in the face of financial hardship. Consideration works when there is little competition, but capitulates in the face of sustained difficulty. Real commitments are harder to come by. They are more costly to maintain but well worth the time. At the Sister Fund, we are not afraid of love.

NOTES

1. Sarah Forten Purvis, a member of the Philadelphia Female Slavery Society, wrote poems and essays for the *Liberator* under the pseudonym Ada. Her 1831 poem the "Lady of Philadelphia" was set to music by the black composer, Francis Johnson. ("The Forten Women: 1805–1883," *Africans in America*, PBS, September 12, 2003.)

2. The kneeling woman, initially used by the Ladies Negro's Friend Society of Birmingham, England, first appeared in print in America in the May 1830 issue of Benjamin Lundy's *Genius of Universal Emancipation*. By 1836, the image was adopted as the emblem of the American women's anti-slavery movement (*Africans in America*, PBS, September 17, 2003).

3. *American Heritage Dictionary*, 4th ed., s.v. "sister" (Boston: Houghton Mifflin, 2000).

4. Leah Wise, quoted in *A Grantmaker's Journey: The Sister Fund: A Report on the First Five Years*, (1998), 12.

5. The Sister Fund collaborated with the Ms. Foundation for Women in providing a grant to support research being done by Angela Bonavoglia on Catholic women's endeavors toward gender equity in the Church. The Sister Fund made two grants to Muslim feminist theologian Dr. Riffat Hassah, director of the International Network for the Rights of Female Victims of Violence in Pakistan.

6. *A Grantmaker's Journey: The Sister Fund: A Report on the First Five Years*, p. 14.

7. Nelle K. Morton, "The Rising of Woman's Consciousness in a Male Language Structure," *Andover Newton Quarterly* 12, no. 4 (March 1972): 177–190.

8. Charlotte Bunch, "Whose Security? Challenges Ahead for Global Feminism," *The Nation*, September 2002.

9. Source of M. J. Gage quote: Elizabeth Cady Stanton, Susan B. Anthony, and Matilda Joslyn Gage, eds. *The History of Woman Suffrage* vol. 1, 1848–1861 (Rochester, N.Y.: Charles Mann, 1889 [1881]) 742–743.

10. Luchina Fisher, "Foundations Dig Up Their Own Data on Girls, Women," *Women'sENews*, May 20, 2003.

11. "I am because we are" is the most elegant translation I've heard of the Nguni word "Ubuntu," where Nguni is the collective name for a group of Southern African languages including Xhosa and Zulu. It's a beautiful sentiment, sometimes also translated as "humanity to others," with implications that extend much further. It lies behind much that is deeply appealing about African culture. Source of "We are therefore I am" http://www.elca.org/jle/articles/contemporary-issues/article.perry-richard.html.Ubuntu.

12. Imago Relationships International is a nonprofit organization with affiliations worldwide.

13. Patriocinio P. Schweickart, "Speech is Silver, Silence is Gold: The Asymmetrical Intersubjectivity of Communicative Action," in *Knowledge, Difference and Power: Essays Inspired by Women's Ways of Knowing*, ed. Nancy Rule Goldberger, et al. (New York: Basic Books, 1996), 306.

THE FUTURE OF FUNDING

E-Philanthropy and Other Innovations

CHRISTINE KWAK, GAIL MCCLURE,
AND ANNE C. PETERSEN

June 20, 2002. New York City — Americans gave an estimated $212 billion to charity in 2001, according to research findings in Giving USA. . . . "Commitment to philanthropy remained strong even in the face of downward economic pressures. The $212 billion total is the highest level of giving ever reported. Even adjusted for inflation, the total is the second-highest on record."

Giving USA Foundation annual report, American
Association of Funding Council Press Release

Every year since 1955, we are given one yardstick of American generosity through the Giving USA survey. Every year, we watch the mark on that yardstick rise, in spite of inflation or economic downturn. Impressive growth, and yet this yardstick cannot begin to measure the informal giving taking place in neighborhoods and along backcountry roads. When asked, most people don't even know what the word "philanthropy" means. But what they do know in their bones is that they've been on both the giving and receiving end most of their lives and that it's crucial to our way of life.

Across all boundaries of race, class, gender, age, or ability, giving is an ongoing part of the human experience. Increasingly, giving in the United States is being examined through various lenses. We've long known the giving levels and practices of large private foundations or corporations, but—once nonexistent—studies of giving by women, cultural communities, and youth are on the rise. There is an increasing recognition of the important contributions made by these groups to philanthropy.

Trends of the Future and the Role of Women

This chapter paints a broad brushstroke of future trends in philanthropy and acknowledges specifically the role and contributions being made by women to the creation of that future. Women and girls are both contributing to philanthropy and benefiting from it. As benefactors, women of wealth increasingly are becoming major donors while grassroots efforts increasingly organize giving by women. The proportion of women employed and holding trustee positions in foundations is growing, with the newest addition being foundations funded by girls for girls. Women increasingly are holding executive positions in the foundation world. As more corporations understand the need to reach out to the communities they serve, women are being given the opportunity to use their relational capacities to start new corporate outreach programs and foundations, or to step into fund development positions in smaller community foundations. As these positions once held for men are filled by women, the collective skill base and stature of women is uplifted. Both philanthropy, and the women contributing to and within it, are forever changed.

At the Kellogg Foundation, we define philanthropy as the giving of time, money, and know-how to advance the common good, and we believe that philanthropy is a habit that must be practiced early and often. We acknowledge that one chapter cannot do justice to the complexity of this field that is reinventing itself as it grows. Yet, from our experience of funding women's philanthropy, we can highlight examples of effective giving by and for women and girls. Some of these examples are innovative, some traditional, but all are given with the conviction that effective giving involves applying a gender lens. Universal giving to everyone often fails to meet specific needs—particularly the needs of women and girls. The old saying echoed by grandmothers and corporations alike has a particular ring here: By serving everyone, you serve no one. Perhaps more important, and a theme reiterated in this book, is a recognition of women as historical social change agents worldwide. The resounding theme is, if you want to change the world, fund women. A confluence of social, economic, and cultural trends is driving change in philanthropy and the "winds of this change" are being felt across the foundation community. So says Lucy Bernholz in her paper, *The Industry of Philanthropy: Highlights from Key Industry Analyses*, as she discusses six trends in play at this time.[1]

The first trend is the *growth of the philanthropic sector*, which is projected to double within the next ten years. Phenomena such as the intergenerational transfer of wealth, the creation of new wealth, and the formation of new "conversion foundations" as formerly nonprofit organizations become privatized are a few of the forces behind this growth. The exponential growth has spurred an era of affiliation and association, with foundations aligning in a patchwork of common characteristics ranging from geography, to interest areas, to demographic identities. Advocates for women and girls are well represented here in such organizations as Women and Philanthropy, the Women's Funding Network, and the Women's Donor's Network.

The second trend is *the burgeoning availability of new tools and services* to facilitate giving, such as e-philanthropy and the explosion of charitable management by financial services firms, such as Fidelity. Community foundations, women's funds, and other regional entities are being pushed into changes by the growth and aggressiveness of charitable management services in the private financial sector that use the Internet with great fluidity. Once looked upon with skepticism, Internet-based giving and Internet services for donors, foundations, and nonprofits have skyrocketed in the last five years, with individual givers serving as the target population for e-philanthropy.

The third trend involves the advent of *business ideology and influence* into the philanthropic sector. Philanthropy has been and will continue to be shaped and pushed by the culture of entrepreneurship that now characterizes the American economy, particularly the technology arena. Unheard of a decade ago, social entrepreneurs and venture philanthropists challenge the traditional operating assumptions of foundations. Venture philanthropy has become a popular approach used by market sector entrepreneurs to apply their own savvy and knowledge to the work of those social entrepreneurs they deem worthy of their investment. This blurring of lines, which historically separated the public, private, and nonprofit sectors, challenges philanthropy's operating principles and in some cases, legal mandates.

Changes in the nation's demographic base represent the fourth trend at play. The growth in numbers of elderly Americans, people of color, and the rise of second- and third-generation professional women is changing both the landscape and the dynamics of life in communities across the nation. A "democratization of philanthropy" is occurring, with new forms and tools opening the doors to people of lesser means than the traditional wealthy associated with charitable giving. The diversity of people participating in philanthropy is on the rise, with women and young people benefiting more from efforts to diversify. Estimates of the intergenerational transfer of wealth from aging baby boomers to their heirs range from $40 to $150 trillion, with no surefire models for predicting how and to what extent some of this wealth will be dedicated to philanthropic endeavors.

The fifth trend is marked by *changes in public funding practices*, such as the devolution of decision making and financial support from the federal government to state and local jurisdictions. Many forms of local and regional charities are emerging, organized by interest areas, geographic community, or simply the similarities of their donors. The Kellogg Foundation, along with other national and regional funders, collectively assessed the impact of this devolution process and collectively supported active civic participation and policy education by those most affected by the proposed changes. (For example, once silent mothers on welfare became involved in the welfare reform process.)

Finally, the sixth trend involves the *increasing visibility of philanthropy*. Public awareness has grown in response to stepped-up media coverage of notable donors such as Bill and Melinda Gates and Paul Newman, increased attention to hospital conversion foundations, as well as an increased effort on the part of foundations to communicate the work of their grantees. As visibility increases, so does scrutiny. The recent economic downturn and Congressional investigation into tax evasion by corporations has raised questions and concerns about philanthropy and its role, rights, and responsibilities, with the creation of new legislation regarding charitable giving underway.

A Not-So-Deliberate Evolution

These trends as well as others have spurred adaptation and evolution in philanthropy; sometimes easily and other times with great angst. Yet in times of both economic boom and bust, amidst the growing pressure to do better in responding to human need and in spite of the many valid criticisms often leveled at philanthropy, many are working hard to do better. These efforts comprise the best of philanthropy's attempts to reinvent itself in a fast-changing world. Reinvention efforts are found in all types of philanthropy, and often are being led by many of the new players, those not traditionally associated with philanthropy of the "golden age" such the Carnegies and Rockefellers. Innovation often is found at the ragged edges of a well-established field, and so too in philanthropy we find the tireless efforts of cultural funds, community foundations, young donors, small venture firms, and women driving much of the change.

Like spring flowers after an April rain, suddenly we see innovation everywhere. Katherine Fulton of the Global Business Network (GBN) has been tracking a sampling of innovations. GBN admits that not all of these activities will survive due to lack of support or simply not working, "but when looked at as a whole, together, these activities represent the seeds of a very promising new era in philanthropy."[2] Regardless of the predictability of their future, these innovations are worth noting. In the area of social investing, the Acumen Fund is launching an approach akin to a mutual fund for philanthropists. Funders concerned about a particular issue, such as international development, come together around a "portfolio" of organizations dedicated to the same purpose. Another new kid on the block, founded by young donors, the Active Element Foundation promotes "hip hop" philanthropy by supporting young leaders and youth organizations "to save our ass in the twenty-first century."

Although foundations traditionally are looked to for their monetary assets, they hold a wealth of other assets. Information or knowledge assets come from their experience of investing in people, organizations, and communities. Foundations hold timely knowledge about social trends, community change, organizational capacity building, policy education, and other ingredients essential to social change. Other knowledge assets include data on key issues, staff experience with specific strategies and community members, research reports, and evaluation data. Assets also include community relationships, convening skills, and the ability to draw together disparate information and people to address complicated issues.[3]

The Kellogg Foundation is one among many putting more than its monetary assets to work on behalf of philanthropy by and for women and girls. Recognizing the potential of the moment, through its Philanthropy and Volunteerism Program Area, Kellogg launched an Unleashing New Resources Strategy designed to increase the ranks of new givers and nurture emerging forms of philanthropy. Kellogg seeks to support promising innovation. In surveying philanthropy, Kellogg found a large percentage of innovation taking place in six population groups quite often at the cutting edge of social change: new wealth creators, youth, communities of color, corporate social innovators, social entrepreneurs, and—of particular interest here—women. In supporting innovation led by women, Kellogg is working to unleash new resources of time, money, and know-how for social good.

Kellogg has looked to that philanthropy happening on the outside edges of the field—that of populations who have learned that they can advance faster and farther if they move together. It is here that women's philanthropy has much to teach from its own decades of experience. "Necessity is the mother of invention," and women's groups learned many years ago the power of networks, alliances, and knowledge sharing. Here is where Kellogg has placed its investment dollars in the women's philanthropy field; on growing the networks of those that fund women and girls. By focusing on field building along with capacity and asset development, the knowledge and experience base of women's philanthropy can be strengthened and connected to the broader realm of philanthropy as well as to the general population of potential donors.

Capturing innovation and effective implementation of creative approaches to philanthropy and disseminating those findings is also a key purpose of this programming. Active projects underway with the Women's Funding Network to track innovation in the area of fund development with new economy donors, women of color, and giving circles, as well as benchmarking the success of women's funds, will contribute much to the knowledge base of women's philanthropy.

Women's Role in Philanthropy, Related Employment, and Leadership

The demographics of foundation employees have changed in the last twenty years. Once a field dominated by white males, women are now the majority and almost 20 percent of the program staff are people of color. The numbers of women being hired increased dramatically beginning in 1986. By 1998, women comprised 66 percent of program staff. Women were slower to enter CEO positions until the mid-1990s. By 1998, approximately half of all CEOs were women. People of color represented 6 percent of all CEOs in 1998, rising from 1.6 percent in 1982.[4]

These statistics have lent themselves to an interest in assisting women of color to rise to leadership positions in foundations. An example of one such leadership and training program is the Women of Color Development Incubator being piloted by the Women's Funding Network. The incubator is a fast-track program for women of color focusing on capacity building in the fund development arena. Fluency and a record of success in this single area is a well-known high priority in searches for both foundation executives and trustees. Contributing to the growth of female foundation CEOs was the burgeoning number of women's funds sprouting up across the United States during the same twenty-year period.

By way of more than numbers, women throughout the United States have shown themselves to be leaders in philanthropy's reinvention of itself. In every area of philanthropy, we see women stepping up to the plate

In 1980, there were nine women's funds in the United States. By 1985, thirty-four funds existed and the combined assets of ten funds reporting yielded $1.2 million in assets. By 2001, seventy-eight women had been added to the list of foundation CEOs. The seventy-eight funds led by these CEOs collectively held $213 million in assets, and in that year distributed $30 million in grants and raised over $79 million for the cause of women and girls.

Women's Funding Network, www.wfnet.org

and serving as the early adopters who spur innovation. Marie Wilson of the Ms. Foundation fought early on to gain the confidence of investors to "bank on poor women," developing successful micro-enterprise with low-income women when it was not popular to do so. Upon the sudden death of her husband, Irene Diamond took the reigns of the Diamond family funds to invest in AIDS research, civil rights, and the arts when others were afraid. Jean Fairfax, of the Arizona Community Foundation, is beloved in the philanthropy world for her early leadership in increasing gender and racial diversity throughout philanthropy and the nonprofit sector. At a pivotal time, Helen Hunt focused her family fund to support women's and girls' issues, mentored countless other donors to do the same, and repeatedly has stepped up to the plate at crucial times shepherding the women's philanthropy movement into its maturation. Susan Berresford, president of the Ford Foundation, is honored for her work to advance the status of women throughout her career. This short list shows women active across the spectrum of foundations. The list could go on, and it does. For each one named here, there are a thousand others increasing the effectiveness of philanthropy by bringing cutting-edge practice and innovation to the challenge of social change.

New Faces, New Forces, New Forms
E-Philanthropy

By the end of 1999, seventy-eight million adults in the United States had access to the Internet.[5] For millions, it is now an essential tool for everyday life. People use it to get the information they need for work and play, to build and maintain communities, and to buy everything from groceries to cars. As more users are logging on, electronic commerce ("e-commerce") is exploding. Researchers estimate that consumer online spending topped $24 billion in the United States in 1999 and will go to $65 billion by 2004 (www.comscore.com).

At the same time, social activism is emerging online. Internet use is becoming more diverse, with women making up 49 percent of active users by the end of 1999.[6] As the volume and diversity of users increase, the Internet is becoming a fertile meeting place for people who have the desire to support social change—and the means to contribute to it. It allows individuals and organizations to communicate cheaply and efficiently over great distances, making it easier to connect causes to advocates, volunteers, and donors. The Internet explosion is creating exciting possibilities for proponents of positive social change. With the right tools, the Web can become a new populist venue where ease of access attracts new donors, including women, to the nonprofit sector.[7]

A growing sector of e-commerce is called "e-philanthropy." It uses the Internet as a tool for charitable and cause-related giving. Large and mid-sized nonprofits are asking for donations online. Profit-making corporations are finding that mixing charity with sales can be a powerful marketing tool. Many companies promise shoppers an automatic charitable contribution when they buy a product or browse an advertisement-laden Web site. Other for-profit companies offer "charity malls" in which they collect donations online and pass them on to recipients for free as a lost-leader for providing lucrative online donation services to corporations and large nonprofits.

Companies proposing to help fundraise on the Internet tend to fall into three categories. The first category is the "charity portal" Web sites that offer a directory of nonprofits. They work to attract traffic to their sites and encourage visitors to make contributions to the nonprofits listed. Often, the listing is free and the portal accepts secured credit card contributions. These portals make their money either from advertising on their site or through the fees they charge the nonprofit. The second category is the "payment service providers" who specialize in handling secure credit card systems for nonprofits. They earn profits through a fee structure based on the contributions received by nonprofits. The nonprofit puts a button on its site so that when a visitor is ready to give, they are switched over for the transaction to take place. The third category are the "e-commerce commission portals," where members are actively encouraged to do their e-commerce shopping through a portal, with a percentage of the purchases going to the buyer's nonprofit of choice.[8]

Beyond merely raising more dollars for nonprofits, the Internet can spread the concepts of philanthropy to a broader spectrum of the public. It opens avenues for empowering a new generation of donors and millions of others—not just encouraging them to give, but helping them to do it wisely, effectively, and strategically. Today's communication technology also can enable nonprofit organizations to recruit new allies who will help achieve their missions. The Network for Good currently is considered by many to be the Internet's largest charitable resource—an e-philanthropy site where individuals can donate, volunteer, and speak out on the issues they care about. Network for Good is bringing electronic philanthropy into the mainstream of the Internet and helping nonprofits obtain online fundraising.

While the potential is great and the timing is right, this new medium also presents major obstacles for nonprofit organizations and those donors trying to pursue a thoughtful approach to philanthropy. Such obstacles include:

- *Entry costs and the digital divide.* New e-commerce technologies are costly to start up and maintain. Although even smaller organizations are finding ways to create a basic Web page, the next level of infrastructure is more difficult to manage. The poorest of the poor with the least access to the new economy are falling farther and farther behind. It is estimated that the average asset base of African American and Hispanic families is $4,500 or less. With many of these families headed by women, the issues of both gender and race come into play as factors in the new economy.[9]

- *Skills needed to navigate the Internet; state registration laws.* Currently, most states have expensive and time-consuming registration requirements for organizations doing fundraising on the Internet. Any organization seeking online donations risks expensive legal challenges from those states if it does not register.

- *Emerging conflicts and privacy standards.* Currently, the field of e-philanthropy is dominated by for-profit entities funded by venture capitalists. Many have the best of motives, but there can be conflicts between the needs of business and the interests of altruism.

Yet, not all small grassroots nonprofits are being left out. The Tides Foundation of San Francisco is bringing the basics of e-philanthropy to grassroots organizations and the women's funding community, directly addressing some of the challenges mentioned above. In 2000, the Kellogg Foundation funded what was then a new and innovative effort by Tides to incorporate women's philanthropy organizations into a new e-philanthropy program designed to match donors and nonprofit organizations via the Internet. A rapid explosion of such sites would soon follow.

Seizing an opportunity to expand social change philanthropy dramatically, Tides created eGrants.org, a charity portal to promote "best practices"

Table 1. Differences between E-Philanthropy and Charity

	Traditional Charity	E-Philanthropy
Who	the wealthy	everyone
What	donating money	investing their time, skills, and money
How	centralized organizations	directly with people who need assistance
Why	broad humanitarian goals	personalized projects, with direct feedback
Result	impersonal aid	highly focused tools and resources

Source: Greenstar Foundation

in philanthropy on the Internet. Internet technology allowed eGrants to assist nonprofit organizations and donors in a way that had not been possible before. The protal was positioned uniquely to bring a new model of philanthropy to the Internet in a program that would: identify and screen progressive charitable organizations doing important and effective work, present clear information on those organizations to potential donors in a compelling and easy-to-use format on the Internet, and efficiently collect contributions from the donors, passing them on to appropriate nonprofit recipients who may lack the technical expertise to raise that revenue directly. Part of the eGrants program was geared to work with key women's philanthropy organizations such as the Women's Funding Network, its member funds, and Women and Philanthropy. These organizations could use eGrants to take online donations directly from their Web sites, allowing them to educate, solicit donations from, and build relationships with previous and new donors without the need for each to develop its own e-commerce technology or to meet onerous and complex state charitable registration requirements.

Today, eGrants, now named Groundspring, segregates its grantees into sixteen issues areas ranging from arts, culture, and the media to social justice. It is one of the few such services that break out women as a separate issue area or cause. A sample of organizational users in the "Women's issues" area of cause listings includes: Dallas Women's Foundation; GirlSource; Third Wave Foundation; Women's Funding Network; and Women's WORLD.

The growth in online fundraising mirrors the surge in political activity on the Internet. A new political digest, *NBC's First Read* (FirstRead@ MSNBC.com, daily memo-date not known) observes: "We are struck by how the Internet has more than arrived in American politics. The proliferation of online organizing/fundraising, and of online campaign coverage, involves more people in the process and picks it apart like never before." Those looking to make a difference by "empowering women in politics, media, society, the economy, and cyberspace" are turning to www.WLO.org, using the Web to do it. Women Leaders Online is one of the largest women's activist groups on the Net. Their mission is to educate voters on women's issues and to encourage pro-woman candidates to seek office. WLO.org is committed to voter education—educating the public on women's issues. The group uses its Web site to provide "netizens" with a broad array of voter guides, feminine activist links, political news links, and other online resources. Periodic e-mail Action Alerts keep members aware of the latest WLO.org news. Women Leaders Online is building an advocacy community of one million members through an extensive e-mail network. The power of this network was shown when the group mounted an e-mail campaign challenging Amazon.com's ad support of Rush Limbaugh's radio program. As a result, Amazon.com pulled its ads from the program. Women Leaders Online has shown that women's issues have a loud voice and fundraising potential on the Internet.[10]

Another example of campaign Internet fundraising is EMILY's List, a political network for pro-choice Democratic women candidates that raises early money to make women credible contenders. EMILY stands for "Early Money Is Like Yeast" ("we help the 'dough' rise"). Mothers Against Drunk Driving (MADD), the nation's preeminent group fighting drunk driving and underage drinking while supporting victims regularly upgrades its Internet infrastructure to ensure that its online fundraising, influencing public policy, raising awareness, and developing strong relationships with supporters is as simple as possible.[11]

A Kellogg Foundation report, "e-Philanthropy 2001: From Entrepreneurial Adventure to an Online Community," highlights a few other trends:

- While many sites have failed to continue, or struggle because of inadequate investment or philanthropic support, insufficient revenue, or poor business plans, others sites have emerged from the tumultuous "dot-conomy." These tend to offer a variety of services with a robust offline network of supporters and members.
- Larger sites specializing in donor and nonprofit relationships have experienced successful growth. In 1999, the AOL Foundation's helping .org raised $300,000 in donations for a multitude of charities; it raised $1.6 million in 2000.
- Click-to-give campaigns flourished in 2000, with sites such as endcancernow.com expanding on the successful Hunger Site model, with online shopping malls growing in number, but being less financially successful.
- Key services are being created daily—the "killer app" (killer technology application) will be the one that weaves together diverse services and unifies numerous needs and opportunities in one accessible place; in effect an "eco-system" for the sector with give-and-take dynamics in action for all users.
- Finally, the Kellogg report suggests that nonprofits still need more tools to understand the online "business to business" services available, and nonprofits themselves need to be willing to invest more in technology solutions to increase the efficacy of their operations.

Online fundraising for nonprofits still has a long way to go before it makes a dent in revenue projections, but those watching the growth say that we can safely assume, as with e-commerce, that people will eventually become more familiar and more comfortable making donations online. Although women were significantly less likely than men to use the Internet in the mid 1990s, this gender gap disappeared by 2000.[12] Today, women and their organizations are aggressively taking advantage of the opportunities afforded both for fundraising and giving online as well as applying their talents in organizing. The "telephone tree," long-tested through time as a way for women to mobilize, has now transformed into a "technology tree." Lightening quick and wide in reach, the Internet is helping women connect and join forces faster and farther than ever before.

New Twists on Traditional Forms of Giving

In recent years, new and innovative forms of philanthropy have emerged in response to the social and economic factors discussed earlier in this chapter. Often these new forms of giving are twists on more traditional giving methods, or they can be complete departures from what most people think of as philanthropy.

Venture Philanthropy

One such twist that has gathered momentum over the last five years is venture philanthropy. Venture philanthropy came of age during the boom of the New Economy and borrows both language and approach from the venture capital world, with the fundamental difference being an emphasis on the social return of investment. With a focus on donors who give both financial resources and intellectual capital, venture philanthropy often seeks to fund intensively to build capacity and grow strong nonprofit organizations.

An emerging trend in venture philanthropy is the "social venture fund," a type of giving circle or pooled fund involving a number of donors who invest in nonprofits through collaborative grantmaking. There are a number of venture philanthropy funds that an individual can join. Each is different in what it asks from donors, in terms of involvement in grantmaking, and intellectual capital provided to selected nonprofits. There are also individuals who are venture philanthropists and who, through their private foundations or direct gifts, make strategic donations that are often multi-year, capacity-building, or operational in nature. Venture philanthropists fund organizations that support enterprising nonprofits and social entrepreneurs with financial resources as well as technical support over a sustained period. Investors make long-term funding commitments, closely monitor performance objectives through pre-defined measurement tools, and problem-solve jointly with the nonprofit leadership team on a regular basis. Like private sector entrepreneurs, this often means bringing to-gether people and resources, including funding from other sources.

Some social venture fund models include New Profit Inc., founded by two young women in their twenties to attract new financial and intellec-tual capital to the nonprofit sector and to develop new financing mecha-nisms for investing in social entrepreneurs; and Social Venture Partners, which seeks to build a focused, committed, and effective philanthropic community in the Puget Sound region by tapping into the personal and financial resources of a new generation of high-tech professionals.

An early player in the field, the Roberts Enterprise Development Fund (REDF) focuses wealth creation and economic development for the homeless using a social venture capital practice with social entrepreneurs to achieve impact. The process of change that has led to the emergence of the "new social entrepreneur" and the "social venture capitalist" has taken place not as a result of the efforts of one or the other. It has happened through a process of individuals on both sides of the table concluding that the traditional approach is lacking.[13] The practice of using a concept like "social venture capital" requires a new language to describe this blended approach of both business and community constructs. The shift in lan-guage represents a fundamental re-definition of roles, responsibilities, and approaches to the funding relationship.

In their article "Virtuous Capital," Christine Letts, William Ryan, and Allen Grossman propose that recent traditions of philanthropy have been based on "program efficacy" and that new approaches to philanthropy are more focused on "organizational capacity."[14] As a result, new approaches to philanthropy, especially venture philanthropy, are moving away from an emphasis on demonstration programs as solutions and moving toward an investment model for innovative ideas and solid organizations that can

Table 2. Venture Philanthropy Shifts the Language of Giving

Old	New
Grants	Grant equity
Funder	Investor
Grantee	Investee
Evaluation	Measurement
Grant proposal	Business Plan

Source: Stanford Graudate School of Business case study "The Roberts Enterprise Development Fund: Implementing a Social Venture Capital Approach to Philanthropy," October, 1998. Avaliable through the Roberts Enterprise Development Foundation office (www.redf.org).

get the innovations "to market." Harvard University's Letts is among many women who are considered thought leaders in philanthropy. Keeping an eye on both compassion and capacity, Letts's current research includes the impact of donor behavior and funding models on nonprofit organizational capacity.

More than a new approach or method of giving, however, the new donors are underwriting a remarkable era of creativity and innovation. Many of them left corporate or entrepreneurial pasts to turn their attention to the nonprofit sector. Catherine Muther quit her job as marketing vice-president at Cisco Systems in 1994. With her high-tech marketing experience, Stanford University MBA, and $2 million from Cisco stock options, she started her own private foundation, calling it the Three Guineas Fund after the 1938 book by Virginia Woolf. The book takes the form of three letters, each a reply to the request for a guinea: one to prevent war and preserve intellectual liberty; one to educate women; and one to promote their employment. In it, Woolf lays out a vision of women's education and economic independence as the foundation of social equity and justice. Muther founded Three Guineas in the same spirit, to create economic opportunity for women and girls.

Three Guineas strategy, criteria, and philanthropy programs are designed to achieve social justice gains that enable women and girls to earn an independent living, participate fully in the economy, and give back to their communities. Muther first created a San Francisco incubator, the Women's Technology Cluster (WTC), to support high-tech start-ups by women entrepreneurs and has since taken the incubator concept a step further—recently launching one to help nonprofit start-ups.

The central objective of the WTC is to facilitate access to capital by women entrepreneurs. While the rate of new business formation by women has grown at a rapid rate, barriers to access to capital persist as a systemic problem for women entrepreneurs. The National Foundation of Women Business Owners reports that of the nearly eight million women-owned businesses in the United States, only 1 percent has used venture capital financing. The WTC is designed as a model for breaking structural and cultural barriers by accelerating the growth, reducing the perceived risk, and facilitating access to angel and venture capital financing for women technology entrepreneurs. A second objective of the WTC is to educate entrepreneurs to give back to the community. The WTC is establishing a culture and value system of giving back, influencing entrepreneurs in the formative stages of their businesses.

Those philanthropists emerging from new fortunes define themselves as social entrepreneurs; some of the most outstanding among them are women. They want to solve defined problems in a specific way. They don't want to simply earmark money for "some vaguely benevolent purpose." They focus on performance. They try to make projects self-sustaining. If manufacturing products has been part of their wealth creation, they often make these products part of their giving. They believe strongly that equipping people with tools and investing in them to go out and create "wealth" is a vital part of their philanthropy. Their interpretation of the age-old equity and access challenge revolves around information and knowledge as the new currency and driving equalizer. Their philanthropy often is targeted to economic development first, with the belief that other forms of social and spiritual wealth will follow. "Through high-tech computer and biotech industries, entrepreneurs have had a transformative impact on the economy and on the society," says Catherine Muther. "When these entrepreneurs turn their attention to social issues and philanthropy, nothing less than transformative social change is expected."[15] Muther is only one of many women helping to redefine philanthropy. For every big-money donor, there are hundreds of others below the radar screen who have embraced philanthropy in creative new ways, and among those the numbers of women are rising.

Youth Philanthropy

While venture philanthropists are reinventing how philanthropy is played, some new and important players are entering the funding game. The Michigan Women's Foundation is the architect of one of the nation's first, and growing, girls-as-grantmakers youth philanthropy programs. Launched in 1995, Young Women for Change is organized to maximize girls' experiences in gender-focused philanthropy and grantmaking and to provide leadership development and team-building training in a culturally diverse setting. Young Women for Change grants funds to programs specifically serving young women and girls and addresses gender correlation to poverty, low self-esteem, health and healthcare, access to jobs, domestic violence, and sexual assault.

The program's focus on gender issues not only increases the amount of funding that reaches young women and girls; it also increases awareness of these issues in its young women participants. The young women determine funding priorities, meeting agendas, proposal evaluations, and funding decisions. Each committee grants a minimum of $20,000 annually to nonprofit groups serving the needs of young women and girls in their geographic area. Committee members range in age from fourteen to eighteen years, are drawn from rural, urban, and suburban schools, and represent a range of socioeconomic and racial groups with fifteen to twenty individuals serving at each site. Recruitment strategies support the Michigan Women's Foundation commitment to providing opportunities and direct hands-on experiences that encourage and instill understanding of racial, ethnic, and economic differences as these intersect gender and empower young girls to effect the social change necessary to address disparity and discrimination. Committee members typically serve a two-year term, then select new committee members to succeed themselves. The girls implement the entire grantmaking process, from writing and releasing the Request for Proposals, to conducting site visits, to selecting the final grant recipients.

The need for effective, high-quality girls' programs coupled with the under-funded status of initiatives that directly address issues that affect girls and women serves as the primary foundation for Young Women for Change. In addition, the program teaches philanthropy as a habit and a life-long tool for social change. Youth philanthropy programs have been replicated nationally and internationally, especially in the young women's philanthropy arena. Of the women's funds currently in operation, there are now twelve girls-as-grantmakers programs, with many more in development.

Giving Circles

Women have long exercised the power of collective service to society. Yet, women today are not limiting themselves to contributions of time alone. In many communities, women are creating giving circles, sometimes called donor circles, to fund projects that improve the quality of life in their communities. And while women traditionally have been generous with their inherited wealth, there's a new generation of women with sizable earned income to contribute. Controlling an increasing share of the nation's wealth, women are in a position to take on greater philanthropic responsibilities. "Giving Circles—a kind of social investment club—are an enormously powerful way to impact social change and pave the way for a new frontier in philanthropy," says author Sondra Shaw Hardy, author of a book on the subject.[16] Giving circles enable people to give voice collectively to their values. The difference between most traditional philanthropic efforts and giving circles is that these groups are designed to inspire, educate, and encourage people to become more effective philanthropists.

A 2001 article in the *Boston Globe* examines the growth of giving circles as a philanthropic vehicle for women donors in the Boston area. The article interviews Beth Schultz Klarman, who started a giving circle of her own as a way of finding philanthropic options that go beyond "quietly writing checks with my husband." Klarman and roughly sixty other women

> The Boston Women's Fund's 2000 Club Endowment Fund has nearly reached its million-dollar mark. Among the Club's 1,680 members are a student intern, the dean of a college, a foster parent who decided to set aside $10 a month for five years, immigrant women, a midwife, a legislator, a Seder group, a nine-year-old girl who used savings from her piggy bank, and a group of women honoring their friend's eightieth birthday.
>
> Boston Women's Fund Web site

are contributing at least $10,000 each over five years through the Boston Jewish Community Women's Fund to organizations that focus on issues affecting Jewish women and girls. Each woman who contributes funds through the group is given a vote on how the money is distributed.

Another approach can be found at the Ms. Foundation, which in the past has created highly successful "collaboratives" of foundations funding a social issue such as women's economic development. Their Democracy Funding Circle was formed in 1996 in response to the increasingly conservative political climate that threatened to "roll back" gains made by the women's and civil right's movements. This small circle of nine or so members supports projects that promote a progressive vision of democracy and encourages collaboration among women's groups and other progressive forces to address challenges from the right.[17]

Finally, the Boston Women's Fund's 2000 Club endowment represents an unusual approach to endowment fundraising. Unlike most endowment campaigns targeted to wealthy supporters, the Boston Fund has created a structure enabling people from all walks of life to contribute. The Fund aims to recruit two thousand individuals of diverse economic means who will each donate $500; many give $100 a year for five years. The donors represent a cross-section including those from low, moderate, and middle-income groups as well as those with inherited wealth. Donors are diverse by age, gender, sexual orientation, race, and culture. The 2000 Club is part of a deliberate strategy to build a multi-racial organization and to increase the diversity of the Fund's individual donor base by expanding the numbers of contributors who are women of color, and women of low, moderate, and middle-income groups.

The advantages of forming giving circles are many, including the fact that pooled dollars invested toward a key issue can have a far greater impact than smaller individual donations. Collective "know-how" of a group adds value and impact to volunteerism, and charitable investments and creating partnerships with a smaller number of charities create a deeper level of involvement to better gauge a return on investment.[18]

Global Giving

According to the 2002 edition of *Foundation Giving Trends: Update on Funding Priorities*, growth in international giving—both in the United States and overseas—surpassed gains in domestic support.

One example of global giving on behalf of women is a $1 million grant from the Gates Foundation awarded to the San Francisco–based Global Fund for Women, a public charity that funds grassroots women's groups in the developing world, to provide small strategic grants to other women's groups. Aiming to transform their communities, these women work to improve access to quality healthcare, education, and economic opportunity for women. Worldwide, sexually transmitted diseases afflict five times as many women as men, and in parts of Africa, where many women lack access to quality healthcare, adolescent girls are six times more likely to be infected with HIV/AIDS than boys. The grant from the Gates Foundation aims to further the work of the Global Fund by making it possible for them to support organizations such as Kenya-based Women Fighting AIDS, which organizes home-based teams of nurses, caregivers, and counselors to help women caring for family members with HIV/AIDS.[19]

With grants ranging between $500 and $15,000 and averaging $6,500, recipients are not required to provide detailed documentation on how the grant money will be spent. Kavita Ramdas, president and CEO of the fund, emphasizes, "Our philosophy is trust, trust, trust, respect, respect, respect. We want to empower women and help them exercise their rights. If you trust that women know what they're doing, you don't need to micromanage the projects. We're saying 'You can use this money however you think will best help your organization.'" The fund is the brainchild of Anne Firth Murray, who had worked at large charitable foundations and in the mid-1980s wanted to create a funding resource for women who had their own ideas about how to help their communities. "What was needed was not just a source of money, but a source that would respond to what women themselves wanted rather than the agendas of the foundations. . . .

> Support for overseas recipients and for international programs in the United States climbed 86.4 percent between 1999 and 2000, from $1.3 billion to roughly $2.5 billion. As a result, international giving as a share of overall foundation funding in the sample rose from 11.3 to 16.3 percent—the highest share on record. Growth in support for overseas recipients surpassed the overall gain with a more than doubling in grant dollars from $430.1 million to $901.3 million.
>
> *Foundation Giving Trends*

The idea of women actually making change in their society was very powerful and it really caught people's imagination."[20]

Cultural Funds

As the face of America is changing, so is the face of philanthropy. With the number of millionaires in the United States on the rise, corporate executives, entertainers, authors, sports figures, and other successful individuals from communities of color take their place among them. And at the same time, the percentage of African American, Latino, and Asian American households with rising incomes is growing, while tribal enterprises are improving the economic circumstances of many Native Americans. In the years ahead, the baby boomers in these groups stand to inherit their parents' holdings as well. These changes represent an opportunity to increase the stability and independence of communities of color by increasing the assets of these communities designated for philanthropic purposes. Each of these communities has cherished traditions of caring for others—-"helping out" . . . "giving back" . . . "just what you do." An awareness of these traditions and how they shape giving behavior is vital to the success of understanding how best to support efforts taking place around the country to grow formal philanthropy in each cultural community.

Beginning in 1996, the Kellogg, Ford, Packard, and Mott foundations, along with the Council on Foundations, launched a project to foster the growth of philanthropy and volunteerism in communities of color. The Emerging Funds for Communities of Color project worked to seek out and develop practices and policies that support philanthropy in communities of color, including programming for sustainable funding. Underlying the effort to develop greater capacity for each community to grow philanthropic activity is the community ownership and management of charitable resources through ethnic funds and related charitable vehicles. Through a promotion of goodwill and improved understanding among all ethnic and racial communities that support asset accumulation as a common challenge, a commitment to new forms and diverse values that broadly reflect multiple cultures emerged.

The Emerging Funds project identified and strengthened creative national and local efforts across all ethnic and racial communities. For instance, in New York City, local Latino community-based organizations have little time and few resources to solicit individual contributions actively. This lack of success in individual fundraising has resulted in a number of innovative initiatives. On a national scale, the Ford Foundation and others have supported an initiative by the nation's largest Latino organization, the National Council of La Raza, to expand membership and thus increase individual contributions as a source of revenue. More locally, an effort led by the Hispanic Federation and supported by the Avon Products Foundation and the New York Community Trust, has had a demonstrable impact on the success of Latino organizations in securing individual contributions.

Of particular interest to the topic of women's philanthropy is the existence of a fund representing both race and gender in its focus: the African American Women's Fund at the Twenty-First Century Foundation (AAWF) in New York. The Twenty-First Century Foundation is one of the few public foundations focused on the African American community. Founded in 1971, the foundation has made grants to more than 250 organizations working on black community development and renewal, as well as youth leadership and education. AAWF supports organizations and individuals working for the education and empowerment of African American women. Organized as a Field of Interest Fund, AAWF is a forward-thinking approach for mobilizing the untapped resources of the black community to support black women's initiatives. The fund is designed to harness the resources and talents of African American women to effect change, social justice, and economic development locally and nationally.

The African American Women's Fund uses the networks of its leadership to expand the circle of giving that already exists. They highlight the contributions of financial analyst, Bonita Burrell, who uses her expertise and passion for art to create an economic development opportunity for African artisans by selling their artwork and artifacts at a biannual fundraising event she organizes. The proceeds are donated to the AAWF for grantmaking purposes. This unique fundraising strategy usually generates more than $20,000 at each event.

Yet, wealth alone is not an indicator of the extent of charitable giving among cultural communities. Low- and moderate-income individuals are often very generous when it comes to making financial donations. Oseola McCarty, a cleaning woman at the University of Mississippi, made headlines when it became known that she had donated her life savings of $150,000 to the school for scholarships for minority students. With more than $500 billion in buying power, over 60 percent of African American households give to charity.[21]

Rapid Growth of Small Foundations

The fastest growing area in U.S.-based philanthropy is among small foundations. A majority of these foundations are family foundations, with the National Center for Family Philanthropy estimating that approximately two-thirds of private foundations are family-managed. While the largest family foundations have endowments well over $5 billion, three-quarters have under $1 million in assets.[22]

Given their often-small staff and single-family origins, family foundations are least likely to be diverse in terms of race, class, ethnicity, sexual orientation, and disability when compared to other categories of grant-making institutions, such as large private foundations. They generally appear less compelled to be accountable to outside forces or to comply with societal pressure to conform to changing practices in governance and operations. Their boards, however, do have the best representation of women trustees in the field due to the participation of family members. Among Council on Foundations members with good records of diversity, more women serve on family foundation boards than other types, whereas few people of color are trustees or staff members.[23]

According to the Association for Small Foundations (ASF), small foundations account for half of total foundation funding in the United States, and yet these foundations often feel isolated from the philanthropic community of larger, more-established foundations. As a result, ASF was formed in 1996 to help small foundations with ten or fewer staff members and small budgets succeed in their work. In the past five years, ASF's membership has grown to more than twenty-six hundred organizations. About half of those are operated entirely by volunteers and have endowments of less than $5 million. Collectively, the members manage $50 billion in endowment, and their twenty-five hundred staff members and fourteen thousand trustees distributed more than $2.6 billion in 2000.[24]

No discussion of small foundations would be complete if it did not include women's funds as one type of small public foundation. To distinguish them from other small foundations, women's and girls' funds make it a point to fund undersupported and emerging programs that fund women and girls. These programs are often not yet on the radar of the larger philanthropic community. The funds are ahead of the curve in testing and refining programs and policies that improve the lives of girls and women in the United States and around the world. In so doing, women's and girls' grantmakers chart a new model of social change philanthropy by partnering with their grantees, often creating dynamic collaborative relationships that lessen the distinction between the grantor and grantee.

Trends in Corporate Social Giving

Pressures from an active and vocal civil society along with enlightened corporate leadership are motivating many in the market sector to reconsider how they might be responsible to both their stockholders and the communities in which they live. Needing help with the heavy lifting of social reform, nonprofits long have focused on the corporation's role in society and have worked tirelessly in recent years to establish worldwide standards for corporate social accountability. In their paper, "Misery Loves Companies: Whither Social Initiatives by Business?" Joshua Margolis and James Walsh of Harvard University and the University of Michigan reference a list of forty-seven such initiatives.[25] These corporations endorsing the above examples of principles are part of a vanguard leading the way to a new appreciation between doing business and doing the right thing. Increasingly, companies are reporting efforts to understand and improve their overall impact in society and in the environment.

Foundations also are using their money to advance a business-led social change agenda through such efforts as the Aspen Institute's Initiative for Social Innovation Through Business. The Council on Foundation's Corporate Philanthropy Index helps companies to measure the business value of their corporate philanthropy. The index rates the attitudes of employees, customers, and civic leaders about a company's philanthropic activities as well as showing how attitudes can affect a company's profitability.

Corporate foundations, also called company-sponsored foundations, derive their grantmaking funds from the contributions of a profit-making business. The company-sponsored foundation is a legal organization separate from the company and is subject to the same regulations as other private foundations. As of 2000, there were 2,018 corporate foundations in the United States. Many corporations also are creating philanthropy lookalikes. Fidelity's Charitable Gift Fund and Merrill Lynch's and Vanguard's donor services are similar to donor-directed funds that have been developed by community foundations. While the funds are popular with donors, they have their share of critics, who see them competing perhaps unfairly with local entities such as women's funds and community foundations.[26]

In its Summer 1998 issue, *The American Benefactor* criticized private industry as a whole for allocating only 1.3 percent of pre-tax earnings for charitable purposes. However, the journal found some positive trends in the making, among them that women entrepreneurs are especially generous, contributing an average of 5.2 percent of pre-tax profits to charity.[27]

Business academics long have examined the relationship between business and society. The annual set of essays collected in *Research in Corporate Social Performance and Policy* has been published since 1984. Business school students have organized a social responsibility group called Net-Impact, whose membership has grown from 150 members in 1993 to 5,000 members in 2000. Women are well represented in membership with a history of female executive directors at the helm of the organization. Business for Social Responsibility (BSR) now counts more than 1,400 members worldwide. In BSR's most recent annual conference line up, women are upheld as prominent global leaders dedicated to the social responsibility. Among them are Vandana Shiva, founder of the Research Foundation for Science, Technology and Ecology, whose book *Staying Alive*, dramatically shifted the perception of third-world women; and Marina Silva, the youngest senator ever to serve Brazil, who successfully built support for environmental protection, social justice, and sustainable development in the Amazon. In spite of the recent economic downturn, a social movement clearly appers to be underfoot. Although it is difficult to judge the exact ratio of women in the ranks of this movement, women clearly are present in full force, leading the call to do business with a conscience.

It's one of the oldest questions in the field of business ethics: Does socially responsible behavior affect the bottom line? In essence, does it pay off? The measurement of a corporation's social performance is operationalized in so many different ways that aggregating results becomes meaningless. Some approaches have been tried along a set of multi-dimensional screening criteria, such as a survey of business students or business faculty members, or a company's reputation among business executives, as we see in the *Fortune* surveys. Others assess a firm's conduct in South Africa, the presence or absence of women and minority directors, the quality of an organization's environmental management record, and the magnitude of a company's philanthropic contributions.

While scholars continue to debate whether social performance contributes to financial performance, companies continue to invest in a wide range of social initiatives. Margolis and Walsh cite research showing that companies' philanthropic contributions more than quadrupled, in real terms, between 1950 and 2000, and go on to say that the reasons executives give for these investments typically have more to do with "an ineffable sense that this work is the right thing to do than with the anticipated returns that shareholders will reap from these investments."[28]

Companies have much to gain from being good citizens. The *New York Times* reports that corporate branding arrangements are growing in popularity. As cutbacks in public funding for nonprofit groups and activities have challenged nonprofits nationwide, corporations, aware of the benefits of projecting a socially responsible image, have been quick to pick up the slack. Corporate giving to nonprofit groups rose from roughly $8 billion in 1996 to more than $11 billion in 1999, according to Giving USA. Yet, corporate philanthropy is particularly susceptible to the changing state of the economy. Corporate foundation giving grew more than 50 percent in constant dollars between 1995 and 2000, due in large part to the strong performance of the economy. However, a weakened economy is ex-pected to affect giving negatively.[29]

Another aspect to corporate giving is in serving women entrepreneurs, where "doing good" has a direct correlation to new business markets. Women-owned businesses rapidly are becoming a more powerful and com-petitive economic force in America. In 1995, partnering with the National Association for Women Business Owners (NAWBO), Wells Fargo intro-duced the Women's Loan Program—the first of its kind—with the goal of providing capital to women business owners. Since 1995, more than 227,000 women business owners have received loans, with their current lending goal being $10 billion over ten years to women-owned businesses.[30]

And while one company works with entrepreneurs, another works to ensure a pathway to becoming entrepreneurial. To alleviate poverty, indi-viduals must have access to resources and possess the skills to acquire and manage financial assets—yet youth and women continue to struggle against social norms and financial institutions that limit this type of access and discourage education and training. Focusing specifically on indigent women and youth, the Levi Strauss Company and Foundation funds pro-grams that promote micro-business, workforce development, and financial literacy, and encourage individual development/learning accounts leading to economic independence. Where poor youth—in particular girls—are denied access to an education, Levi Strauss funds programs globally that seek to build support among families, teachers, community leaders, and policy makers for these youth to attend school, address barriers to access, and create self-sustaining schools when appropriate and necessary.[31]

In many cases, a corporation's activities are catalyzed by individual women. Goldman Sachs has two such powerhouses—one in the firm and the other heading their foundation. A January 2003 Web news brief by *Women's Enews* highlighted Anne Kaplan of Goldman Sachs as one who "tills fresh soil."[32] *Women's Enews* reported that in 2002, about 28 percent of privately held businesses in the United States were run by women, marking a 14 percent increase in five years. The brief claims that if Kaplan gets her way, that number will continue to rise. To give things a push in the right direction, Kaplan joined forces with Goldman Sachs, one of the most elite investment banks in the United States, to help Smith College launch a women's financial education program with $2.5 million in seed capital. This program is the first of its kind in the United States aimed di-rectly at recruiting and training young women to take leadership positions in the worlds of business and finance.

Endowed with $200 million in 1999, the Goldman Sachs Foundation is led by Stephanie Bell-Rose, who encorporates a high-engagement approach to philanthropy by utilizing venture funding and hands-on community involvement. Bell-Rose comments:

> Building on a rich tradition of leadership and community involvement, professionals from the firm become involved with Foundation grantees in strategically important ways that leverage their skills and leadership abilities. Some have joined the boards of organizations we support and provide needed leadership and business guidance, while others are mentors to the young people served by the organizations. Still others participate in Foundation programs and events as presenters, judges, panelists, and speakers. With one foot on Wall Street and another in the world of philanthropy, the Foundation plays an important role as a bridge between the private and nonprofit sectors. We combine traditional grant-making with careful business analysis to optimize the performance of supported organizations.[33]

More recently, twenty nonprofit organizations presented business plans at the first Yale School of Management/Goldman Sachs Nonprofit Ventures competition for revenue-generating enterprise, vying for four final prizes of $100,000 to be used to help them launch their ventures. The competition received 655 entries from nonprofits. One of the four winners was El Puente Community Development of El Paso, Texas, dedicated to the empowerment of low-income Mexican immigrant women and their families that have been affected adversely by global restructuring.

In telephone interviews with Bell-Rose and Juan Sabateur, philanthropic advisor to Goldman Sachs, several themes regarding the role of women in corporate philanthropy were explored. For example, women are increasingly the leaders in corporate philanthropy, but why?

In order to be successful in any demanding field, one needs to be able to cross boundaries and build bridges. In order to become leaders, women have had to learn how to communicate effectively across cultures, barriers, and boundaries. They have learned as "outsiders" how to explore the "other" or "inside" perspective; in effect, crossing into a different culture, whether it be gender, race, or class. In the broadest sense of the word, a woman's "cross-cultural competencies" are strengthened by having this "outsider perspective."

Of the challenges faced by being a woman in corporate philanthropy, Bell-Rose comments that people tend to think that because she is seen as more accessible, softer in her approach, she will be more flexible and easily convinced. "I find myself saying 'No' not just once, but five times to the same person." She believes this is a fact of life for women in her field, and finds it takes more energy to stick to her proactive agenda. "The challenge is defining the parameters of where you are heading." And, according to Sabateur, this is where Bell-Rose has done well. When much of corporate philanthropy was giving smaller grants, she took a more venture-capital approach, giving fewer grants at the $1 million level and focusing the intellectual capital of Goldman Sachs employees to help with the success and sustainability of the grantees. From his advisory capacity with different women over the years, Sabateur believes that women have "mainstreamed themselves in the philanthropic world and have made great strides in introducing social investing to the corporate world," all while holding twin agendas of a "double bottom-line of financial return and social return."

The flurry of activity embraced by corporations in the twenty-first century raises the question again. Does corporate social investing pay off? The jury is still out, and it seems that the public is not without its suspicions while at the same time expressing support for corporate giving. A survey done in 2001 by the public relations firm Hill and Knowlton found that 79 percent of Americans took corporate citizenship into account when deciding whether to buy a particular company's product. However, the vast majority of the public exhibited skepticism about the motivations of corporations for charitable giving. Survey findings suggest that corporations need to do more than simply give away dollars, but need to act in ways that are meaningful to their various shareholders—consumers, investors, employees, and members of the local community—and that genuinely demonstrate their core corporate values. This challenges companies to do more than shell out money, but to place their charitable giving in a broader context of corporate citizenship that will remain a priority in both bull and bear markets.[34]

Opportunities and Challenges

Women's philanthropy organizations demonstrate tremendous ambition— ambition equal to the magnitude of the social problems they seek to address. Violence against women and girls, inequity in education and the workplace, poverty among older women, and a woman's right to choose are just a few of the challenges faced each day. Much has been accomplished, often with few resources. Yet, we believe that the future success of women's philanthropy organizations will depend on their own strength and development; indeed their own capacity for leadership in this new era of philanthropy. Women's funding organizations, seeking to build the capacity of their grantees, must concentrate on building their own. Only from this place of strength can they shine and be recognized as they go about the business of sharing with the broader world of philanthropy and society the gains that they have fought hard to attain over the years. When shared, these gains become gifts to those coming after them; gifts of experience, knowledge, connectedness, and the capacity to hold great vision. Women's funds have long shared their practices among themselves, but sharing beyond the confines of those working in women's philanthropy is territory that still has much to be charted.

With the current interest in foundation effectiveness among grantmakers, women's philanthropy organizations stand in a place to make even greater contributions. This interest in effectiveness by the foundation community is one representation of philanthropy striving to reinvent itself, and in such times windows once slammed shut are open to let in a little fresh air.

The goal of foundation effectiveness is to hold up the best foundation practices as a goal for standard practice in philanthropy. Among practitioners of philanthropy, foundation effectiveness refers to a growing emphasis on grantmaking that is transparent, respectful, and that creates positive and enduring social change. In essence, foundations are held to the same high standards of performance they have long required of their grantees.[35]

The field of women's philanthropy, though relatively small, historically has had a strong track record in the areas of transparency and respectfulness, not to mention positive and enduring change. The creation of women's shelters and safe houses is only one example of such change. Other areas discussed in the broad array of literature on foundation effectiveness suggest that effective foundations strive to have more board and staff diversity; take more risks; recognize emerging priorities more quickly; strive to maintain an open culture; allow for greater staff discretion; take advice from grantees more seriously; be more accountable to communities served; be mission driven while maintaining flexibility in implementation, and be more accountable in documenting the effectiveness of what they do.[36]

If you look closely, you will find that women's philanthropy organizations practice their philanthropy in such a way that their strong track record continues in all of the suggested areas of foundation effectiveness; all but one. They have much to own and share from that which they skillfully and perhaps instinctively evolved over time as "best practice" in working with women, girls and communities in general—what we now know as best practices to effect social change. Yet, the one area still in need of development is that of accountability; not to the communities served, for women's funds are superb at that, but accountability in documenting the effectiveness of what they do.

The issue of accountability for documenting effectiveness in women's philanthropy, like that of so many foundations, is an area that is underdeveloped. Foundations are brilliant at "improving" with their work but struggle to "prove" that their work can be pointed to as making the difference. This inability to prove causal relation to social change is hardly a criticism that can be leveled at women's philanthropy or even philanthropy in general, as the complexity of such measurement has challenged the best of social scientists and evaluation specialists. Nonetheless, efforts must be made to do so to continue to garner the support of investors and society in general. Efforts are underway with a focus on benchmarking by umbrella organizations such as Women's Funding Network and Women and Philanthropy, who realize that women's philanthropy has results to celebrate—if they can be captured adequately.

Women's Philanthropy Organizations as Knowledge Foundations

In her paper *The Industry of Philanthropy*, Lucy Bernholz states her assumptions about change in philanthropy. She believes that philanthropic innovation is stymied by fragmentation and silos in the industry; structural barriers limit the movement of money but not knowledge; readily available technologies and newly positioned enterprises can move ideas through and across the industry; and moving philanthropic knowledge is the lever for industry-wide change.

These assumptions hold much worth noting by women's funds. If moving philanthropic knowledge is the lever for industry-wide philanthropic change and innovation, how can the "mother lode" of knowledge and experience be mined and moved more effectively within the field of women's philanthropy and outside it in the broader world of foundations? One answer is for women's philanthropy organizations to embrace more strongly the concept of being a "knowledge foundation." Bernholz defines a knowledge foundation as a philanthropic institution that views knowledge as a distinct asset and strategically develops, captures, uses, and shares knowledge to achieve its mission.

Although for years women's organizations have used education as a tool for raising consciousness about issues relevant to women and girls, they appear to have not yet claimed their rightful place in teaching and leading others about the effectiveness of their community-based and grassroots philanthropy. Women have much to share in this arena where their egalitarian, relation-oriented approach is well suited.

Despite the economic gains made by women over the last fifty years, they are often still marginalized in the realm of money and philanthropy. What will help women's philanthropy claim that rightful place of leadership and gain a larger seat at the table? Building financial assets is crucial, but we believe an even more timely answer to the question lies in a new commitment to the most important asset of the twenty-first century: knowledge. This means paying serious attention to knowledge development and knowledge exchange; building upon what women's philanthropy organizations *know* works. By creating a stronger knowledge management system that internally communicates important learning, and shares wisdom externally, women's philanthropy will be seen as a knowledge leader in a time of important transition.

All the right concerns about why there's not enough time or resources to focus beyond raising one's own endowment are valid. Women's funds are working hard to grow their asset base and to grow their presence on the philanthropic map. This is critical work, and the Kellogg Foundation has funded many projects to invigorate these efforts. Yet, as many foundations have learned the hard way, money alone is not the answer to sustainable growth and development. As was observed in the explosive growth of Silicon Valley, a shared commitment to networks and collective progress was a critical factor in advances spreading rapidly, and whole industries needed to grow as a precursor to the success of individual firms.

Bernholz predicts that the qualities of communities of interest and networks hold the greatest promise for foundations to lead the way in developing new philanthropy. Women's philanthropy networks are formed, well-functioning, and poised to lead. It will take concerted effort to keep the grants going out the door in response to growing need, raise individual organization endowment levels, and at the same time, collectively build and share knowledge. But each of these are crucial elements to sustainability both for the field and for individual organizations. Far too often, the focus remains on grantmaking, and if not making the grants, raising the money for the grants, with field-building low on the list of priorities. The historic collectivity of the women's philanthropy field must find new levels of mastery. For all boats to rise, the collective water level must be raised.

There is a new edge being shorn in philanthropy. Collectively, women's philanthropy organizations can step onto that edge and own their wealth of knowledge and experience as they increasingly become key actors in reinvention. As this chapter illustrates, women are and always have been on the cutting edge of innovation. The twin engines of larger assets among a strong collective, and a vibrant connected knowledge base, will strengthen the place of women's funding today and into the future. Visible and recognized for their expertise in philanthropy, it will become second nature to coin a phrase from a recent women's philanthropy communications campaign: "Ask a Woman for Directions" (www.ASKaWOMAN.org).

NOTES

1. Lucy Bernholz, *The Industry of Philanthropy: Highlights from Key Industry Analyses* (Oakland, Calif.: BluePrint Research and Design, Inc., 1999–2002) 5–7. The trends section by Bernholz also credits two other sources: Foundations for the Future, University of Southern Calif., Los Angeles, 1999; and New Strategies for New Futures, Charles Stewart Mott Foundation, Fall 2002.

2. Katherine Fulton, *Philanthropy's Future: Pieces of the Emerging Puzzle: A Resource Guide* (San Francisco: Global Business Network, 2001) 1.

3. Bernholz, *The Industry of Philanthropy*, 16–17.

4. Burbridge, Lynn, William Diaz, Teresa Odenhahl, Aileen Shaw, *The Meaning and Impact of Board and Staff Diversity in the Philanthropic Field: Findings from a National Study*; Sourced Chapter—Diversity in Foundations: The Numbers and Their Meanings; Burbridge, Lynn; Joint Affinity Group; 2002. The joint affinity group does not have a website. The Joint Affinity Groups (JAG) is a nationwide coalition of grantmaker associations that engages the field of philanthropy to reach its full potential through practices that support diversity, inclusiveness, and accountability to communities. The LGBT funders website carries the full reprot at: http://www.lgbtfunders.org/lgbtfunders/JAG/diversity_study.htm.

5. MRI CyberStats, Fall 1999, at www.mediamark.com/MRI/docs/TopLineReport.html.

6. Ibid.

7. Craver, Mathews, Smith & Co., "Socially Engaged Internet Users: Prospects for Online Philanthropy and Activism," September 1999, at www.craveronline.com. CMS is a fundraising and membership development firm for progressive nonprofits and philanthropy in the United States.

8. Michael Stein, "Elementary E-Philanthropy" *NetAction Notes — A Project of the Tides Center* 53 (December 27, 1999, http://www.netaction.org/notes/notes53.html.

9. Just Economics, 1999. Tides Foundation, unpublished report.

10. Women Leaders Online Spring 2003, Website, www.wlo.org.

11. Ibid

12. Ono, Hiroshi and Zavodny, Madeline; *Gender and the Internet*; SSE/EFI Working Paper Series in Economics and Finance, no. 495; July 2002; Social Science Quarterly, 2003.

13. Stanford Graduate School of Business case study "The Roberts Enterprise Development Fund: Implementing a Social Venture Capital Approach to Philanthropy," October, 1998. Available through the Roberts Enterprise Development Foundation office (www.redf.org).

14. Christine Letts, William Ryan, Allen Grossman, "Virtuous Capital: What Foundations Can Learn from Venture Capitalists," *Harvard Business Review*, 1997.

15. Thomas Reis, *Unleashing New Resources and Entrepreneurship for the Common Good: Scan, Synthesis, and Scenario for Action*, W. K. Kellogg Foundation, December 1998.

16. Sondra Shaw-Hardy, *Creating a Women's Giving Circle: A Handbook* [pub info]

17. Julie Petersen, *The Collaborative Fund Model: Effective Strategies for Grantmaking*, The Ms. Foundation for Women, 2002, Web site [URL].

18. Baltimore Giving Project Web site, www.baltimoregivingproject.org.

19. Bill and Melinda Gates Foundation, "Bill and Melinda Gates Foundation Announces Global Fund for Women Grant to Improve Women's Health in Developing Countries," press release, September 30, 2002.

20., Heather Knight "Palo Alto Group Donates Millions Worldwide, No Strings Attached," *San Francisco Chronicle*, May 28, 1999.

21. *African American Philanthropy: A Legacy of Giving,* an online publication of the Twenty-First Century Foundation, [URL].

22. National Center for Family Philanthropy, Web site, 2002 [URL]

23. Joint Affinity Group Report, *Diversity in Foundations: The Numbers and Their Meaning,* Web site, [URL] 140

24. Association of Small Foundations Website, www.smallfoundations.org, November 13, 2001.

25. Joshua D. Margolis and James P. Walsh, "Misery Loves Companies: Whither Social Initiatives by Business?" Harvard/University of Michigan, unpublished, working paper, June 22, 2002.

26. Aileen Shaw, *Corporate Philanthropy: The Business of Diversity,* Joint Affinity Group Report, www.lgbtfunders.org/lgbtfunders/JAG/jag08.pdf.

27. Thomas Reis, *Unleashing New Resources and Entrepreneurship for the Common Good: Scan, Synthesis, and Scenario for Action* (W. K. Kellogg Foundation, unpublished, internal working paper, December 1998).

28. Margolis and Walsh, "Misery Loves Companies."

29. Loren Renz, Vice President for Research, and Steven Lawrence, Director of Research, "Foundation Growth and Giving Estimates—2001 Preview," The Foundation Center, Website: http://www.fdncenter.org, 2002.

30. Wells Fargo Website, www.wellsfargo.com, 2003.

31. Julie Leupold, "From Seven Who Till Fresh Ground," *Women's Enews,* [URL], January 1, 2003. Website: www.levistrauss.com/responsibility/foundation/index/htm, February 2003.

32. Goldman Sachs Foundation website: www.gs.com/foundation.

33. Renz and Lawrence, *Joint Affinity Report.*

34. Dorothy Johnson Center for Philanthropy and Nonprofit Leadership, "Forward," *Agile Philanthropy: Understanding Foundation Effectiveness* ([place]: Grand Valley State University, August 2002).

35. Hill and Knowlton, Inc. "Americans are Looking for Good Corporate Citizens But Are Not Finding Them According to Hill and Knowlton 2001 Corporate Citizen Watch." http://www.hillandknowlton.com/index.php?section1=news&section2=news.archive&period=2001-07&id=31, 2001.

36. Bernholz, *The Industry of Philanthropy,* 5–7.

THE NEXT WAVE

Feminism, Philanthropy, and the Future

KALPANA KRISHNAMURTHY

I was born in 1976, the year America celebrated its two hundredth anniversary, the year that *Roots* was published, the year that Jimmy Carter and Walter Mondale were elected to the White House, the year the Supreme Court reinstated the death penalty. By definition, my birth in 1976 puts me at the tail end of the so-called Generation X, the generation after the Baby Boomers. Where that places me and my generation on the scale of feminist history is an entirely more complicated question.

As a young woman growing up in the Pacific Northwest, the way I perceived women in the world changed every day. Watching my mother go to her medical practice each day, answering our home phone, "Which Dr. Krishnamurthy would you like—Mr. Dr. Krishnamurthy or Mrs. Dr. Krishnamurthy?" helped me know that I could be anything. In the early 1980s when Sandra Day O'Connor became the first woman on the Supreme Court and Sally Ride the first woman in space, I knew that the doors of possibility were opening for women

Many in my generation grew up watching women break through barriers in our society because of the victories of the women's movement. While we all grew up knowing that women still faced discrimination, most of us were fairly confident that our generation would continue accomplishing "firsts." while eventually building to a point where we weren't counting women anymore.

Getting on the Radar

In the early 1990s, young women around the country began to talk about their dissatisfaction with the world and the current state of affairs. The early 1990s were packed with events that riveted and shocked young people, such as the Rodney King trial and decision, the William Kennedy

Smith rape trial, the U.S. Supreme Court confirmation of Clarence Thomas, and the Supreme Court decision on *Planned Parenthood vs. Casey,* which upheld mandatory twenty-four-hour waiting periods and other restrictions to abortion. What did all of these events have in common? They were about pressing issues that affect young women: sexual harassment, rape, race in America, reproductive health, economics, class.

And yet, when you turned on the television, read the news, or listened to the radio, no one was talking or listening to young women. The pundits and experts were almost always white men discussing the ramifications of various legal arguments, not the reality of these issues, not the impact on young women's lives.

In January 1992, Rebecca Walker wrote an article for Ms. Magazine examining the impact of the Clarence Thomas confirmation. Her article was entitled "Becoming the Third Wave." Walker ended her piece with a call to action:

> So I write this as a plea to all women, especially women of my generation: Let Thomas's confirmation serve to remind you, as it did me, that the fight is far from over. Let this dismissal of a woman's experience move you to anger. Turn that outrage into political power. Do not vote for them unless they work for us. Do not have sex with them, do not break bread with them, do not nurture them if they don't prioritize our freedom to control our bodies and our lives. I am not a post-feminist feminist. I am the Third Wave."[1]

Walker articulated a rage, anger, and hunger for action that resonated with young women and men across the country, who wrote to Ms. Magazine declaring themselves part of the Third Wave. By May 1992, Walker and Shannon Liss had started the Third Wave Direct Action Corporation. The organization's initial mission was to fill a void in young women's leadership and to mobilize young people to become more involved socially and politically in their communities.

Creating Her-Story

Before the organization had time to solidify, it was already at work on its inaugural project, Freedom Summer '92. Recognizing that the upcoming presidential election would offer a unique opportunity to bring the voices of young people into the political debate, Freedom Summer '92 was a cross-county voter registration and education drive. Organized by a handful of youth, the tour took 120 young people around the country in twenty-three days to register voters in twenty-one under served communities. In addition to registering or reaching out to more than twenty thousand new voters, the result was a strong sense of community, empowerment, and leadership among the Freedom Summer Riders.

In a telephone interview in 2002, Amy Richards, a key organizer of Freedom Summer '92 said, "One of the best measures of the success of Freedom Summer is that I still run into alumni, people who went on the bus tour ten years ago, who introduce themselves and say, 'I went on Freedom Summer in 1992, and it helped change my life.' The ideas behind Freedom Summer have continued to inform Third Wave—we know that the best way to reach people is to reach out to them, and not presume that they will come to us."

For the next two years, Third Wave Direct Action Corporation continued to work with the nucleus of Freedom Summer alumni and other young women and men. As more and more letters poured in from young women around the country energetically stating, "I want to join the Third Wave," the organization began to define itself as a member-driven organization, run by a thirteen-member board of directors.

By 1995, Third Wave Direct Action's priorities were responding to letters from young feminists around the country, trying to enlarge the organization's membership base, responding to the media's misrepresentation of Gen X, and creating a lasting organization. In addition, much of Third Wave's energy went toward finding creative ways to raise money for projects led by and for young women.

Where's the Money?

At the same time that Third Wave Direct Action was getting up and running, research from the philanthropic world was showing the dismal percentage of dollars going to women and girls. In the early 1990s, less than 4 percent of all philanthropic dollars were directed to programs serving women and girls. Recognizing that even fewer dollars were making it to the innovative programs that Third Wave Direct Action members were leading across the country, Amy Richards and Rebecca Walker began having conversations with Catherine Gund and Dawn Martin about the need to have a fund for young women.

Catherine Gund, a third-generation trustee of the George Gund Foundation, was raised by a feminist and philanthropically minded mother who instilled in her a tradition of philanthropy. "My mother taught me from an early age about the core values of philanthropy. Creating a fund to support young women seemed like a logical step in ensuring that the vision and voices of young women would receive the funding to flourish and grow," said Gund in a speech (June 4, 1999) to Americans for the Arts.

Dawn Lundy Martin, a staff person at the Astraea Lesbian Foundation for Justice, had worked with Catherine through her role as an Astraea board member. "Interestingly, Catherine's and my very different cultural and economic backgrounds brought us to similar thinking about the need to provide financial, activist, and technical assistance for young women to do social justice work. We saw feminism as having the possibility to become an all-encompassing framework that could apply to the activism being done at a local level. We saw feminism as something that would continue to evolve in the hands of a diverse group of young women. We also saw an absence, there were no national organizations—feminist or otherwise—that sought to bring young women together around the issues that concerned them," said Martin.

The original idea was to keep the Third Wave Fund and the Third Wave Direct Action Corporation as two separate organizations—linked in the goal of supporting the leadership of young women—but each maintaining a different mission, different boards, and different means toward similar goals. The fund's program areas were developed through concerns shared with the Third Wave Direct Action members: economic empowerment, reproductive rights, education, and a general fund for activism and organizing.

The Third Wave Fund's twenty-five member board of advisors was convened at the first board retreat in the summer of 1996. The group that came together at this first meeting was a multi-class, multi-gendered, multi-racial group of young people; it included some of the most dynamic young activists in the country. Writer Farai Chideya, filmmaker Sandy Dubowski, and others joined individuals such as Internet entrepreneur Omar Wasow at the first meeting. The young people at the table were uniquely positioned in a broad range of communities to spread the word of the new Third Wave movement.

The retreat brought together a cross-class, cross-race group of young women and men to explore the goals, vision, and structure for the fund. At the opening of the retreat, board members were asked to talk about what skills or experiences they brought to the specific challenges of fundraising and grantmaking. "Board members who had applied for scholarships in college—who had never considered themselves grantwriters—realized that, in fact, they already had the skills to craft a compelling request for funding. Others who grew up attending fancy cocktail parties realized that they could accompany those who were uncomfortable at our higher-end benefits, introducing them, and teaching them the fine art of shmoozing," said Gund.

During that first year, Third Wave raised $100,000 from the support of individuals and foundations. The philanthropic community was generous in sharing its time and expertise with a new "little sister" organization. The Funding Exchange, a national network of activist funds, handled all the finances while the Sister Fund gave Third Wave our very first foundation grant. Just as foundations took a leap of faith, individual donors went out on a limb to support Third Wave. Donors recognized the missing link: There were no organizations that were helping to develop the political and cultural activism of the next wave of feminism. If the movement was going to develop and grow, there needed to be an organization to help make it happen. And Third Wave Fund filled that need by supporting groups around the country who were cultivating the next generation of feminist activists.

The Third Wave Foundation Is Born

Because of waning energy on the part of Third Wave Direct Action board members, it was decided that both Third Wave Direct Action and the Third Wave Fund would be better served by becoming the Third Wave Foundation. As the Third Wave Foundation, the organization combined the activist spirit of Direct Action with the philanthropic focus of the Fund, creating a dynamic activist foundation focusing on young women from fifteen to thirty.

Hiring Vivien Labaton as the first parttime staff person, Third Wave awarded almost $13,000 in grants during 1997. The initial individuals and groups that the fund supported laid the base upon which future grantmaking would be built: emergency funding for abortions, scholarships, building young-women-led reproductive rights organizations, and general operating support for young-women-led groups and projects.

From the beginning, it was clear that Third Wave was a multi-issue feminist organization. The experiences of board members as activists, the calls from our membership, and the types of requests we received all indicated that Third Wave would support the leadership of young women as they worked on issues such as environmental justice, prison reform, living wage campaigns, as well as on the more traditional feminist issues. Third Wave's definition of feminism explicitly would connect women's issues to issues of race, heterosexism, class, and other forms of oppression.

Over the next two years, the Third Wave Foundation experienced rapid growth and increased public recognition. We held one of our biggest fundraisers, the premier of the movie *Girl's Town*, which raised over $40,000. We also secured a number of large individual donors, most of whom have continued to support us over the years. In addition, the media began to turn to Third Wave as an organization that represented a "new branch of feminism" and one that could serve as the voice of young women around the country. As our public recognition grew, our programmatic priorities also were beginning to gel, and we became one of the first institutional funders of a number of young-women-led, progressive organizations. Groups such as the School of Unity and Liberation (SOUL), an

Oakland-based organizer training project, or film projects like *Live! Nude! Girls! Unite!* about organizing sex workers in San Francisco were awarded Third Wave grants—when in all likelihood, they might not have found funding at a traditional feminist foundation.

Where We Are Today

During the first five years of our development, Third Wave broke new ground in supporting the voices of young women. Our accomplishments include:

- *Grantmaking*. In our first five years, Third Wave gave over $350,000 to individual organizations led by young women across the country. In our Organizing and Advocacy Fund, Third Wave supports efforts to challenge sexism, racism, homophobia, economic injustice, and other forms of oppression. Our Reproductive Health and Justice Fund supports activities that directly expand the scope and definition of reproductive justice and promotes reproductive health for young women. Finally, our Scholarship Fund is available to full- or part-time women students thirty and under who are activists, artists, or cultural workers engaged in dismantling racism, sexism, homophobia, and other forms of inequality.
- *Networking*. Since the summer of 2000, Third Wave has brought together young women activists to exchange ideas and share information with groups in philanthropically underserved regions of the country. ROAMS (Reaching Out Across MovementS) was developed to serve two purposes: informing Third Wave of the challenges facing progressive grassroots organizations and the strategies they have employed to address them, and simultaneously helping strengthen the networking connections among progressive groups in a region. Since 2000, Third Wave has taken more than twenty-five young women to visit fifteen states, meeting with over seventy-five progressive organizations in the Southeast, Pacific Northwest, and Southwest.
- *Public education*. Third Wave reaches out to both individual young women and the overall field of philanthropy through public education efforts. To raise awareness of sexism and provide an opportunity for young women to speak out, Third Wave's "I Spy Sexism" campaign gives tools to young women that help begin conversations in their community about the effects of sexism. Within philanthropy, Third Wave aims to increase charitable dollars that support young women in social justice work; our activities include speaking at philanthropic conferences, hosting the Making Money Make Change (a gathering for progressive young people with wealth), and other strategic means.

Leadership

At Third Wave, we are the community we serve. The Third Wave board of directors is made up of fifteen young women and men activists and allies. As a multi-issue organization committed to developing a broad race, class, and sexuality analysis in the next generation of feminists, Third Wave is deliberately structured to incorporate diversity in identity and ideology. An official board resolution states that we seek a board that is at least 50 percent people of color, 50 percent gay, lesbian, bisexual, or transgendered, and no more than 30 percent men. Third Wave is also committed to developing the leadership of young women, thus our board primarily is composed of women in their early and mid-twenties.

That means that our board work can be challenging. We bring individuals to the table who have a wide array of experience and expertise—one board member may be a student pursuing a PhD, another may have no formal higher education; board members are activists, donors, low income, transgendered, and men. Put all these ideas, identities, expertise, and opinions in one room, and you have a dynamic and sometimes contentious mix. Board meetings frequently evolve into free-form discussions on topics in the media, political discourse, ideas about how to improve the movement. At the same time, board members do not all have the same experience working with staff, managing a budget, or making grant decisions. In recent years, the organization has made a commitment to providing more regular training to board members, including trainings on fundraising, communications, and organizational management. Building the skills of the women and men at the table is an important part of leadership development at Third Wave.

Our dedication to placing young women at the center of leadership also includes our commitment to the staff. Third Wave has a responsibility to be an organization by and for young women, thus the staff are all young women under thirty. With three fulltime and one parttime staff members, plus a host of young women interns and volunteers, Third Wave has made a commitment to providing young women and young women of color leadership opportunities that do not exist within the larger, traditional feminist or philanthropic movements.

The Culture of Third-Wave Feminism

As an organization of young feminists, Third Wave often is called upon to speak for the next generation. Inevitably, when speaking with women's organizations, we are asked a series of questions along the following lines:

- Why are young women today afraid of using the word "feminist"?
- What are the political goals of the third-wave movement?

- Why are young women today more obsessed with expanding personal freedoms instead of creating systemic change?
- Why aren't young women concerned about the issue of abortion?
- Does anyone in your generation know who Gloria Steinem is?

Third Wave has tried to answer these questions at each turn in respectful and engaging ways that encourage dialogue among second- and third-wave feminists. A number of books and anthologies have been published in recent years that attempt to answer similar questions, bringing the voices of young women from different communities and activist backgrounds together in an attempt to articulate an individual and collective identity for our generation of feminists. But still the uncertainty lingers, and as time passes, the questions from our foremothers get louder and more concerned. The questions are symptomatic of a much larger generational divide that must be bridged in order to ensure the health and vibrancy of the feminist movement in the future.

Ours is a generation that grew up with the victories of the civil rights movement, the feminist movement, the gay and lesbian movement. This context gives our work and our analysis a different flavor—we are multi-issue in our approach, we are inclusive of men, we are working within a global economic framework, we are incorporating *all* of a person's identities into the work we do. Third Wave's feminism begins from a place of interconnectedness, a place that many older feminists view as a lack of focus. We understand this interconnectedness to be one of our core strengths.[2]

And so, young women work on the issues using a different framework than our foremothers. Third Wave articulates a feminism that speaks to the interconnectedness of political issues in the world. Instead of putting issues that are more "recognizably feminist" at the forefront, we bring to the forefront a diversity of progressive issues that we can investigate using a gender lens; these issues range from economic globalization and its many effects on Third World women to prison reform here in the United States, from sweatshop labor to environmental devastation, from reproductive justice to racial profiling. We see that the issues of race, class, environmental justice, and prisons are linked to one another, and we work to address these issues from within many social justice movements.

The Third Wave Foundation's job is to support young women bringing a feminist lens to social justice work—regardless of whether that work is within traditionally defined women's issues or not. A list of Third Wave's grantees includes organizations such as Danzine, an organization for women sex-workers and exotic dancers in Portland, Oregon; the film *Tulia, TX: Scenes from the Drug War*, which explores the effects of a drug bust in a small African American community; and From the Holler to the Hood, a grassroots project in Whitesburg, Kentucky, that explores the impact of the prison industrial complex on women in Appalachia.

Working with Young Donors

Young people in philanthropy are viewed very differently than young women in feminist circles. Rather than being questioned for their analysis, philanthropy looks at young donors as an enigma: What exactly do young donors want? What types of issues engage and interest them? And of course, how do we get young donors to give to our organizations and groups?

Much has been written about the upcoming transfer of wealth that the philanthropic sector will see over the next few years and decades. By some estimates, nearly $10 trillion will be transferred from one generation to the next over the coming thirty years.[3] As the Baby-Boom generation inherits its wealth, many families with young people in their twenties and thirties have found their children wanting to play a more active role in helping determine how and where the giving happens. "Philanthropy today is a form of activism, it's about more than just sitting on sidelines," says Catherine Gund.

In the past five years, many organizations and networks have been created to support young people engaging in philanthropy. One of the first support systems was the Making Money Make Change gathering, started by Third Wave in 1998. MMMC is a national gathering that brings together approximately seventy women and men ages fifteen through thirty-five each year to explore wealth issues within the context of progressive social change. There is no other national gathering like Making Money Make Change—one that is specifically organized by and for young progressive people of wealth.

Through community-building activities, workshops, and discussions, participants inform, support, inspire, challenge, and share ideas with each other about various aspects of wealth and social change philanthropy. Whether attendees are already innovative philanthropists, or just beginning to learn about these issues, MMMC provides a unique space in which the diversity of perspectives, knowledge, background, and experience are valued at the gathering. The event is now cosponsored by Third Wave, Active Element Foundation, Tides Foundation, the Funding Exchange, and Resource Generation.

Making Money Make Change has been joined by a host of programs, giving circles, and networks that make up a new generation of young donor organizing. "Young donor organizing grew out of past waves of progressive philanthropy, including the efforts of wealthy donors and activists who helped created the Funding Exchange," says Alison Goldberg, creator and director of Foundations for Change in Boston.[4] "The innovations of past generations are central to the work that young donors are doing now. Activist-advised/controlled grantmaking is a central theme, as is developing a peer-support network for wealthy individuals."

Engaging young donors may mean challenging assumptions around language, issues, collaboration, and decision making. The bottom line? Young donors are seeking new ways of participating in philanthropy. They want to be engaged, they want to be at the table, they want to help frame the issues, and they want to work in collaboration with one another and other activists. "Traditional philanthropy, and women's philanthropy, need to actively woo the next generation by putting young people on boards, offering leadership training, and involving younger people in governance and management. [Many young people] bring a fresh eye to the work, a willingness to take risks, a passion for organizing and advocacy, and an openness that [foundations] should look at as assets," says Gund.[5]

Moving Forward

Young feminists and young donors face similar challenges as they work with their older counterparts. The widening gap between generations in both communities highlights a need for open intergenerational dialogue, with listening on both sides of the table. The process of building a collective vision for social justice that incorporates the perspectives of both generations is vitally important for moving a progressive agenda, and we must continue to work together to build a larger and more expansive definition of both feminism and philanthropy.

NOTES

1. Rebecca Walker, "Becoming the Third Wave," Ms. *Magazine* ll, no. 4 (January/February 1992).

2. Vivien Labaton, and Dawn Lundy Martin, eds. *The Fire This Time* (New York: Anchor Books, 2003).

3. Paul Van Slambrouck, "Entering a Golden Era of Giving," *The Christian Science Monitor*, September 15, 1998.

4. Newsletter, National Council on Responsive Philanthropy, Summer 2002.

5. Catherine Gund, "The Education of Young Donors: A Two-Way Street," *The Chronicle of Philanthropy*, January 14, 1999.

AFTERWORD

JING LYMAN

Women the world over always have been entrepreneurs—in their families, in their work lives, in their communities. In fact, frequently women's creativity, flexibility, resourcefulness, and commitment have kept these units intact. Women's ingenuity often has bridged the gap between social need and economic reality.

Women have built these bridges through the development of nonprofit organizations that foster and support the well-being of communities; they've done it through the cash and barter businesses that help to sustain them and their families; and they are doing it now through their philanthropy. It has been only in the last two to three decades that we have begun to recognize *all* this activity as true entrepreneurship. In fact, we now have a fancy title for this phenomenon: social entrepreneurism. The trendiness of this phrase, however, still under-credits the survival techniques used by women throughout time to keep their families and their communities afloat.

Look back at the chapters in this book—at the myriad initiatives and the authors who have helped to spawn them—and you will understand the breadth and spirit of women's entrepreneurism. Over and over, in so many different ways, these authors are describing their own or another woman's way of creating a new initiative to help women and girls close the gap between their societal and their economic worlds.

Many years ago, when attention first was being paid to the potential of women's business ownership in this country, a telling point was made in one of the new enterprise magazines: Men go into business as a strategy; women enter business as a way of life. It is staggering to note now the number of women's businesses that are based on some aspect of service-to-the-community. For example:

- A woman's bookstore in Kansas City gives new-purchase bonus points for bringing back used books that can then be recycled to nonprofits serving low-income children.

- A pottery business in West Philadelphia offers senior women status while paying them to paint glazes. They also can take home some of their products to sell in church fairs or to friends for supplemental cash.
- An eighteen-year-old envisions healthy fruit-based sodas; researches how to make appropriate syrups and begins making them in her Brooklyn kitchen. She then persuades a bottler to take her on as a customer and eventually sells her thriving business for millions of dollars after besting a Goliath alcoholic beverage company trying to pirate her syrups and her distinctive label. She then invests in one of the early socially responsible money market funds, now flourishing as a whole family of mutual funds.

Perhaps the most astonishing and inspiring stories are those of the hair care/cosmetology businesses started by such model entrepreneurs as Mme. C. J. Walker and Annie Malone (who both rose from abject poverty to become two of America's first female self-made millionaires.)

As a trustee of the Mary McLeod Bethune Museum and Archive for Black Women's History, I was enthralled to discover that each of these women, having started with a personal need to stem hair damage and loss, developed ointments that soon interested friends, then friends-of-friends, until they had established successful business enterprises. But they didn't stop there. They expanded their businesses and gave jobs to people in their neighborhoods, providing job training for others. They built their factories to be a combination of community center and (in today's parlance) incubator facilities—places where small businesses could start up in a supportive environment. These factories had auditoria (used for concerts and community performances, as well as for business) and classrooms. Small shops surrounded the factory exteriors so that new or expanding businesses could become established while serving the community. These women, and many more like them, were both social *and* economic entrepreneurs. They did well by doing good.

Cate Muther's Three Guineas Fund and its companion, Women's Technology Cluster, both located in San Francisco, are a modern-day variant of this concept. Having done well, Muther is now doing good. Kwak, McClure, and Peterson refer to women like Muther in their chapter: "Those philanthropists emerging from new fortunes define themselves as social entrepreneurs; some of the most outstanding of them are women." These women's efforts represent one important form of social enterprise—the philanthropy that flows from newly earned or acquired wealth. But my own definition of this phrase is much broader and includes women with little or no monetary resources but much creative vision, resourcefulness, common sense, and determination. These are the women who as individuals, but often working in communities, can make "mountains out of molehills."

And the world of women's philanthropy is beginning to take note. As Grumm and her co-authors write: "For Women's Funding Network members, it is inefficient to leave out the voices and valuable contributions of every community member, even if it means that progress is somewhat slower than it might have been had a more segmented approach been taken."

In this context, yet a different kind of entrepreneurism is evident in the extraordinary models of such "third world" programs as the Grameen Bank in Bangladesh, India's Self-Employed Women's Association (SEWA), and the U.S.-based Trickle Up, all programs in which grassroots women, given access to tiny amounts of capital, have established the validity of a peer-group equivalent of loan security. Since they use the resources provided by their new businesses for more adequate food and education for themselves and their children, they are again building that bridge between social justice and economic vitality.

The adaptation in the United States of successful micro-enterprise programs in the developing world has galvanized attention and focused the potential for reversing the negative cycle of poverty for low-income women and their families. It is the recognition of this entrepreneurism among women, and their tradition of inclusive peer-group support, that has brought such strength to the field of micro-enterprise generally, for women, men, and youth.

Again this important point is underscored in the chapter by Kwak et al. They stress that: "the future success of women's philanthropy organizations will depend on their strength and development; indeed their own capacity for leadership in this new era of philanthropy. Women's funding organizations, seeking to build the capacity of their grantees, must concentrate on building their own. Only from this place of strength can they shine and be recognized as they go about the business of sharing with the broader world of philanthropy and society the gains that they have fought hard to attain over the years. When shared, these gains become gifts to those coming after them; gifts of knowledge, connectedness, and the capacity to hold great vision. Women's funds have long shared their practices among themselves, but sharing beyond the confines of those working in women's philanthropy is territory that still has much to be charted."

Perhaps the Third Wave Foundation will be next in charting this course. As Krishnamurthy says: "Ours is a generation that grew up with the victories of the civil rights movement, the feminist movement, the gay and lesbian movement. This context gives our work a different flavor—we are multi-issue in our approach, we are inclusive of men, we are working within a global economic framework, we are incorporating *all* of a persons identities into the work we do. Third Wave's feminism begins from a place of interconnectedness . . ."

I believe that "women are and always have been at the cutting edge of innovation . . ." This book reminds us of that, and represents a hopeful and inclusive future. For that reason alone, it is a fine contribution to the growing body of literature on women, philanthropy, and social change.

WORKING WONDERS

DAVI WALDERS

If you want to feel proud of yourself, you've got to do things you can be proud of.

Oseola McCarty, 1908–1999

So large, so real, so present,
Oseola McCarty might just speak
from the Annie Leibovitz portrait
in the museum gallery. Sweaters
a kilter, hair a crown of uncontrolled
silver, she stares into the camera,
lips set, almost smiling. She stands
in Hattiesurg heat, her yard and
wood-frame house a background blur
behind her large eyes and steady gaze.

So many nevers—never finished
Eureka Elementary, never drove,
never traveled, never explored
or earned more than nine thousand
dollars each of the seventy-five
years she took in laundry before
arthritis crippled her. Washing
each dropped-off bundle, ironing,
folding, tying up her small deposits
week after week, year after year.

And then the decision. Summoning up
from her own deprivation a vision
of determined imagination. Walking

to the bank, making the withdrawal.
The long, slow bus trip across town.
Waiting. Waiting all afternoon
to startle, to hand over one hundred
fifty thousand dollars to Southern Miss.
Waiting to speak, to give, to educate
others. Waiting with that same look
as she stands in her level yard,
her level eyes daring you to cry.

In 1995, Ms. McCarty donated $150,000 to establish the Oseola McCarty Endowed Scholarship Fund, which provides assistance to financially needy students at the University of Southern Mississippi.

ABOUT THE
CONTRIBUTORS

Katherine Acey is executive director of the Astrea Lesbian Foundation for Justice. She is a founding member and past chair of the Funders for Lesbian and Gay Issues and former board member and chair of the Women's Funding Network. The recipient of several awards for community and philanthropic leadership, she has participated in numerous international delegations focusing on women's issues and human rights in Africa, Asia, Latin America, and the Middle East.

Judy Bloom is currently development officer and director of imprint giving for the Jewish Community Endowment Fund in the San Francisco Bay Area. She was formerly the executive director of Resourceful Women, a nonprofit membership organization. A founding president of Professional and Business Women of California and director of employer services at Jewish Vocational Services, she served for ten years as district director for Assemblywoman Jackie Speier, who now serves in the U.S. Senate.

Mary Ellen S. Capek is a philanthropic and nonprofit consultant, author, and speaker. A founding officer and former head of the National Council for Research on Women, she is based at the University of New Mexico Anderson Schools of Management as a Research Scholar.

Patti Chang has been the president and CEO of the Women's Foundation since 1995. She has served as the president of the San Francisco Commission on the Status of Women and now serves on the boards of the Women's Funding Network, the Women's Leadership Alliance, and the National Advisory Board for GenderPAC.

Kanyere F. Eaton joined the Sister Fund as its executive director in 2000. An ordained minister and social worker, she has served as director of social services at the Riverside Church in New York City and worked with grassroots women in nonprofit and faith institutions that emphasize the link between the health of a community and the spiritual wellbeing of each of its members.

Sunny Fischer was director of the Sophia Fund, the first private women's foundation in the country devoted exclusively to women's issues. She is a co-founder of the Chicago Foundation for Women, and an early leader in the Women's Funding Network and Chicago Women in Philanthropy. Currently she serves as executive director of the Richard H. Driehaus Foundation and is board chair of the Family Violence Prevention Fund.

Tracy Gary has been a feminist philanthropist and activist advisor to donors, institutions, and grassroots organizations that build social change for over thirty years. She founded more than a dozen nonprofit organizations and has served on numerous boards of directors of philanthropic and social change organizations, helping them to raise or leverage over $250 million. She is the co-author of *Inspired Philanthropy: Your Step by Step Guide to Creating a Giving Plan* (Jossey Bass, 2002) and is widely published in her field.

Christine Helen Grumm is executive director of the Women's Funding Network. She has served as the executive director of the Chicago Foundation for Women, and deputy general secretary of the Lutheran World Federation in Geneva. She also served as executive director of Education Program Associates, Inc.

Helen LaKelly Hunt is founder and president of the Sister Fund. She helped found many other women's funding institutions, including the Dallas Women's Foundation, the New York Women's Foundation and the Women's Funding Network. She has served on the boards of several foundations, including the Ms. Foundation for Women, Women and Philanthropy, and the New York City Women's Agenda. She is the recipient of numerous awards including the National Creative Philanthropy Award and Gloria Steinem's Women of Vision Award from the Ms. Foundation for Women. An inductee of the National Women's Hall of Fame in Seneca Falls, New York, she holds a Doctorate from Union Theological Seminary.

Emily Katz Kishawi is the director of membership and communications for the Women's Funding Network. She was previously the director of communications and public affairs for Equal Rights Advocates, director of development and communications for the YWCA of Rochester, New York, and vice president of communications and develoment at California Emergency Foodlink.

Kalpana Krishnamurthy is director of the Third Wave Foundation, where her work focuses on development and communications. An activist and advocate, she was a national organizer for the Take Our Daughters to Work Program.

Christine Kwak is a program director in the Philanthropy and Volunteerism Programing Area of the W.K. Kellogg Foundation. Trained as a therapist, she has devoted much of her career to positive youth development. Currently she provides leadership in the areas of women's philanthropy, national and community service, and program learning.

Diane Horey Leonard, a 2002 graduate of Cornell University, is a program officer at the Michigan Women's Foundation.

Jing Lyman, a founder of Women and Philanthropy and currently a Trustee of the Enterprise Foundation, is a social entrepreneur who has spent her life working on various aspects of community-building including fair and affordable housing, community economic development, and issues related to minorities and women. She has spent twenty-five years actively promoting philanthropy for and by women and girls

Gail D. McClure, PhD, vice president for programs at the W.F. Kellogg Foundation, was formerly vice president for social development programs at the Academy for Educational Development in Washington, D.C. Her PhD is in higher education and public policy.

Carol Mollner, formerly a planning and evaluation consultant to philanthropic and nonprofit organizations, is currently Development Director for the Headwaters Foundation for Justice in Minneapolis. She was the first executive director of Women's Funding Network and she has served on the boards of National Network of Grantmakers, National Committee for Responsive Philanthropy, and Minnesota Council of Nonprofits, among other organizations. She is the recipient of numerous awards, including a Jessie Bernard Wise Woman Award by the Center for Women's Policy Studies in Washington, D.C.

Jo Gruidly Moore has extensive experience in capacity building for nonprofit organizations. She has served as founder, staff, board chair, and campaign chair as well as in advisory and consulting capacities where her focus is board development, creating individual donor programs, and fundraising strategies that target specific communities. She has worked with such organizations as EMILY's List, the National Center on Poverty Law, and the Council for a Parliament of the World's Religions.

Anne B. Mosle is president of the Washington Area Women's Foundation and former co-chair of its board. She served as senior vice president at the Center for Policy Alternatives, where she led their national campaign, "America's Economic Agenda: Women's Voices for Solutions," and has been recognized as a leading woman activist by *Jane* and *Working Woman* magazines.

Kimberly Otis is president and CEO of Women and Philanthropy. She was the founding executive director of the Sister Fund and is former chair of the New York Regional Association of Grantmakers. She is also a past board member of the Women's Funding Network. She has held numerous positions in fundraising, research, and management with several nonprofit and social justice organizations.

Anne C. Petersen, PhD, is senior vice president for programs at the W.K. Kellogg Foundation. Previously, she was deputy director of the National Science Foundation. She has been a university researcher and administrator and a consultant to major foundations. She is the author of several books and articles on adolescent and gender issues.

Marianne Philbin is a consultant to nonprofit organizations and foundations specializing in new project start-up, organizational development, program development, and evaluation. Formerly executive director of the Chicago Foundation for Women and executive director of the Peace Museum in Chicago, she has served on numerous nonprofit organization boards of directors and she is a member of the Greater Chicago Philanthropy Initiative.

Barbara Y. Phillips, program officer of the Ford Foundation, is responsible for the portfolio of grants and other activities related to women's rights and gender equity within the Human Rights Unit of the Peace and Social Justice program. Currently a member of the board of directors of Women and Philanthropy, she has been engaged with the women's movement since 1971 when she joined the Women's Coalition of Jackson, Mississippi. A lawyer, she was previously a partner in the San Francisco firm Rosen & Phillips and staff attorney with the national Lawyers' Committee for Civil Rights Under Law.

Deborah L. Puntenney, PhD, holds the positions of research associate at the Institute for Policy Research, and director of research and publications at the Asset-Based Community Development Institute, both at Northwestern University in Evanston, Illinois.

Kavita N. Ramdas is president and CEO of the Global Fund for Women. Previously, she was a program officer at the John D. And Catherine T. MacArthur Foundation, where she worked on issues of poverty in the United States, economic development, and international population issues.

She was named Woman of the Year in 2002 by the Santa Clara Women and Law Society and also received the "Choosing to Lead" award at the National Women's Leadership Summit that year. She is a founding member of the board and past chair of Asian Americans and Pacific Islanders in Philanthropy.

Marsha Shapiro Rose, PhD is associate professor of sociology at Florida Atlantic University. She is the author of several articles on women and wealth, including "Philanthropy in a Different Voice: The Women's Funds," and "Southern Feminism and Social Change: Sallie Bingham and the Kentucky Foundation for Women."

Cynthia Ryan is principal of the Schooner Foundation, a private family foundation based in Boston, which has an international focus on human rights, peace, and security. She serves on several related boards of directors, and she is a member of the Peace and Security Funders Group, the International Human Rights Funders Group, and Grantmakers Without Borders. She earned her master's degree from the University of London School of Oriental and African Studies.

Zaineb Salbi founded Women for Women International, which was recognized in 1995 by President Clinton for its support to women survivors of war and conflict. She has written and spoken extensively on the role of women in war and post-conflict situations and her work has been featured widely in the media. She holds a master's degree in economics and development from the London School of Economics.

Margaret Talburtt, PhD is executive director of the James A. and Faith Knight Foundation, the largest funder of women's and girls programs in Southeast Michigan. Formerly president and CEO of the Michigan Women's Foundation for eight years, she was a co-founder of Formative Evaluation Research Associates, where her clients included the W.K. Kellogg Foundation, Ford Foundation, Exxon Foundation, and several colleges and universities. She co-chairs Michigan Grantmakers for Women and Girls and serves as chair of the board of trustees of the Women's Funding Network.

Marie C. Wilson is co-founder and president of the White House Project/Women's Leadership Fund, which was established in 1998 to advance women's leadership in all spheres. President of the MS. Foundation for Women since 1985, she is the 2002 recipient of the Robert W. Scrivner Award for Creative Grantmaking as well as other awards from the Network of Women's Funds and Women in Philanthropy.

Stephanie Yang is a senior program officer at the Women's Foundation of California, where she directs the Sisterhood Fund, among other programs. She is author of *The World Belongs to Us: Young Women, Leadership and Philanthropy*, a program guide, and she helped develop the first *Girls as Grantmakers Tool Kit*. She holds a master's degree in French literature from Tulane University, where she specialized in feminist and film theory.

ABOUT THE EDITOR

Elayne Clift is an award-winning writer and journalist whose articles have appeared in various publications in the United States and abroad. In addition to writing and teaching women's studies at several New England colleges and universities, she has worked internationally in the fields of women, health, communication, and development. A Vermont Humanities Council Scholar and author of several essay and fiction collections, she serves on the Governing Council of the Vermont Women's Fund. Her latest book is *Hester's Daughters*, a contemporary, feminist re-telling of *The Scarlet Letter*. She lives in Saxtons River, Vermont.